HARVARD HISTORICAL MONOGRAPHS   LXIX

Published under the direction of the Department of History
from the income of the Robert Louis Stroock Fund

Nota di tutte le Anime esistenti nella Città di Venezia nell' Anno 1586.

Nota di tutte le Anime esistenti nella Città di Venezia nell' Anno 1655.

The Population of Venice in 1586 and in 1655. Biblioteca Nazionale Marciana, Ital. VII, Cod. 2211 (10049).

Industry and Economic Decline in Seventeenth-Century Venice

RICHARD TILDEN RAPP

Harvard University Press
Cambridge, Massachusetts, and London, England   1976

Library of Congress Cataloging in Publication Data

Rapp, Richard T
  Industry and economic decline in seventeenth-century
Venice.

  (Harvard historical monographs; 69)
  Bibliography: p.
  Includes index.
  1. Venice—Economic conditions. I. Title.
II. Series.
HC308.V4R36   330.9'45'31   75-16149
ISBN 0-674-44545-7

For Wilma

PREFACE

The craft of economic history has undergone a transformation in the recent past. Methods once alien to history have become routine for today's researcher. Historical statistics, formerly used for casual illustration, now form the basis of much investigation. For modern studies this new approach has borne much fruit, yet, surprisingly, early modern economic history has benefited less from the new methodology. It is not easy to understand why this should be. As several historians have shown, data are available, even if difficult to locate and transcribe. Certainly the problems posed by the study of economic change in preindustrial society are worthy of interest. Perhaps it is the fear of revisiting grounds already well trodden (a fear which does not daunt historians of the modern era) which has retarded the application of new methods to early modern history. The purpose of this book is to shed new light on one long-studied problem: the decline of Venice.

For more than a century historians have striven to understand how and to what extent the city of Venice fell from the heights of commercial primacy to insignificance. It is one of the most commanding topics in early modern economic history—the supreme case-study of an economy experiencing the very opposite of "development." The problem is, in a sense, undisguised and this enhances its appeal. The economic fortunes of early modern Venice did not swing wildly with exogenous events such as invasions or political upheaval. The Serene Republic, to be sure, had its episodes of piracy, plague, and war, but as serious as they were, they did not alter the course of the secular trend. This is a fact which contemporary Venetians seemed to appreciate very well—a remarkable insight, considering that those "exogenous" events of the seventeenth century were full of drama and portent in the life and history of the city. Still, economic observers were aware that the effects of the piracy problems early in the century, the plague of 1630-1631, and even the long War of Candia (1645-1669) were transitory. Their reports pay brief, pro forma attention to these problems and then nearly always abandon temptingly simple excuses in recognition of more real and more complex sources of economic difficulty: international competition, failures in productivity, or falling aggregate demand. They saw as we see now that production, consumption, and the level of international trade are the factors that count.

In this study I have chosen to concentrate on production, without ignoring commerce and consumption. The response of industry to adverse market conditions is the key to understanding Venice's fight for competitive survival.

Instead of reviewing the separate industries of Venice one by one (an impractical but often-used method) I have chosen to focus on the factors common to all manufacturing enterprises: labor supply, capital employment and technology, foreign demand, and the influence of government on industrial activity. A statistical census of employment is the backbone of this inquiry for the reactions of Venice to a threatened commerce can best be revealed by measuring the changing allocation of labor. In this fashion one may study structural change in the economy of seventeenth-century Venice in much the same fashion as change of a more general nature in a modern economy might be analysed.

What emerges is not a radical reinterpretation of Venetian history so much as a confirmation of what many scholars have begun to suspect already: that the catch-all phrase, "the decline of Venice," embodies a myth.

I am indebted to the U. S. Government Fulbright-Hays Program and the Kent Fellowship Program of the Danforth Foundation for generously providing me with the resources to conduct two years of uninterrupted research in Venice and the United States.

Professor James C. Davis introduced me to the study of Venetian history, and from the very onset of my interest in this subject I have benefited from his constant advice and criticism.

I am particularly grateful also to Professor Martin Wolfe for his advice and encouragement throughout the course of this project.

Professors William G. Whitney, Richard A. Easterlin, and Stefano

PREFACE

Fenoaltea of the Department of Economics of the University of Pennsylvania were kind enough to read parts of the manuscript and offer valuable suggestions. Generous criticism from Mrs. Florence Edler de Roover, Professor William Bouwsma, and Mrs. Madeleine R. Gleason inspired many late revisions of the text.

It was Professor Frederic C. Lane who directed me to guild census materials in Venice which ultimately led to the exploration of the Naval Personnel Administration archive (*Milizia da Mar*). This repository has provided the most fruitful body of data on the labor force of Venice. For this and countless other kindnesses I am deeply grateful.

The late Professor Raymond de Roover was an unflagging source of guidance to me ever since my introduction to economic history at his hand. His untimely death in 1972 deprived me of the long-awaited chance to express publicly my thanks to him, and for me this is the most bitter disappointment of the project.

I thank the staff of the Archivio di Stato di Venezia for extending to me their traditional combination of helpful assistance and goodwill.

CONTENTS

TABLES

FIGURES

Industry and Economic Decline in Seventeenth-Century Venice

1

Introduction

Decadenza is a word with which historians have, without hesitation, explained away the late history of the city of Venice. Nineteenth-century authors, mindful of her reputation as a city of license and prideful of the high morals of their own civilization, called the fall of the Serenissima an example of the wages of sin. They linked the decay of maritime energy and the shrinkage of sovereignty that befell Venice to moral decay, debauchery, and ennui. Historians in a recent and less self-righteous era have been more methodical in seeking out the causes of Venice's fall from her place in history, but they have neglected to re-examine the old criteria of decline. Consequently, the prejudices of moralistic forebears survive to some degree in modern studies. Loss of status, shrinkage of empire, and forfeiture of hegemony in trade are still the main elements of the current formula for evaluating economic failure, at least in Venice.

But what do these conditions measure? That France and Holland were gaining ground and Venice losing? That England's sphere of influence was enlarging at Venetian expense? Clearly these assessments of *relative* decline are impressionistic at best. *Status, empire,* and *hegemony* are words that say nothing about the support of the population of Venice, the ultimate and absolute consequence of that city's economic change. We do not measure modern economic growth in this way, evaluating progress on a comparative basis. Today especially, in an age when the realization is growing that world leadership is no synonym for harmony and well-being, this formula is in need of a new assessment.

By the end of the seventeenth century French industry had surpassed Venetian industry in productivity and Dutch and English shipping had wrested control of Mediterranean trade from the Rialto market. This is well known. But the main question is: Was Venice worse off?

The historiography of the decline of Venice is a tale in itself. In the past, the main focus was on the question: "When did it happen?" Earliest examinations of the issue associated the beginnings of the commercial downfall of Venice with the conquest of Constantinople and the interruption of the routes of Oriental trade by the Ottoman Turks in the mid-fifteenth century.[1] An important revision was made by A. H. Lybyer in 1915. He argued that effective disruption of Venetian trade did not take place until the beginning of the sixteenth century when the Portuguese, using the Cape route to the Indies, checked the flow of spices across the Levant, attacking the foundation of Venice's most profitable trade.[2] Two decades later, this argument was in turn refuted by Frederic C. Lane who demonstrated that the Portuguese derived no real economic advantage from the new trade route, and that the short-term interruption of pepper flows in the East was merely the result of short-lived artificial obstacles posed by the Portuguese.[3] Lane further showed that previous historical assessments of Venice's carrying trade were mistakenly depressed because they overlooked the replacement of galleys by round ships in Venetian fleets during the sixteenth century. Actually the volume of trade did not fall until the very end of the sixteenth century, and thus the date of the commercial decline of Venice was driven into the seventeenth century. Following Lane, other students of the problem have authoritatively established this as the period when Venice lost her commercial hegemony in Europe.[4]

---

1. See, for example, W. Heyd, *Histoire du commerce du Levant au moyen-age* (Leipzig, 1885-1886).

2. A. H. Lybyer, "The Ottoman Turks and the Routes of Oriental Trade," *English Historical Review,* 30 (1915), 577-588.

3. Frederic C. Lane, "Venetian Shipping during the Commercial Revolution," *American Historical Review,* 38 (1933), 219-239; and "The Mediterranean Spice Trade: Further Evidence of its Revival in the Sixteenth Century," *ibid.,* 45 (1940), 581-590. Both articles are reprinted in *Venice and History: The Collected Papers of Frederic C. Lane* (Baltimore, 1966), and also in Brian Pullan, ed., *Crisis and Change in the Venetian Economy in the Sixteenth and Seventeenth Centuries* (London, 1968). My references are to this useful collection, hereafter cited as *"C & C."*

4. See Lane, "Mediterranean Spice Trade," *C & C,* p. 38; Domenico Sella, "Crisis and Transformation in Venetian Trade," *C & C,* p. 94; and Gino Luzzatto, "La decadenza di Venezia dopo le scoperte geografiche nella tradizione e nella realtà," *Archivio Veneto,* 5th ser. 54 (1954), 162-181.

Venice is hardly a remote island, in a geographic sense, and yet she maintained few ties with other Italian states. Her insularity and the independence of her religious and governmental traditions had long been cultivated. But because the geographic and economic unity of the Mediterranean region cannot be ignored, it would be an error to treat the story of the Venetian economy in isolation. It was the genius of Fernand Braudel that brought into focus a confluence of economic factors that began to adversely affect the entire Mediterranean community during the late sixteenth century.[5] Carlo Cipolla continued this line of inquiry into the seventeenth century showing the collective difficulty of producers of the Italian peninsula in competition with the expanding Atlantic community.[6]

Another major step was taken by Domenico Sella who first explained the importance of the export industry to the economic fortunes of Venice. When Venice was in her prime as an entrepôt, much of the merchandise she sold to her customers in the Levant and in Europe was of her own manufacture. Sella demonstrated that in the seventeenth century the failures in trade and in productivity were interrelated.[7]

Summarizing the results of a half-century of debate, Brian Pullan states,

Research in the economic history of Venice over the past thirty or forty years has shifted the period of decisive decline forward from the early sixteenth to the early seventeenth century. The Portuguese did not finally destroy the prosperity of Venice: the credit or blame for this must lie with the northwestern maritime nations of England and the United Provinces, with Amsterdam and London rather than with Lisbon and Antwerp.[8]

This is the current state of our understanding of the economic history of Venice in its most crucial period. But Pullan writes of the destruction of the prosperity of Venice. Where is the evidence of that?

---

5. Fernand Braudel, *La Méditerranée et le monde méditerranéan à l'époque de Philippe II,* 2d ed. (2 vols., Paris, 1966).
6. Carlo M. Cipolla, "The Economic Decline of Italy," *C & C,* pp. 127-145.
7. Domenico Sella, *Commerci e industrie a Venezia nel secolo XVII* (Venice-Rome, 1961).
8. Pullan, *C & C,* Introduction, p. 20.

INTRODUCTION

The assumption that has uniformly colored the study of this problem is that the loss of hegemony necessarily implies loss of prosperity.

To unravel the tangle of assumptions, let us stipulate two definitions of economic decline.

(1) *Relative decline* means loss of hegemony or position with respect to other nations in the economic community. This may be accompanied by loss of the carrying trade and of port traffic, competitive failures in industry, and dissolution of formal or informal sovereignties (i.e., empire or sphere of influence). Venice—indeed the entire Mediterranean region—experienced decline relative to the North Atlantic commercial powers during the Commercial Revolution of the seventeenth century.

(2) *Absolute decline* can only mean a reduction in the capacity of an economy to support its population at a given standard of living. This capacity may correspond to net national product (or income) so long as it is understood that population must be taken into account. A static per capita national product which results from proportional falling-off in both productivity and population must not be confused with mere economic stability; it is surely symptomatic of diminishing capacity to sustain economic support. What this means is that for absolute decline to occur, (a) the standard of living must fall; or (b) the size of the population must fall; or (c) both (a) and (b) must happen together. These failures, if they are to qualify as decline, cannot be temporary or short-run events. Relative and absolute decline can conceivably happen together (as in the case of the Roman Empire) but one may also occur without the other.

One difference between relative and absolute decline is that absolute decline compares economic activity in a region with past performance, while relative decline involves comparisons with other regions. Citizens of early modern Venice—or any threatened country for that matter—may have been more sensitive to relative changes (the fall of their national economy in relation to others) than to absolute decline (awareness of which requires some intimacy with the past). For this reason written records relate primarily to manifestations of relative decline and distort the historian's perspective. Loss of empire is a more palpable blow than a steady erosion of the real wage.

Economic historians sometimes aver that by antithesis the study of economic growth includes economic decline, yet there exists generally an unwillingness to deal with both growth and decline in a similar fashion. Growth is measured in terms of productivity or per capita real income. Comparison is by time series. But when decline is the subject the treatment often changes. Loss of status, commercial defeat, and other matters rather more psychological than economic become paramount.[9] This approach is not unprofitable but neither is it comprehensive. Absolute decline is measured by more fundamental considerations: population, productivity, and the standard of living, each of which we shall address in investigating the "decline of Venice."

The chapters that follow deal with the story of Venetian industry during the years of challenge in the seventeenth century. They represent an attempt to see beneath the individual fortunes of the firms by examining the common factors that ultimately control the productive capability of the economy. Foremost among these fundamentals is the labor force: its size, organization, and allocation among the sectors of the economy. Labor was the most important factor of production in early modern manufacturing, and changes in employment patterns reveal the changing economic structure of the city. The construction of an employment census from guild conscription records is the device I have used to measure structural shifts (chapter 3). Attention has been given as well to the application of capital in Venetian industrial processes and to the effects of the economic policies of the state. But capital was a distinctly minor factor of production in the static technology of early modern industry, and although the government's policies had great impact upon costs, movements of the work-force, above all, caused the basic changes in the economy.

This new look at the Venetian economy in the seventeenth century has produced some surprising results. It has demonstrated that, in an absolute sense, the economy of the city did not decline. The level of Venetian participation in international commerce did tumble. The

---

9. Carlo Cipolla prefers economic decline to mean "a loss of pre-eminence," in *The Economic Decline of Empires* (London, 1970), pp. 1-2. The distinction between absolute and relative decline has been made implicitly in Brian Pullan, *Rich and Poor in Renaissance Venice; The Social Institutions of a Catholic State, to 1620* (Cambridge, Mass., 1971), and Ernesto Sestan, "La politica veneziana del seicento," in *La civiltà veneziana nell'età barocca* (Venice, 1959), pp. 37-45.

output of the major industries did fall off. Yet, by adjustment of employment away from export industries into occupations which serviced the domestic market, no appreciable loss in population or in living standard was sustained.

This remarkable adjustment to *relative* decline bespeaks greater flexibility than we generally suppose is possible in an economy where guilds control the organization of labor. Guilds have typically been represented as agencies of rigidity and conservatism. In Venice at least, this was not the case. Alterations in the basic nature of guilds during the years of crisis facilitated shifts in the allocation of labor without encumbrance. Moreover, guilds did not promote stagnation in technology. Pressure against innovation came largely from the government. A Senate of nobles, long bereft of their role in the commercial destiny of the city, was the most vigorous opponent of innovation in methods of production and marketing. Fearful of compromising the Venetian reputation for quality merchandise, the state forbade cost-cutting measures that could have breathed life into Venice's chance for competitive survival. Because of government conservatism Venice lost her leadership to newcomers who borrowed her techniques, modified them, and used them with considerable success to oust Venice from international trade. Even the provinces of the Venetian mainland (terraferma) grew at Venice's expense, for they were not subject to the industrial regulations which stifled innovation in the island industries.

A Survey of Venetian Industries

At one time, Venice was the greatest industrial power in Europe. The cinquecento was the heyday of Venetian manufacturing. It would be difficult to overestimate the power and diversity of the Venetian manufacturing sector, especially in comparison to other European states. Of all sixteenth-century European manufactured goods, only a few were made in a way that could be called "industrial" in the modern sense—employing considerable capital equipment, factory-type production, and division of labor. Naval construction, textile manufacture, glassmaking, and some chemical and metallurgical industries could qualify. Venice was a world leader in every one.

One of the earliest and greatest of Venetian industrial products was textiles. The manufacture of woolens had undoubtedly been established in Venice since the end of the thirteenth century,[10] and the city's reputation for making the finest quality of woolen fabrics was international. But the period of industrial growth in the sixteenth century witnessed an unprecedented expansion in this area, from an annual output of about 2,000 pieces of cloth early in the 1500's to an approximate average of 20,000 pieces during the last third of the century.[11] The manufacture of silk cloth, introduced to Venice—so tradition says—in the thirteenth century by families from Lucca,[12] had become one of the largest and most profitable industries in Venice, employing over 2,100 guild members and 2,000 looms at the end of the sixteenth century.[13] Other smaller, important branches of the textile industry were cotton, linen, and fustian and canvas making.

Older even than the manufacture of textiles in Venice was the art of glassmaking which moved to the island of Murano in the late thirteenth century but which antedated that by at least a century, probably more, in Venice.[14] Venice's reputation for glassmaking was foremost in Europe, again because of a long-standing tradition of high quality and because of the unique colors that the masters of Murano managed to achieve. An infinite variety of glassware—including specialties such as stemware, bottles, ornamental serving pieces, glass beads, artificial pearls and jewels, scientific instruments, plate, rosary beads, and mirrors—was made in Murano and sold world-wide. During the sixteenth-century boom years no industry enjoyed greater growth than mirrormaking. Venice was at this time the only place in Europe where a first-class mirror could be bought—a century before the French competition fostered by Colbert began to cut into the monopoly. We have no statistics on glass production to tell whether the entire industry shared in the sixteenth-century expansion, but glass products, especially beads and glass pearls, appear in quantity in cargo lists of the period.[15]

---

10. Gino Luzzatto, *Storia economica di Venezia dall'XI al XVI secolo* (Venice, 1961), p. 69.

11. Sella, *Commerci*, App. E, pp. 117-118.

12. Luzzato (*Storia,* p. 70) says that silkworking in Venice preceded the immigration.

13. See below, table 3.10, and Sella, "Crisis and Transformation," *C & C,* p. 90.

14. Luzzatto, *Storia,* p. 68; Astone Gasparetto, *Il vetro di Murano dalle origini ad oggi* (Venice, 1958), p. 49.

15. For examples of sixteenth-century cargo lists see Marino Sanuto, *I Diarii* (58 vols., Venice, 1879-1903), III, 1187-1189; IX, 536-537; XII, 77-78; XL, 176-177. All lists contain boxes of crystal or glass beads or rosaries. The citations are given in Lane, "Mediterranean Spice Trade," p. 48.

INTRODUCTION

Of all her industrial specialties, shipbuilding was the most critical for Venice. For centuries the viability of the trading economy as well as the military power of Venice depended on her capacity to launch superior sailing vessels. From the time of its foundation in the early twelfth century, the state shipyard—the *arsenale*—was the site of the most advanced technology in Europe. Aside from the arsenal, many private shipyards or *squeri* contributed to the Venetian trading fleet. To summarize briefly the condition of shipbuilding in the sixteenth century is a difficult task. Activity in the arsenal was unstable, fluctuating with the military requirements of the moment. Employment in the arsenal and ship construction were both at their peaks between 1534 and 1574, but soon thereafter, shortages of timber drove the industry into permanent decline. By 1606 more than half the fleet was of foreign manufacture.[16]

The production of luxury merchandise for export had long been a mainstay of Venetian trade. For many of these products the element of superior quality was their distinctive coloration. Venice had, in a certain sense, a monopoly on color, for the secret and exclusive dyes and color-properties of many of her luxury items made their reputation unique in the world. Such was the case with glass, and also with silk and wool fabrics. The finest of these cloths were dyed by secret process in scarlets and crimsons made from fabulously expensive imported dyestuffs. The chemical industry of the city was one of its most important commercial assets for not only did it supply materials to domestic industries but it also produced a variety of processed dyestuffs, paints and other chemicals for export. Among the chemical industries were two more Venetian luxury specialties: sugar refining and soapmaking. Venice was established as one of Europe's key refinery cities and distribution centers for sugar as early as the fifteenth century.[17] Many pounds of sugar came to Venice prerefined at the site of the cane fields, but much processing was also done on a small scale in the city by members of the spicers' guild who specialized in confectionery articles. The manufacture of soaps from imported soda ash, quicklime, and olive oil—dating back to at least

16. Frederic C. Lane, *Navires et constructeurs à Venise pendant la Renaissance* (Paris, 1965), pp. 102, 138; Lane, "Venetian Shipping," pp. 38-43.
17. Sella, *Commerci,* p. 4; Luzzatto, *Storia,* p. 71.

the fourteenth century in Venice—became one of the city's more lucrative export industries. It was closely regulated by the government and went largely unchallenged by foreign competition until the seventeenth century.

The youngest industry to grow in the fertile medium of the sixteenth-century expansion was printing, which had been carried by Germans to Venice in the late fifteenth century. The heyday of the Venetian press followed the turn of the century, and Venice immediately became the center of the world book trade under the leadership of the great printing houses like the Giunta and the house of Aldus.

The many guilds of the leather industry (there were about seven) worked leather for both domestic and export use. The butchers supplied hides to tanners, whose product went to the various guilds of shoemakers. Finer imported skins were traded by leather merchants and put out to processors and finishers. The most exacting of the leather crafts was leather engraving and gilding. Workers at this trade were members of the guild of artists.

Other more minor manufactures whose products found their way into Venetian ships bound for every European port were waxworking (candle making), goldworking and jewelry making, wood and bone carving, coopering, and the making of trimmings (ribbons, fringes, etc.). Although industries serving only the domestic market were insignificant by comparison, there were noteworthy ones, among them distilling, woodworking (furniture and framing), metalworking, and various types of food processing.

This brief catalogue of enterprises active in the city of Venice before the beginning of the crisis of the seventeenth century is impressive testimony to the sophistication of the Venetian industrial sector. The English industries, which were subject during the years 1540-1640 to the technological change called by John U. Nef the "first industrial revolution," seem almost primitive in contrast to the industrial panorama of Venice.[18] A certain number of the "new" industries appearing on the English scene—large scale founding, metallurgical

---

18. John U. Nef, "The Progress of Technology and the Growth of Large-Scale Industry in Great Britain, 1540-1640," *Economic History Review,* 5 (1934), 3-24. Nef's point, of course, was that the technology of English industry was changing, not that industry was particularly advanced or diverse.

industries and sugar refining—were old and established Venetian (and mainland) specialties. The entire industrial complex of the British Isles during the sixteenth century was much less advanced than that of Venice alone. English industry was only just beginning to service an international trade whereas Venice had been at it for centuries.

As the sixteenth century ended, the Venetian expansion slowed and the commercial combat with the North Atlantic nations intensified. The industries of Venice found themselves faced with contracting quantity demand as the new competitors, selling similar merchandise at greatly reduced prices, went about winning her old markets. In Constantinople, a market that was at one time Venice's alone, the Venetian share of the trade in the 1630's was only about a quarter of the total while England, with more than 40 percent, was the new leader.[19] Venice's German market was cut away by the Flemings, English, and French who with their newfound supremacy in the carrying trade brought Eastern goods directly from the Levant to the German fairs.[20]

Venice, of course, was suffering a fate common to all the corners of the industrial quadrilateral: Genoa, Milan, and Florence, as well as Venice herself. These territories all enjoyed the bountiful middle years of the sixteenth century, only later to be threatened on every side. Well before the turn of the century a flood of northern-made textiles, the sayettes of Flanders and the kerseys of England, had seemed about to submerge the Mediterranean market.[21] Florence tried to match the cheap, light northern fabrics with her local country woolens but the city was long past her industrial prime. Venice hung on and in fact did well, for her products were a cut above the competition. But the

---

19. This estimate comes from a litigation among the mercantile communities in Constantinople that was resolved by contributions proportional to the "capital" employed in trade there over three years. The final distribution was of eight parts: " . . . three to the English, two to the French, two to the Venetians, and one half to the Flemings, the remaining half being divided into eight portions, three to England, two each to Venice and Flanders and one to France . . . " According to this division Venice was left with only a quarter of the Constantinople trade, surpassed by England's forty percent. *Calendar of State Papers and Manuscripts Relating to English Affairs, Existing in the Archives and Collections of Venice, and in Other Libraries of Northern Italy,* ed. Rawdon Brown et al. (London, 1864-1895), vol. 23, nos. 310 and 320, June 23 and July 15, 1634, pp. 236-237, 246.

20. Sella, "Crisis and Transformation," p. 94.

21. Braudel, *La Méditerranée,* I, 354-361, 397, 424, 559-562.

kerseys and sayettes were only a first blow—they never passed as substitutes for first-quality Mediterranean city-made cloth. It was only in the early seventeenth century that the new fully-finished English fabrics—blatant imitations of Venetian woolens—began to drive the home products even from the southern European market.[22]

Industry in northern Italy generally was staggered by new competition at this time. In Milan and neighboring Brescia the manufacture of arms and other metalcrafts suffered, and in Genoa what artisan production remained was slowly being lost.[23] Farther afield, in the great Mediterranean empires of Habsburg Spain and Ottoman Turkey the stagnation which set in developed into absolute decline with failing productivity of the soil and of urban industry, and with falling population levels.[24]

There were bright spots in the southern emporium but they owed their brief luminescence to the favor of the northern commercial powers. It is noteworthy that the two minor ports of Leghorn and Ancona began a flourishing trade in the seventeenth century as a result of the purposeful diversion of shipping away from older ports by the English, Dutch, and French. The motive was to escape high customs duties and to circumvent Venetian and other Mediterranean intermediaries (merchants, brokers, transshippers) in order to make direct contact with the Turkish and Balkan markets. Leghorn became a virtual English colony and Ancona was the preferred spot for trading with Greeks and Dalmatians in cotton, wax, wool, hides, but mostly in wool and silk cloths.[25] Although Ancona and Leghorn each had certain minor advantages in location, the patronage they received was due largely to the commercial contest waged by the northerners against Venice.

22. See Ralph Davis, "England and the Mediterranean, 1570-1670," in F. J. Fisher, ed., *Essays in the Economic and Social History of Tudor and Stuart England* (Cambridge, 1961), p. 120, and Barry Supple, *Commercial Crisis and Change in England 1600-1642* (Cambridge, 1964), pp. 147-152.

23. Braudel, *La Méditerranée,* I, 395-396.

24. See Cipolla, *Economic Decline of Empires,* pp. 121-234.

25. On the new trade of Ancona, see Archivio di Stato di Venezia (henceforth A.S.V.), *Senato, Deliberazioni, Rettori,* filza 5, *Decreto* of Sept. 10, 1633 and attached memorandum (*scrittura*) of Sept. 2, 1633, by the *Cinque Savi alla Mercanzia*; also *Cal. S. P. Ven.,* IX, no. 1119, Jan. 15, 1602, *m.v.* [i.e., Venetian-style dating]. On Leghorn, see *ibid.,* XXI, no. 55, Mar. 31, 1628.

INTRODUCTION

The new competitors from the north, practicing the tenets of mercantilism, force-fed new home industries to give independence from imports and to expand sales abroad. Textile manufacture, glassmaking, shipbuilding, and printing grew in northern Europe and robbed Venice of the market for industrial products. Indeed, industrial competition was the chief cause of Venice's commercial failure—more important even than the navigational aspects of the "Commercial Revolution," the change in European market structure away from the Mediterranean to the North Atlantic trade. The timing of events suggests this. The Commercial Revolution was a sixteenth-century phenomenon; yet when Antwerp was at the apex of her newfound commercial leadership, Venetian trade was still active and profitable. In fact, when the commercial defeat of Venice was accomplished, during the first third of the seventeenth century, it was done largely in Venice's own territory, the Mediterranean. In the Levant, for example, Venetian cloths were displaced by English and Dutch cheap fabrics. Ultimately, the major effect of the Commercial Revolution on Venetian industry was that potential competitors achieved the capacity to bypass Venice and her services entirely.

Had Venice but maintained the initiative in manufacturing, her products could have sold in the new continental markets as well as they had in the days when customers came to Venice's door. But during the seventeenth century she lost her industrial supremacy. Indeed, for Venice the most unfortunate aspect of the growth of the North Atlantic powers was their success as industrial competitors, not their capture of the carrying trade. The benefits of trade for Venice could only diminish as she was left with less and less to sell.[26]

One cannot deny that old market relationships had given way to new ones or reject the obvious fact that advantages of location such as Venice enjoyed will erode with time. Venice was painfully subject to

---

26. The commercial failure and the industrial failure of Venice cannot be considered identical or completely interrelated phenomena. It is likely that the port of Venice would inevitably have been passed over as Europe turned westward to the Atlantic trade. When this might have happened in the absence of northern competitive incursions in the Mediterranean is entirely a matter for conjecture. The decline of Venice's function as entrepôt did not cause industrial failure. A more complex set of factors created impediments to the marketing of manufactured goods for Venice (chap. 5)—factors which do not suggest that industrial decline was merely a side-effect of the diminished importance of the port.

these trends. But the immediate causes of the relative decline in Venetian economic power lie elsewhere.

It is therefore unwise to be content with an explanation of Venice's crisis that would be based solely on the growth of new European markets or on changing patterns of trade.

To understand fully the complexity of circumstances that caused commercial and industrial collapse of Venice but left her population and standard of living intact is in itself a challenge. We must direct our attention to labor and capital in Venetian production, and to the responses of the economy in general to the commercial reverses of the seventeenth century.

2

The Labor Force of Venice in the Seventeenth Century

The Guild Organization of the Labor Force*

By the seventeenth century the organization of the Venetian labor force into *arti* or guilds was an institution more than three hundred years old. The Venetian arti shared characteristics with their counterparts in other European cities to make them correspond well to the archetypal European guild, typically combining economic, religious, and confraternal functions.

The Venetian guilds were the result of an amalgamation of two institutions distinct in purpose and origin. The earlier was the *scuola,* a society of devotion. The *scuola* existed for common worship, assistance, and banqueting. The second was the *arte,* an association for maintaining craft discipline, for regulating the professional activity of the workers and settling minor disputes among them, and for insuring the performance of the labor which was owed to the Doge or commune. The institution of the *arti* had been effected by the state in order that the craftsmen might all be supervised by the Justices who were appointed by the state for that purpose. The *scuole* had existed long before as societies of devotion. But when the *arti* were created the two institutions became fused.[1]

This amalgamation was complete by the end of the thirteenth century.

---

* A glossary of the principal Venetian guilds is given in Appendix I.
1. Frederic C. Lane, *Venetian Ships and Shipbuilders of the Renaissance* (Baltimore, 1934), p. 72. In the revised edition of this work previously cited (*Navires et constructeurs*), p. 68.

The guilds exercised surveillance over the entry and progress of workers into their labor pools, attended to the business of regulating quality control, and attempted by the exercise of monopoly power to foster the economic well-being of the membership.

Individual guilds owed their particular characteristics to the technological organization of production in the respective professions. In most uncomplicated occupations the guild encompassed the entire work force of the craft. For those industries whose production process was of sufficient complexity to require marked division of labor, independent guilds existed for the workers in each separate process. There were guilds of independent petty artisans and guilds of industrial magnates. In these respects the Venetian arti follow the general European pattern. But the remarkable thing about the Venetian system is that it far outlived its counterparts in other cities—persisting without drastic change for over five centuries and surviving even the venerable Republic itself by a few years.

One important element in the guild system of Venice, uncommon elsewhere, was the overriding presence of the government in guild affairs, for the state was determined to control every aspect of production so as to insure the financial well-being of the city. Among the economic functions of each arte, therefore, was its critical role as spokesman of the industry before the government.

Guilds had no governing power in Venice, unlike in Florence. There was no room for legislative or administrative representation of labor in the aristocratic government. The guilds rarely, if ever, acted in concert. This is not to say, however, that there was no communication of information and demands for action between the individual arti and the state. Such communication was a constant feature of any guild's activity. Larger and wealthier arti wielded strong suasive power too, but ultimately more important from the standpoint of the viability of the guild system was the right of every guild to present grievances and request redress from many receptive government agencies. These procedures were invoked continuously, and the records of the government indicate a high degree of responsiveness. The very fact that there is no incidence of any major upheaval by workers suggests that this system of government by appeal was successful.[2]

---

2. This record of tranquility might possibly have indicated a high degree of success in the art of suppression. But the large body of documents that record countless minor

THE LABOR FORCE OF VENICE

Considering the capacity of the industrial sector to respond to change—an essential quality of the seventeenth century in Venice—the most significant element of the organization of production was the widespread use of controlled piecerates. The intended effect of the piecerate system was to buffer the cost of labor, the major factor of production, against the short-term vagaries of a free labor market and place it as much as possible under government control. Rates, or *mercedi,* were fixed by the government overseer agency, or even legislated by the Senate, and were enforced with sufficient rigor that the cost of production attributable to labor would in no way fluctuate with the supply of labor or with the demand for the final product.[3] In those industries where intermediate processes were divided among several guilds, all workers were paid at a piecework rate. Fees were changed only by authority of the state—specifically the agency that governed the industry—and after litigation between the manufacturing guilds who were the recipients of piecerates and the merchant guilds who were the payers. Often, when the direction of changes in the pay rate ran contrary to actual labor market circumstances, the method had adverse results. "We impoverished and miserable workers of the guild of *fustagneri* have suffered as much as we can without having the chance to shed these, our wretched tears before the singular justice of [you] the most illustrious *Provveditori alla Giustizia Vecchia.* "[4] So begins the appeal of the fustian weavers whose craft is reduced to such a state in 1621 that the members are almost at the point of abandoning home and children. For many years, they say, their piecerates have remained unchanged while expenses continued to rise. The suit was successful: the weavers were permitted to raise their

conflicts, adequately resolved by appeal to administrative or judicial agencies of the government, suggests otherwise. Principal state agencies dealing in guild matters were the *Giustizia Vecchia, Cinque Savi alla Mercanzia, Provveditori di Comun*, and *Collegio alle Arti.* The Giustizia Vecchia was the major regulatory agency and judicial body for guild matters; the Cinque Savi alla Mercanzia or "Board of Trade" was the overseer of general economic issues, involving itself in guild business when the commercial well-being of the city was at stake; the Provveditori di Comun, among a variety of responsibilities, managed major industries (wool and silk cloth manufacture); the Collegio alle Arti was composed of these three magistracies meeting in joint session to adjudicate inter-guild disputes and to alter guild statutes.

3. The appropriate commission was in most cases the Giustizia Vecchia. However, the wool and silk industries and the state shipyard, the Arsenale, were under the special jurisdiction of other agencies.

4. A.S.V., *Giustizia Vecchia,* b. 223, reg. 291, pp. 21-23, Nov. 4, 1621.

fees by about 2 lire for each piece of cloth woven, and the *bombaseri,* the fustian and cotton cloth merchants, were obliged to buy cloth at the new price.[5] Nine months later the weavers were back before the Giustizia Vecchia: "We are mindful of the great error that we the fustian weavers have committed before the merchants regarding the manufacture of cloth and canvas . . . [charging] a greater price than the cloth is worth because the merchant says he cannot afford to have cloth woven at that price, calling himself unable to support the price conceded by the *Collegietto* . . . "[6] After the old prices had been boosted by 2 lire by the decision of the *Collegio alle Arti,* the merchants either chose or had been forced to curtail production and so the issue had come back to 'court' so that the humiliated weavers could apply for a return to the old schedule of prices.

A similar plaint in 1586 from the woolworkers guild, the *laneri,* demonstrates the difficulties of the mercede system in inflationary times.

The extreme and incredible poverty and misery of us unfortunate wool beaters, carders and combers is such that we are compelled to seek shelter from our hunger, and that of our families who are starving, by appearing before Your Excellencies, the *Cinque Savi* and *Provveditori di Comun,* confident of obtaining your justice and compassion like that just relief that this Serene Republic has granted to other workers in the woolen industry. Your Excellencies know that for some years the things needed to live and dress and to rent a house are growing such that prices have doubled. So to continue with our miserable lives, double the expenditure is necessary, and further, the tools and instruments of our trade have likewise doubled in price in such a way that the combs used to work the warp threads which used to cost about 12 lire sold for 24 to 30 lire, and to adjust the teeth which must be done at least monthly used to cost 1 soldo—now one must spend 2½ soldi each, and to remake them instead of the former 40 soldi now one must pay 4 lire. Similarly the cards used for working the weft wool

---

5. It appears that in some cases mercedi were other than simple piecerates. The cotton merchants were putting-out entrepreneurs for they procured raw materials and put them in the hands of the clothworkers and weavers, shepherding the cloth through various stages of production. In the cotton-fustian-canvas industry, transactions between merchants and craftsmen were considered sales, however, and the amount for which the finished cloth was returned to the merchant was a fixed price, not technically either a wage or a piecerate.

6. A.S.V., *Giustizia Vecchia,* b. 223, reg. 291, pp. 68-69, July 3, 1622.

THE LABOR FORCE OF VENICE

for which one used to pay 36 to 38 soldi now cost 66 to 78 soldi, and these are good only for about a month, often less. And the beating rods which once sold for 50 soldi per hundred now cost 6 lire per hundred. To add to our woes the merchants have recently required the practice of working the wool to such fineness and with such caution that the job which formerly took a day now with the greatest effort takes two. So expenses to live, dress, pay rent, and supply ourselves with tools have doubled and tripled and our effort and loss of time has grown, but in no way have our own fees increased, being limited without any raises, except when some merchant seeing our misery and the merits of our labors and the benefits he receives from them gives something over and above this limit, but for the most part they refuse to give this extra measure, the price of our blood and toil . . . We are sure that in the same manner that this Illustrious Dominion has granted its justice to the weavers, shearers and other woolen workers by raising their *mercedi,* applying the same charity and justice you will relieve our aforementioned urgent and true travail and grant the just request which we have come to make . . . Offering to justify the above-mentioned things so that when it seems certain to Your Excellencies that the things we have said are true, we further humbly recommend to Your Excellencies the prices we ask below.[7]

The *gastaldo,* the chief guild officer, submitted the petition of his woolworkers to the government agencies mentioned in the document. Exactly one month later the wool merchants presented their rebuttal but the fee hike was sanctioned over their objections. Within two years the increase was revoked and woolworkers' mercedi in 1588 were back at the old level.[8] The extended description of the doubling of the cost of living in this document gives weight to the widely held belief that in Italy the most severe period of the long-term inflation known as the "price revolution" occurred during the last quarter of the sixteenth century.[9]

By contrast, a similar fee dispute between wool weavers and merchants in 1603 produced this complaint: "It has been a particular misfortune of the vitally important wool trade that in these times, when

7. Museo Civico Corret (hereafter referred to as "Correr"), *Mariegola Lanificio,* Dec. 3, 1586. In the document a list of services follows, together with newly proposed piecerates.

8. Biblioteca Marciana, Venice (hereafter referred to as "Bibl. Marc."), *Parti Veneziani* (131.D. 158), "Regolazione dell'Arte della Lana di Questa Città e Terraferma fatta dalli Clarissimi Sigri Cinque Savi sopra la mercantia, e Provveditori di Commun, Collegio a cio deputato," Mar. 27, 1588.

9. See Braudel, *La Méditerranee,* I, 468; Fernand Braudel and Frank Spooner,

the worker is probably better off than he ever has been, and when the bread from which the poor man feeds is cheaper than it has been for many years, votes should have tied over the most unjust request of the weavers for a pay increase, which has gravely affected this trade."[10] Piecerates in other industries were adjusted on numerous occasions throughout the seventeenth century, usually in keeping with a general slow rise in the money wage. For the industries most critical to the city's economy, such as wool, silk, dyeing, and shipbuilding, this was accomplished as part of revisions in industrial regulations decreed by the Senate. But the procedure was still the same: litigation between payer and payee before lower authorities whose recommendations were then enacted into law. By controlling costs in this manner the government, in keeping with its policy of overseeing the economy, hoped to preclude 'unnecessary' rises in costs or, in the opposite event, diminution of the real wage below the subsistence level.

The emerging economic powers had launched successful assaults on the commercial and industrial primacy of Venice in the Mediterranean. The result was a general shrinking of the effective demand for Venetian industrial products and a corresponding contraction in the demand for industrial labor. While the major objective of the Venetian guilds was, as always, to try to insure the well-being of their members by controlling production, the task became more difficult because of the general economic misfortunes that befell the city. The organizational result of this sustained economic trauma was the partial collapse of the arti themselves involving a long-term exodus of workers from the city, debilitation of many guilds and consolidation of weak guilds into large agglomerates,[11] and the partial but signifi-

---

"Prices in Europe from 1450 to 1750," *Cambridge Economic History of Europe,* IV (Cambridge, 1967), 404; Amintore Fanfani, *Storia del lavoro in Italia dalla fine del secolo XV agli inizi del XVIII* (Milan, 1943), p. 44.

10. Trans. by Pullan (*C & C,* p. 14), from A.S.V., *Senato, terra,* f. 166, Apr. 21, 1603.

On the dating of the price revolution in Venice, see Fernand Braudel, "La vita economica di Venezia nel secolo XVI," *Civiltà veneziana del Rinascimento* (Venice, 1958), pp. 92-96. Here Braudel puts the start of the inflation in Venice at 1560 although wheat prices (p. 94) do not reflect the price rise until 1590. By 1603 the price of wheat had returned to pre-inflation levels.

11. The absorption of small guilds into larger ones—a process that had begun before the years of industrial crisis—may admittedly have had administrative expediency as its chief cause. By the end of the sixteenth century the *Collegio di Milizia da Mar,* the Naval Personnel Administration, had subtended many smaller guilds under a few main

THE LABOR FORCE OF VENICE

cant abandonment of the unitary guild system.[12]

Severe decline in demand for Venetian industrial products, along with most of the city's other economic miseries, actually started in the second decade of the seventeenth century. The individual industrial guilds in their *scritture* speak invariably of the shrinkage in their numbers in relation to the days of plenty in the sixteenth century. They say that many of their remaining members, unable to find sufficient employment, are among the ranks of the poor. The guilds were so depleted of men that following the plague of 1630 the Senate nullified with a stroke all arti regulations against the entry of non-Venetians into the guilds, with the expressed purpose of replenishing the supply of labor. The opening of the arti was to last for three years and any mainlander or foreigner was permitted to exercise any craft so long as he paid the *ben entrada* (entrance fee) and *luminaria* (candle fee).[13] While recovery from the plague was rapid, employment within the major industrial guilds continued to diminish through the century. And while overall guild membership remained at a fairly constant level, lack of work in export industries forced many workers into situations where they might work only a few months during the year. Many abandoned manufacturing guilds in favor of professions where livelihood depended less on the vagaries of the export market. Migration to the terraferma and out of the Veneto altogether became sufficiently serious to debilitate many of the arti. Lack of work, the guilds explained to the government, was the cause of all these changes.

Of all the arti, the woolworkers were the most heavily affected by the fall in demand and their ranks thinned most rapidly. In 1660 the cloth shearers complained of gradual but steady reductions in membership as members left the craft and sought employment elsewhere

---

ones for the purpose of more efficient tax collection, thereby effectively unifying them. The largest of the agglomerate arti were the woolworkers (*laneri*), dry-goods retailers (*marzeri*), painters (*depentori*), and metalworkers (*fabbri*). In some cases the absorption did not go smoothly. While, for example, the coppersmiths (*caldereri*) joined the ironworkers guild during the fifteenth century, litigation about taxes and guild fees persisted between the two groups well into the next century by which time the caldereri numbered only about 15 percent of the total fabbri agglomerate (A.S.V., *Archivio degli Arti, fabbri,* b. 110, *Registro termination e sententie*).

12. By "unitary guild system" I mean that a man typically joined one guild and adopted its singular profession for the duration of his life. This was the usual case for European guild systems, Venice included, until the seventeenth century.

13. A.S.V., *Inquisitorato alle Arti,* b. 4, Nov. 18, 1631. Similar steps were taken after the 1575 plague (Brian Pullan, "Wage-Earners and the Venetian Economy, 1550-1630," *C & C,* p. 160).

because of lack of work.[14] By the end of the century they were about one-fifth of their 1660 numbers. Members had abandoned the wool guilds to become hatters, boatmen, servants, carpenters, and silk weavers.[15] Silk weavers, meanwhile, became brokers, boatmen, grain sellers, and boxmakers.[16] Other occupations favored by those who could no longer find satisfactory employment in the industries geared to the export trade were: selling and making foodstuffs, brokering and portering, retail selling, and the navy. Many workers retained membership in both the old and the newly adopted guild either in the hope of regaining their original trade, or because its seasonal nature permitted them to engage in their old craft for part of the year.

The many instances of multiple professions and the increase of the practice during the course of the century is most clearly visible in the growing number of apprenticeship contracts over the century which name *maestri* having as many as four or five separate occupations.[17] Guild rolls too list cases of double professions. In 1672 there were 145 mercers who shared occupations with other guilds such as cloth weavers, combmakers, and chemists. Even some glassworkers branched out into coopering, glovemaking, fruit and wine selling, and other vending trades.[18] A side-effect of the mixing of professions was that many guilds began to have trouble enforcing the exclusive rights to sell their wares. Coopers complained of a used-barrel market conducted by wine merchants. Mercers encroached upon the selling rights of the stationers, soapmakers, and glass blowers.[19]

---

14. A.S.V., *Milizia da Mar*, no. 722, *Scrittura cimadori*, Aug. 4, 1660.

15. A.S.V., *Provveditori di Comun*, b. 54, *Scrittura garzotti*, May 29, 1663.

16. A.S.V., *Arte della Seta*, b. 106, *fasc.* 143 *extra*, Sept. 16, 1682.

17. See A.S.V., *Giustizia Vecchia*, ser. 14, *Accordi dei Garzoni*. The incidence of maestri having many separate occupations (in the sense of guild affiliations) increases through the seventeenth century and through the eighteenth. The following contract exemplifies this trend:

Bernardo q. Giacomo da Friul d'ani 12 in circa s'acorda per Garzon con Antonio Caronello Maestre de oglio saon Biavarol Mandoler Maestre Doltiore e Salumier per ani sei . . . [A.S.V., *Giustizia Vecchia*, ser. 14, b. 124, reg. 175, p. 79, Nov. 23, 1681].

In former days Maestro Caronello would surely have had to limit himself to membership in only one of the professions mentioned in the contract. By 1681, however, the situation was such that his name could appear on all the guild rolls: the soapmakers, grainsellers, almond and dried fruit sellers, and salt-fish sellers. Perhaps he was merely a grocer in today's terms, but the combination of functions he served would have been improbable before the seventeenth-century dissolution of the unitary guild system in Venice.

18. A.S.V., *Milizia da Mar*, no. 547, fasc. *marzeri*; *ibid.*, no. 542, fasc. *cristalleri e paternostreri da vetro*.

19. A.S.V., *Giustizia Vecchia*, ser. 15, b. 131, July 1, 1643.

THE LABOR FORCE OF VENICE

The developments caused further problems for the state, which depended on the arti for taxes, particularly those levies associated with maintaining naval strength. The changes in the guild structure made the repartition and collection of the tax burden more difficult.[20] While the agglomeration of guilds and the partial abandonment of the unitary guild system are significant from the standpoint of understanding organizational changes in the guild system, they are little more than a side-issue to the major labor problems of the century: the reallocation of labor in the face of changed market demand and the debilitation of the industrial work force.

The Size of the Labor Force

The total labor force of the city of Venice neither grew nor diminished to any significant extent during the seventeenth century, nor did the number of men enrolled in the guilds, except under the short-term influences of plague and war. The general population level of the city showed some decrease from sixteenth-century levels from the turn of the century up to the decimation of the 1630 plague. Within twenty years the population had restabilized at 140,000-160,000 which may be said to represent the normal level. The protracted War of Candia (1645-1669) had no perceivable effect on total population figures, and the number of people inhabiting the city of Venice remained more or less stable from mid-century through the 1700's (table 2.1).

Table 2.1 Population of Venice

Year	Population	Year	Population
1552	158,069	1624	141,625
1555	159,467	1633	102,243
1563	168,627	1642	120,307
1581	134,871	1655	158,772
1586	148,097	1696	138,067

Sources: 1586 and 1655, Bibl. Marc., *Ital.* VII, *Cod.* 2211 (10049), p. 42 (see Appendix 2, below). For all other estimates, see Daniele Beltrami, *Storia della popolazione di Venezia dalla fine del secolo XVI alla caduta della Repubblica* (Padua, 1954), p. 59.

20. A.S.V., *Senato, terra,* filza 687, Jan. 24, 1660, *m.v.*

About 14-18 percent of the total city population, or approximately two-thirds of the work force, belong to guilds (table 2.2). The residual third of the work force includes members of certain guilds who were not listed in the conscription rolls of the *Milizia da Mar* from which this information was drawn. The other important component of the residual or non-guild work force are workers in unincorporated professions. Of the former category—the statistical omissions from the guild censuses—by far the largest single bloc of workers were the members of the fully incorporated arsenal guilds: the ship carpenters (*marangoni all'arsenale*), caulkers (*calafati*), and oarmakers (*remeri*). These defense workers were called to the arsenal daily—in time of war as well as peace—by the great bell of the city, the *Marangona,* and when needed they were obliged to serve as officers on the galleys.[21] Thus the *arsenalotti* were exempt from any consideration as conscripts or payers of conscription taxes and were therefore omitted from the guild census of the Milizia da Mar. 1500 (± 25%) is a safe estimate of the combined membership of the arsenal guilds in the sixteenth and seventeenth centuries.[22] Some 300 to 500 guildsmen who were trained as cannoneers also were exempt from conscription as oarsmen and thus not included in the guild census.

Other incorporated professions that are missing from the total membership statistic are guilds which held exemptions from conscription for various other reasons, usually because of small or temporarily depleted membership or by virtue of some permanent privilege. Wool merchants and hatters never appear on the guild lists. And in 1595 for instance, some of the other exempt guilds were: lawyers, notaries, trimmings makers, beef slaughterers, distillers, oil porters, iron sellers, glass-bead makers, dried-fish sellers, compositors, lumber merchants, and some boatmen.[23]

Then there are the sailors, about whom very little is known. They had a scuola, founded in 1573, and all ships' companies were obliged to enroll—officers and crewmen alike. At the time of the guild's formation 56 noble captains and 929 marineri were enrolled, but by the

---

21. Lane, *Venetian Ships,* pp. 185-186.
22. See Ruggiero Romano, "Economic Aspects of the Construction of Warships in Venice in the Sixteenth Century," *C & C,* pp. 71-75; Lane, *Navires,* p. 165; and Beltrami, *Storia,* p. 212.
23. A.S.V., *Senato, mar,* filza 129, Nov. 25, 1595.

24

THE LABOR FORCE OF VENICE

Table 2.2 Population and the work force

	1586-1595	1655-1660	1690-1696
A. Total population	148,097	158,772	138,067
B. Males over 18	41,742	44,257	-
C. Male nobles	2,147	1,844	-
D. Male *cittadini*	2,312	2,620	-
E. Male *popolani*	37,283	39,793	-
F. Male clergy and Jews	2,638	4,521	-
G. Eligible work force	34,645	35,272	
H. Institutionalized male poor	793	632	-
I. Work force	33,852	34,640	-
J. Guild membership	22,504	21,051	24,049
K. Residual work force	11,348	13,589	-
Percentage of population in the work force	22.9%	21.8%	-
Percentage of population in guilds subject to census	15.2%	13.3%	17.4%

Sources: for 1586 and 1655, Bibl. Marc., *Ital.* VII, *Cod.* 2211 (10049), p.42; for 1696, Beltrami, *Storia,* p.59

Notes on derivations:

B. B = C + D + F + H + I

E. E = B - (C + D)

F. For 1586: male clergy = 1,774; all Jews = 1,694; male Jews = (1,694 x .51) = 864. For 1655: male clergy = 2,135; all Jews = 4,870; male Jews = (4,870 x .49) = 2,386. Sex ratios of .51 and .49 from Beltrami, *Storia,* p. 80.

G. G = E - F

H. For 1586: total institutionalized poor = 1,555; males = (1,555 x .51) = 793. For 1655: total institutionalized poor = 1,290; males = (1,290 x.49) = 632.

I. I = G - H. The title of the category in the document corresponding to "work force" is *Artesani e Bottegeri.* The exclusion of nobles and cittadini from the work force category follows the administrative convention of the documents but does not imply that these classes did not work. Together they comprise the bulk of the professional and managerial class of the city, in government and in the private sector. Among the cittadini we find the great majority of Venice's medical doctors, lawyers, accountants, and non-noble merchants. That the term *work force* is not meant to be comprehensive of all productive citizens is signalled too by the exclusion of women, Jews, and the clergy.

J. Below, table 3.1. These are the totals of the guild censuses of the Naval Personnel Administration (*Milizia da Mar*) for the years 1595, 1660, 1690. Guild membership, therefore, refers only to those guilds subject to the

(cont.)

censuses. Exempt guilds fall into the residual work force category.

K. K = I - J. This includes those engaged in professions not incorporated into guilds as well as members of guilds which were exempt from the *Milizia da Mar* survey. See below, chap. 3.

---

end of the seventeenth century membership was down to only 17 nobles and 269 sailors.[24] There were 212 households headed by marineri in 1642 in the quarter of Castello, and probably not as many again in the rest of the city.[25] These fragments of information notwithstanding, the actual numbers and origins of sailors in early modern Venice are obscure. There is evidence that many who were driven out of other jobs for lack of work turned to the sea as a livelihood, but this still cannot account for more than a small proportion of the professional seamen who had always been one of the city's chief prides. There are indications that by the seventeenth century that pride may have been less justified than in past eras. It was the opinion of the English that the chief cause of Venice's commercial backsliding was the loss of navigational skills and the low quality of her sailors.[26] If this was accurate, it may be further indication that Venetian ships were being manned by increasing proportions of the unemployed who abandoned old occupations to become non-professional seamen. "Andato per marinaro" was a common notation on the guild rolls.

The second component of the residual work force—the unincorporated crafts—consists of the so-called street professions and the unskilled industrial work force. The former were itinerant purveyors of foods, assorted drygoods, and minor services from door to door within the city—occupations too humble to merit formal organization for the most part. *Conzalavezi* (tinkers and cat-castrators!) were members of the *arte dei fabbri,* and the guild of *pestrineri* sold milk door-to-door, but most itinerants belonged to no guild. It would be hard to imagine what the sum total of all the food peddlers, inksellers, lamp carriers, keywardens, street sweepers, and so forth might be.[27]

The last, most important, and most elusive category of unorganized workers is that of the unskilled industrial work force. Employed prin-

---

24. Mario Nani-Mocenigo, *Storia della marina veneziana da Lepanto alla caduta della Repubblica* (Rome, 1935), p. 77.

25. A.S.V., *Provveditori alla Sanità,* b. 570.

26. *Cal. S. P. Ven.,* vol. 12, no. 383, p. 249, Dec. 2, 1611.

27. For a poetic and pictorial catalog of these occupations, G. Zompini, *Le Arti che vanno per via nella città di Venezia* (Venice, 1785).

THE LABOR FORCE OF VENICE

cipally by large-scale industries—the arsenal and textiles—this group represents what must have been a fairly large but unmeasurable force of men who were employed on either a short-term or seasonal basis. It has been estimated that for every member of the major arsenal guilds there was on hand at least one unaffiliated workman.[28] There was also in the woolen industry a large force of workers who belonged to no one guild; they were used in the early stages of production—the preparation of raw wool for spinning. Although preliminary processes required little in the way of specialization or training, the trades were controlled by the three sub-guilds of the *lanificio*: the beaters, carders, and combers. In a complaint about the tax burden on its members, the laneri assert that there are 3,000 woolworkers of whom only 600 are enrolled in the guild; the rest, not being guild members, do not share the heavy financial burden placed upon the arte by the state.[29] So in this case the proportion of non-guild workers was one to four, which is much higher than that of the arsenal. On the other hand it is almost certain that the unorganized workers were employed for only part of the year, especially in the strongly seasonal textile industries.

For other textile industries the situation was similar. The only official silkworkers guilds were the throwsters, weavers, silk merchants, and gold thread makers, but none of these covered the "assembly line" workers who handled the routine jobs in the production process: those who worked the raw silk, those who steamed, boiled and wound the threads; those who assisted in the weaving process by warping the loom and adjusting the heddles and combs, and the silk cloth finishers.[30] While the spokesmen of the industry were willing to put the

28. Romano, "Economic Aspects," p. 75.

29. A.S.V., *Milizia da Mar*, no. 545, fasc. *laneri*, n.d. (probably 1597), "Una querella da presentar a la Avogaria da Comun": " . . . come nel arte nostra; si atrova da hominij tremille in circa, cio'è seicento descriti in scolla, et il resto non descriti, li quali non descriti, non sono sottoposti agravezza di sorti alcune di essa scolla . . . " From time to time a document of this nature turns up claiming that the guild *supports* many hundreds more persons than its membership, which usually means members and their families. It is therefore prudent to mention that this statement of the *laneri* does not refer to families but to woolworkers themselves, 600 in the guild, and about 2400 unaffiliated workers.

30. A.S.V., *Senato, terra*, filza 883, "Copia di scrittura presentata dalli Prov[ri] alla Seta al Mag[co] Ecc[mo] di Cinque Savij," Dec. 16, 1672; and A.S.V., *Arte della Seta*, b. 123, fasc. 394 *extra*, p. 11, n.d.:

Essendovi ancora molte altre particolari persone fuori delle sudette Arti [toschani, testori, filatogi, tentori, manganeri, battioro, filaoro] Le quali cavano il suo vivere da

number of persons supported by the manufacture of silk cloth at 40,000, or about one-third of the entire city population, a more reasonable estimate would still be double the 2,000 workers represented by the silk guilds.[31] The real misfortune of not knowing the magnitude of that part of the silk industry's work force unrepresented by the arti is that indications point to much modification in these areas of the production process over the seventeenth century. To quote Domenico Sella:

> The shift of the silk industry to new localities affected spinning to an even greater extent than weaving: the seventeenth century, in fact, witnessed the complete relocation of the making of silk thread (even in its finer variety, organzine) from the towns to the countryside. What took place then was indeed more than a mere change of location: it was also a change from hand-made to mechanical spinning thanks to the generalized adoption of the so-called "Bolognese silk mill."[32]

While Sella is speaking of northern Italy in general, his description of the decentralization of silk-thread making applies especially well to Venice, for throughout the seventeenth century the production of both silk thread and silk cloth itself was escaping the city of Venice into the terraferma. Indeed, so far as the city silk industry was concerned, the chief cause of its decline early in the seventeenth century was Veneto competition—this despite the city's control of the mainland and her occasional efforts to suppress this trend.

Two other categories within the labor force of Venice warrant at least passing mention: female labor and the poor. The role of the former group at the distaff has traditionally been emphasized in con-

---

più minimi affari, e pur non sono meno importanti, che bisogni nella medesima Arte, che sono quelle che trazzono le sette, altre che le binano per far orsogli sette da oro, et da Cuser, altre che incanano le trame e orsogli tenti, altre che construiscono li ordimenti, altre che li rimettono nelli lizzi, e pettini, altre che inviano li lazzi alli lavori in opera, si che sono numero infinito il popolo che ritraze il suo alimento dalla detta Arte della Seda.

31. The exaggerated estimate of 40,000 comes from the scrittura of Dec. 16, 1672 (above). The figure of 2,000 silk-guild members is for the year 1660 and includes the guilds of gold thread beaters, silk throwers, dyers, silkweavers, and silk merchants (see below, table 3.10).

32. Domenico Sella, "Industrial Production in Seventeenth-Century Italy: A Reappraisal," *Explorations in Entrepreneurial History,* 2nd ser., 6 (1969). 240.

THE LABOR FORCE OF VENICE

sideration of the domestic aspects of preindustrial textile production. Beltrami says: "Especially in the wool and silk guilds, some phases of the work were effected in domestic circumstances and many feminine hands, of every age, and for most of the year, were applied to the task."[33] Fanfani, in his history of Italian labor, concurs, mentioning the admission of women as journeymen and, on occasion, as masters in the guild of fustagneri and recalling the female sailmakers who were employed by the arsenal.[34] There are cases on record of female master mirrormakers[35] and even silk weavers;[36] but these are rare instances.

Female labor is acknowledged to have been an important aspect of premodern "domestic industry" in Europe. While as a generalization, there is no reason to take exception to the picture of preindustrial domestic labor, I believe it applies less to Venice than to other textile centers for, as we have mentioned, the Venetian merchants, forced to reduce costs, had turned to the mainland for threadmaking and other preliminary processes. A document of the year 1682 investigating the unique problem of a temporary labor shortage in the Venetian silk industry says that wives and daughters of maestri are an unimportant consideration because they just do household work, cleaning up and occasionally preparing bobbins or warping the looms, but the bulk of the routine work is done by the journeymen and apprentices.[37] This refers to weaving. However, preliminary processes in silkmaking—reeling, winding, throwing, and boiling silk filament—were done more by women than by men, and to the extent that these jobs remained in the city they were an important source of employment for female heads of household.[38]

For industries other than textiles, I have found few references to the employment of women though it is difficult to judge whether or not

33. Beltrami, *Storia,* p. 201.
34. Fanfani, *Storia del lavoro,* pp. 123-124.
35. A.S.V., *Giustizia Vecchia.* ser. 14, b. 119, Dec. 22, 1632.
36. *Ibid.,* Dec. 18, 1632. At the end of the eighteenth century when clothmaking was a small and unprofitable craft in Venice, women were employed in all capacities, even as weavers. In the wool industry at that time, the majority of workers were female, "substituted for purposes of economy [*femine sostituite per resparmio*]" (A.S.V., *Inquisitorato alle Arti,* b. 45, report of Andrea Tron, June 23, 1781, insert no. 6).
37. A.S.V., *Arte della Seta,* b. 106, fasc. 143 *extra,* "Informazione in materia della stretteza de Lavoranti e Garzoni accresciuta nell'arte della Testoria."
38. See, for example, Correr, *Cod. Donà dalle Rose,* b. 351, *Ristretto, Dorsoduro.* 1642 under *Arte della Seta.*

this is a fiction of documentation. There were female shopkeepers, barmaids, laundresses, and servants who were not enrolled in guilds, though their training was regarded as some sort of apprenticeship, and contracts for employment of women in such capacities are recorded in the journals of the Giustizia Vecchia. Above the rank of apprentice it is the widows of master craftsmen who are most often registered as full members of the craft guilds. The guild rolls of the Milizia da Mar do not contain many such listings, but in a city where more than one of every ten households was headed by a woman it would be imprudent to discount their presence in the work force.[39]

The final unknown quantity is the number of unemployed in seventeenth-century Venice. The document that has provided our population statistics for table 2.1 in the years 1586 and 1655 fails us here, for it lists only the beggars and poor and sick who are in some respect "official." That is to say, it probably includes only those occupying or enrolled with Venice's charitable institutions, the *ospitali, scuole* or *luoghi pii.* For the year 1586, 1,111 occupy the hospitals and 444 are listed as beggars. In 1655 there are 1,290 persons in the hospitals and no listing for the "questuanti." We can assume with security that these numbers give no indication of the real magnitude of the number of impoverished souls in the city. For purposes of comparison, the more detailed census of the year 1760 conducted by the Provveditori alla Sanità lists over 3,000 *"poveri vergognosi"* and almost 18,000 beggars in a population of virtually the same size as that of the earlier sample years.[40]

Where are the poor hidden in the seventeenth-century breakdown? Most likely in two places. First, it is probable that the majority of the poor were not subscribers to institutional charity, either of the state or of private and religious organizations and thus were not included in the census or in the total population estimates. Not knowing the source of the 1586-1655 document or how the information was gathered, we can only assume that the omission occurred in this fashion.

The poor may also be found among the 20,000 guild members. True

---

39. In 1642 one of every eleven households was headed by a widow in the sestiere of Castello; nearly one of eight in Dorsoduro (A.S.V., *Provveditori alla Sanità,* b. 570; Correr, *Cod. Donà dalle Rose,* b. 351.
40. Beltrami, *Storia,* p. 204; see also Pullan, *Rich and Poor,* pt. 2, chap. 4.

THE LABOR FORCE OF VENICE

to their primary function as confraternities of mutual assistance, the arti maintained in membership those of their profession who could not find sufficient work to support their families and offered what succor they could from special guild funds. When the arti make separate mention of their poor in the guild lists we can get at least some general idea of the prevalence of this condition. Of the 23 master wool-cloth tenterers (*chiodaroli*) left in Venice in 1672, 5 are listed as "poveri"; and by 1690 of 22 masters, 12 are unemployed. There were 63 working tanners (of the guild of *conzacurami*) in 1672—35 others unemployed. Surprisingly, only 11 percent of the silk throwsters (*filatoi*) were listed as "poveri" in 1672, but that proportion had doubled by the last decade of the century. One would have expected a higher proportion of impoverished members in this superannuated guild but perhaps their attrition took the form of abandoning the guild and profession altogether. Equally surprising is the large number of poor and unemployed in the goldsmiths guild (*oresi*): of 688 members a full 200 were absent or impoverished. There is no record of the goldsmiths ever suffering the general economic privations of the century; in circumstances where all the guilds pleaded for relief from their individual tax burdens, the pleas of the oresi are conspicuously in absence. Yet in 1690 this guild, whose absolute numbers and relative share of the labor force grew uninterruptedly throughout the seventeenth century, suffered a full 29 percent unemployment. The picture of unemployment among the guild members is at best fragmentary and inconclusive.[41]

There is some evidence, as we have mentioned, that the sea was the workhouse of Venice. First of all, this appears to have been the official wish of the government, which permitted ship captains to hire *sottomarinai* from the ranks of the poor as a fourth of each crew "with a view toward thus purging the city of the poor and vagabond."[42] Secondly, when men were forced out of certain professions one of the more common recourses was to "go for a sailor."

---

41. The unemployment statistics in this paragraph are from A.S.V., *Milizia da Mar,* nos. 538-557, which contain guild rolls grouped alphabetically. Members listed as "poveri" or "non esercitano" I regard as unemployed; those listed as having changed profession or having left the city were not included in unemployment figures.

42. Fanfani, *Storia del lavoro,* p. 143; see also Pullan, *Rich and Poor,* pp. 145, 366-369.

The state made public works projects and experimental industrial schemes into opportunities for employing the poor. In the middle of the seventeenth century about 4,000 persons were reported at work on public projects.[43] Many patents for new manufactures in Venice were granted with the proviso that inmates of the ospitali be trained in the unskilled tasks of the trade.[44]

Considering the fact that a large proportion of the city's industrial work force was employed by the textile industry (30-40 percent of guild employment), we can expect that seasonal unemployment further eroded the capacity of these workers to support themselves—as in the wool industry, with the limited period for shearing and transporting fleeces to Venice. Figure 1 shows the extremity and regularity of these fluctuations. For several reasons the silk industry suffered less from seasonal disoccupation: most of the raw silk came from local suppliers or at least from Venetian territories. Final demand for silk goods had not fallen off to nearly the extent that Venetian woolens had suffered. Furthermore the silk weavers had, over literally centuries of dispute, secured the right to employ some of their looms "for their own account," that is, independent of the silk merchants. They managed to operate in two markets, producing both for export—the merchant's market—and for domestic consumption, selling privately, and in this way reducing the spottiness of their work year.[45] Finally the partial transition within the silk industry away

---

43. James Howell, *A Survey of the Signorie of Venice* (London, 1651), p. 185.

44. See, for example, a project for using hospital inmates for silk workers (A.S.V., *Arte della Seta,* b. 100, fasc. 68, p. 56, Nov. 4, 1636). Also, the Holland-cloth project of Pietro Comans (see below, chap. 4, text and note 30) was granted approval on condition that "figlioli che sono in ospitali" be taught how to card and spin wool according to his methods.

45. Permission for a weaver to use 2 of 6 looms in his shop for self-employment dates from at least 1554 (*Decreto Senato,* Dec. 15, 1554, mentioned in a resumé of silk legislation, A.S.V., *Cinque Savi,* b. 477, *tomo* 1), but the privilege was constantly being challenged, revoked, and reassigned. One of the most interesting aspects of this practice is the disposal of the goods by the weavers, independently of merchants. Surprisingly, it seems that they retailed these fabrics themselves, not through drapers or mercers, but directly to the consumers, "gentlemen and ladies of high birth." The following document testifies to this unique practice (A.S.V., *Senato, terra, filza* 1095, June 1688):

Facio Fede Io Anzolo Ronzoni Nodaro de L'Off° de Larte de Testori da panni di seda con mio giuramento come sopra li doi teleri a noi reservati fabrichiamo e faciamo fabricare à nostri confratelli della medema Arte per autorita del Ecc.mo Senato panni cossi da oro come di seda benche no siamo descriti nel numero de mercanti et quelli liberamente vendiamo cossi alle case e mezadi [selling tables or areas] capitano alle medeme nostre case e mezadi Cavaliere e Dame e liberamente giornalmte

from coarser qualities of cloth toward finer and more expensive gold-threaded fabrics made the industry more labor intensive. The same looms, implements, and techniques were used for both productions but the larger number of warp threads and the greater attention to quality that was required for the manufacture of the high grade cloth boosted by as much as three times the number of man-hours per cloth.[46]

Population Movements and Labor Supply

The general picture of the labor supply in seventeenth-century Venice clearly portrays long-term stasis. The interval between observations in table 2.1 is so great that the possibility of perceiving short-term fluctuations, or even accurately visualizing a secular trend, does not exist. This does not invalidate the observation that the size of the effective work force of the city was the same in 1655 as it had been seventy years earlier or that total membership in the city's guilds hardly changed from one observation year to the next throughout the course of the century. There is of course documentary evidence which testifies to variation in the size of the work force, principally during years of plague and famine, as for example after the 1630-1631 catastrophe when the work force was so depleted that the guilds were opened to foreigners.

In relating the wage level to labor supply Pullan has measured a

---

vengon a comprar simil lavori ne da niuno siamo per ciò molestati e piu venendo qualche dano per vender simil lavori liberam[te] li compriamo come per leggie si sono permesso.

Data da Lofficio Li 8 Aprile 1688

Anzolo Ronzoni nod°
di de: Off° di mano proprio

This novelty in the silk industry was a major departure from the industrial precedent of enforcing the distinction between merchants and craftsmen. When workers in other industries tried to gain the same arrangement as the silkweavers had won, they were thwarted. Tanners were forbidden to buy and sell leather (A.S.V., *Cinque Savi,* n.s., b. 130, fasc. 208, Sept. 7, 1600). The retailing of wool cloth was forbidden in private shops or houses and was reserved for the stores of the drapers (*ibid.,* b. 127, fasc. 44, pt. 1, Jan. 3, 1659, *m.v.*).

46. See Sella, *Commerci,* pp. 128-131, and "Industrial Production," pp. 238-239. For man-hours of work per cloth, see A.S.V., *Arte della Seta,* b. 106, fasc. 140. For a weaver to make 60 *brazza* of *siviglie ordenari,* a low-quality silk, took 28 days. The best brocades required 90 to 100 days for a similar length.

1. Monthly wool-cloth production
   Source: A.S.V., Militizia da Mar, no. 722, August 23, 1660.

considerable effect of the diminished supplies of workmen in the early 1580's just after the plague, and in the years 1620-1621 and 1628-1629 which were notable for famine. He says, however, "Venice could quickly repair many of its losses." In fact, in the post-plague years of the 1570's, replacement by immigration happened so fast that the effect of the momentarily smaller labor pool on the wage rate was completely nullified for journeymen (*lavoranti*) by the end of the decade, and shortly thereafter for maestri.[47] All indications point to the relative unimportance of exogenously caused short-term variations for determining the course of the secular trend in size of population or of labor force. A brief examination of the factors controlling the size of the labor force—birth and death rates and migration statistics—will serve to corroborate the conclusion that the size of that force experienced almost no change in the seventeenth century.

Table 2.3. Vital rates in Venice

Years	Birth rate	Death rate	Rate of natural increase
1581	34.1	32.5	+ 1.6
1586	31.8	27.5	+ 4.3
1600-10	33.06	33.38	- 0.32
1611-20	26.71	33.93	- 7.22
1621-30	32.67	57.30	- 24.63
1631-40	38.43	43.27	- 4.84
1641-50	33.86	33.33	- 0.53
1651-60	30.87	29.32	+ 1.55
1661-70	34.65	32.32	+ 2.33
1671-80	33.11	32.91	+ 0.20
1681-90	28.80	31.97	- 3.17
1691-1700	29.65	30.37	- 0.72

Source: Beltrami, *Storia,* p. 156.

For this century in Venice, changes in the rate of natural increase go a long way toward explaining movements in the city population. A comparison of the birth and death rates over a period of time (table 2.3) has the effect of amplifying short-term drastic changes caused

47. Pullan, "Wage-Earners," pp. 159-163. See also S. J. Woolf, "Venice and the Terraferma: Problems of the Change from Commercial to Landed Activities," *C & C,* p. 177.

principally by many deaths in a short period, while obscuring longer-range movements. Still it may be observed that as the total population figures for Venice vary around a perceivable "natural" level for the given period and place (about 140,000±20,000), so the rate of natural increase cycle varies around zero (figure 2). Were it a century of population growth, the rate of natural increase would be expected to vary about a positive trend, but Beltrami's decennial birth and death rates (for selected parishes) support the hypothesis of a static city population in the seventeenth century.

Too little is known about the patterns of migration in the Veneto during the early modern period but it is possible to recognize the basic flows to and from the city.[48] The findings of modern students of Venetian history correspond well to recent demographic observations that long-term net flows of populations are directly related to spatial differences in real income, while short-term population movements more nearly coincide with immediate differences in employment opportunities.[49] Beltrami and S. J. Woolf have outlined the prolonged attraction of the mainland both for investment in land and for relocation of persons. By 1690, 50 of the 270 woolworkers remaining on the rolls of the guild of laneri were living and working in the terraferma, mostly in Padua.[50] The guild roll of the *conzacurami* (tanners) for 1713 bears the note that many of the members, unable to find work, have gone to Verona, Brescia, Ancona, Romagna, and elsewhere, or live in foreign countries.[51]

But migration out of the city of Venice was not only to the close mainland possessions. The "push" of diminished relative income and chronic underemployment impelled the departure of Venetians, especially skilled industrial workers, beyond the dominion to other parts of Italy, and in special cases to France and England. The harsh retribution that was often inflicted by the Council of Ten against emigrating masters in certain industries (principally glassmaking, dyeing, soapmaking, silkweaving) are now part of Venice's popular lore. These efforts at punishment point up the basic fact that there was

---

48. Daniele Beltrami, *La penetrazione economica dei Veneziani in Terraferma: forze di lavoro e proprietà fondiaria nelle campagne venete dei secoli XVII e XVIII* (Venice-Rome, 1961), and Woolf, "Venice and the Terraferma."

49. Richard A. Easterlin, *Population, Labor Force, and Long Swings in Economic Growth* (New York, 1968), p. 150.

50. A.S.V., *Milizia da Mar*, no. 545, fasc. *laneri*.

51. *Ibid.*, no. 542, fasc. *conzacurami*, and *Cinque Savi*, n.s., b. 132, fasc. 207.

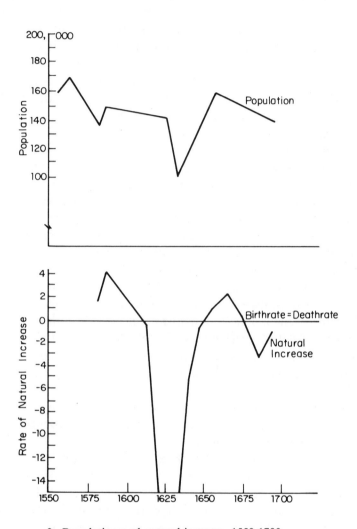

2. Population and natural increase, 1550-1700
Source: Tables 2.1 and 2.3.

a strong temptation to leave for foreign parts because of the opportunities of higher real incomes abroad. For the important soapmaking
industry, the problem had reached the proportions of a major crisis by
the beginning of the seventeenth century. The market for Venice's
exports of soap was being overtaken by new competitors in Genoa and
Livorno—almost all were expatriate Venetian masters and journey-

men.[52] The introduction of gold-cloth weaving at Lyons dates from the settlement of Venetian weavers in that city.[53] Incredibly, hundreds of glassblowers from the remote island of Murano left the confines of the lagoon during the seventeenth century to become *Weltbürger*. Lured by the prospect of enormous profits, they established glass-works in every corner of Europe and even in the New World.[54]

The emigration of industrial workers from Venice cannot properly be called a search for higher wages. Generally the wage level in Venice was higher than elsewhere in Europe, and steadily rising.[55] The departures of industrial tradesmen actually became an *entrepreneurial* exodus in which those who were willing to run the risks of setting up production in a foreign place and of incurring the animosity of the Serenissima stood to gain enormous profits. This long-term pattern was very erratic and selective, striking certain industries more than others, and the overall yearly magnitude of emigration was certainly not large enough to cause governmental concern about depopulation.

Narrowing our perspective to a shorter-term view of how migration affected the supply of labor in Venice, what evidence we possess suggests movements largely in the reverse direction of the long, slow outflow from the city. The nature of short-term migration was that shortages in the city labor market brought people into Venice from the outlying provinces. Although the flow reversed when the city work force became saturated, net migration into the city was always greater than the number of persons returning to the countryside. The ease with which artisans and unskilled workers moved from mainland towns and villages into Venice—thus effectively buffering the island city's work force against demographic crisis of long duration—was one of the most important benefits of the relationship with the terra-ferma.

In early modern Venice, generally speaking, people moved out of the city because prospects for higher real incomes were growing else-where and this trend was slow and prolonged. Movement into the city

---

52. *Ibid.*, b. 56, Senate decree of Jan. 29, 1613, *m.v.* This piece of legislation gave expatriate Venetian soapworkers three months to return to Venice or be declared "banditi."

53. *Cal. S. P. Ven.*, vol. 23, no. 209, p. 161, Nov. 4, 1633.

54. *Ibid.*, vol. 17, nos. 26, 120, 379; vol. 24, no. 498. The complete story of the emigration of Venetian glassmasters may be found in Gasparetto, *Il vetro di Murano*, pp. 101-113.

55. See below, table 4.7.

was more sporadic and "clumpy," responding mostly to the strong pull of opportunities for immediate employment in those years when Venice was in need of workmen. This explains the observed rapid rate of recovery from plague and famine in the city after the years 1576-1577 and 1630-1631. We can, in fact, measure the impact of this migration in restoring the population in the post-plague decades of the seventeenth century.

Proceeding from the premise that a change in population from time 1 to time 2 may be caused only by migration or by natural increase (which for the present case will be the mean annual rate of natural increase in decade 1), where:

$$P_1 = \text{total population in time 1}$$
$$RNI_1 = \text{rate of natural increase in time 1}$$
$$NM_2 = \text{net migration in time 2}$$
$$TI_2 = \text{total population increment in}$$
$$\text{time 2 } (P_2 - P_1)$$

and time 1 to time 2 is 10 years, we have:

$$TI_2 = 10 \left(RNI_1 \frac{P_1}{1000} \right) + NM_2$$

that is, the change in population over the decade is equal to the average rate of natural increase multiplied by the initial population, which gives the increment caused by births and deaths for each year of the decade, plus NM, the residual of population change over the decade unexplained by natural increase and therefore attributable to migration. Thus,

$$NM_2 = TI_2 - 10 \left(RNI_1 \frac{P_1}{1000} \right)$$

Applied to decennial population statistics for Venice this yields the figures set out in table 2.4.

To elaborate on the application of this procedure: for example in the first ten-year period, which comprises the plague years, the population had fallen by 39,350. The natural increase term of the equation is:

$$10 \left(-24.63 \times \frac{141,600}{1000} \right) = -34,876.$$

This indicates that a decrease of 34,876 would be expected just because of the high incidence of deaths over births as specified by the

Table 2.4 Population change by component, 1630-1660

Decade	Mean annual rate of natural increase	Population (year)	Population increment	Increment caused by natural increase	Increment caused by net migration
1621-30	-24.63	141,600(1624)	-	-	-
1631-40	-4.84	102,250(1633)	-39,350	-34,876a	-4,474
1641-50	-0.53	120,300(1642)	+18,050	-4,949	+22,999
1651-60	+1.55	158,800(1655)	+38,500	-638	+39,138

Source: tables 2.1 and 2.2.

aVenetian health authorities listed total deaths in the city during the plague months, July 1630 to October 1631, at 46,490 (*Museo Civico Correr, Cod. Gradenigo,* b. 125, and *Cod. Donà dalle Rose,* b. 354). The natural increase increment is an estimate of *net* population loss attributable to an excess of deaths over births between 1624 and 1633.

rate of natural increase. The remaining loss of 4,474 unexplained by births and deaths is therefore attributable to departure from the city, i.e., net migration over the decade. This result is in keeping with what would be expected as a result of the catastrophic years at the end of this decade. In the next decade we note that almost 5,000 more persons died than were born, no doubt because of the residual effects of the plague: food shortage, sickness, etc. Instead of reflecting this further decline, however, total population has grown by some 18,000, and again we must attribute this to migration— in-migration in this case and in sufficient numbers to make up the loss of 5,000 *and* add 18,000 to the city's population. The recovery process continues through the 1650's, a period marked by a temporarily stable natural increase: a birth for every death, more or less. But the total population figure leaps up between 1642 and 1655 by some 38,500, an amount equal to original losses in the 1630's, bringing the overall figure to well above pre-plague levels. Growth is entirely attributable to migration into the city.

Crude as this method may be, it demonstrates that the speedy recoveries that returned the population and work force of the city to pre-calamity levels after the advent of some natural holocaust cannot be seen as resulting from the indigenous population's reproductive capacity. Migration from the mainland in response to immediate employment opportunities in Venice and encouragement by the state was what replenished Venice's population so dramatically.

Still there is no gainsaying the inaccuracy of this demonstration, depending as it does upon a less-than-wholesome set of statistics. As mentioned above, the rates of natural increase are based upon the mean decennial birth and death rates observed by Beltrami in thirteen of the city's parishes with an effective total of less than 40,000 persons. Also open to possible question is my use of the total population estimate for 1655. This figure (158,722), and its breakdown by sex and social class, appears as an addendum to the universally accepted table entitled, "Nota di tutte le Anime esistenti nella Città di Venezia nell'Anno 1586" found in the Marciana Library. Historians, following the example of Julius Beloch, have distrusted this addendum and made no use of it, but I believe this distrust to be unjustified.[56]

---

56. See Frontispiece and Appendix II.

The other important issue involved in accepting the estimate of 159,000 souls in Venice in 1655 is precisely the matter of recovery from the 1630-1631 plague. It is generally assumed that Venice never fully reached pre-plague population levels until the eighteenth century.[57] If the 1655 figure is accurate, it means that just twenty-five years after the ravages of the plague—when Venice was in the depths of her economic doldrums and in the midst of a major war as well—her population was at the top of a demographic swing, almost equalling that of the prosperous mid-sixteenth century. The absence of any reliable statistics for the second half of the seventeenth century confounds the feasibility of positive corroboration.

Three facts give added credence to the possibility of this rapid recovery: (1) The plague of 1576 was relatively as destructive as that of 1630. Both wiped out between a fourth and a third of the city population. Yet if the recovery within twenty-five years of the 1630 plague is surprising, the post-1577 recovery is spectacular. Within ten years, the population rebounded to over 148,000. This is attributed to the prosperity of the city during the last decades of the sixteenth century, but it still makes the seventeenth-century recovery seem less unlikely.[58] (2) Independent statistics show that by 1660 the guild-incorporated work force had already exceeded in size the pre-plague levels of the earlier part of the century.[59] (3) The pool of persons available to migrate from Venetian dominions was large, and the acknowledged fact that plague struck more heavily in the countryside explains the "push" that, combined with the "pull" of job opportunities in the depopulated city, brought large numbers from the hinterland to

---

57. Woolf, "Venice and the Terraferma," p. 178.

58. The effect of plague on population totals:

	Plague of 1576			Plague of 1630-1631		
	Year	Pop.	Index	Year	Pop.	Index
Pre-plague	(1563)	168,627	100	(1624)	141,625	100
Post-plague	(1577)	120,000	71	(1633)	102,243	72
Recovery	(1586)	148,097	88	(1655)	158,772	112

Source: (1577) Pullan, "Wage-Earners," p. 159; all others, table 2.1.

59. See below, table 3.1. In 1603 there were 20,253 members of the enumerated arti; in 1660 guild membership was back over 21,000.

THE LABOR FORCE OF VENICE

Venice. The plague reduced the total Veneto population from 1,350,000 to about 1,020,000, a drop of about one-fourth.[60] The overall size of the terraferma population even after the plague makes it seem more reasonable that more than 50,000 mainlanders may have migrated to the city over the years 1630-1660.

Between the years 1633 and 1642 when the city populations numbered respectively 102,250 and 120,300 (both statistics are universally accepted), Venice regained some 18,000 persons. Even if the rate of natural increase over this decade had been an impossible 10 per 1,000, which was the rate of modern Europe in 1947, instead of the ascertained negative rate of -4.84 per 1,000, natural increase could still explain only about one-half the total increase in city population. Heavy migration is clearly the key factor.

The stability of the size of the Venetian labor force throughout the 1600's is in large measure due to the compensatory pattern of short-term migration between the Venetian mainland and the island city. There were also long-term out-migrations from Venice caused by a growing difference in real incomes between Venice and the rest of Europe to Venice's disadvantage. This slow pull was somewhat selective to the degree that opportunities for employment abroad were greater only for a minority of skilled workers in new, diffusing European industries. But it could hardly be considered numerically debilitating in the light of the chronic underemployment prevailing in Venice during most of the seventeenth century. For the century on the whole then, considering the stability of total work force and decennial rates of natural increase, and what we know of the countervailing effects of long-run outflows and short-run inflows, the *net* effect of population movements on the labor force was probably small.

The Control of Labor Force Entry

The Venetian labor force had considerable capacity to control the supply of labor by regulating the acceptance and progress of apprentices. For most of the guilds, the original statutes of incorporation (*mariegole*) stipulate the acceptable range of ages for enrollment of

---

60. Woolf, "Venice and the Terraferma," p. 177. Although it is likely that some immigrants came from outside Venetian dominions (the 1642 census of the *piovani* lists many residents of Milanese origin in Venice), ease of passage and settlement was naturally greatest for Venice's mainland subjects.

apprentices and the required number of years of apprenticeship. These criteria were designed to insure that apprentices would enter service at a trainable age and would be required to serve enough time to learn the trade.[61] With the exception of a few guilds which strictly enforced these regulations (such as the *marangoni di casa*) there was widespread deviation whenever labor market exigencies so required. In the 1620's, which were years of temporary contraction in the economy and also in size of population and labor force, the need for workmen in some guilds became acute and was met in peculiar ways.

In a case typical of those years, the masons protested to the Collegio alle Arti in the hope of instituting a punishment for those members who brought overage apprentices into the guild: in at least one guild there was "much confusion . . . over the matter of enrolling apprentices because many of our brothers take on apprentices who are full-grown men, older, in fact than the masters. It is impossible for these apprentices to be subject to their masters."[62] The bargemen complained of a similar problem: the old apprentices who have been coming into the guild are too truculent and besides, when finished with their term, they are too old for the "draft" and cannot serve their guild in the galley call-ups.[63] Maximum draft age was forty-five years; yet the dyers issued a complaint about apprentices of "forty, fifty, sixty years of age and more."[64] The woodcarvers' guild found that the shortage of accomplished masters during this period caused problems as the quality of workmanship progressively deteriorated:

It is clearly visible that the state of our craft is steadily going from bad to worse because there are so few good masters and thus, when apprentices sign up with their masters they don't attend to learning and when they finish their term they enter the guild as masters themselves without knowing how to make one decent thing; then they take an apprentice as if, not withstanding their own incompetence, they could teach someone else; and in this manner we are reduced to a bad state of affairs.[65]

---

61. For lists of ages and terms, as regulated, see A. Pancotto, "Le condizioni dei garzoni a Venezia dalla fine del secolo XVI alla fine del secolo XVIII" (unpub. diss., Istituto Universitario di Economia "Ca'Foscari," Venice, 1945-46), p. 10.

62. A.S.V., *Giustizia Vecchia, Collegio alle Arti,* b. 223, reg. 291, f. 40, Jan. 3, 1620, *m.v.*

63. *Ibid.,* f. 71, Jan. 26, 1622, *m.v.*

64. *Ibid.,* f. 84, Sept. 27, 1623.

65. *Ibid.,* reg. 292, Oct. 1625.

There is not much to suggest that the guilds were actually sealed off in times of temporary glut in the labor market—only one case was reported between 1689 and 1694 when new apprentices were excluded from the glassmakers guild and promotions in rank were frozen, but the reason for this action is obscure.[66] Oversupply of labor in the contracting seventeenth-century economy was fairly chronic and while the individual arti complained of unemployment in their ranks the number of apprenticeship contracts registered with the Giustizia Vecchia did not diminish until the eighteenth century (table 2.5). Likewise there seems to be no change in the average age of the entering apprentice or in the average length of the contractual term of apprenticeship over the course of the century. The reason for this is not adherence to the age and duration limits of the *mariegole.* In most guilds, for any given sample year, the ages of entering apprentices vary widely from the very young to those who only list themselves as being of *età maggior,* and the term of apprenticeship is more closely related to the age of the apprentice at entry than to the stipulated term of the guild statutes. That is to say, the apprentice was taken on for a sufficiently long term that, however young, he could not graduate to lavorante still a child; if the apprentice were old, he would receive a shorter term than usual.

The fact that the individual guilds continued to enroll apprentices, despite their awareness and constant complaints that members were reduced to poverty for lack of employment, is somewhat paradoxical. The explanation, I believe, is that in most industries, in order to accomplish any work at all, the individual master required the services of apprentices and journeymen. For it was naturally the low-grade workers who did the basic tasks necessary to production and beneath the station of the *capo maestro.* The best example is in weaving where traditionally it was the *garzone* who operated the pulley strings that controlled the *lazza* (*licci*) or heddles, raising or lowering the threads of the warp.[67] It was mindless work requiring considerable physical effort[68] and it was totally noncontributory to the education an appren-

66. Pancotto, "Le condizioni," p. 8.
67. A.S.V., *Arte della Seta,* b. 106, fasc. 143 *extra,* Sept. 16, 1682, "Informazione in materia della stretezza di lavoranti e garzoni accresciuta nell' Arte della Testoria."
68. Abbot Payson Usher, *A History of Mechanical Inventions* (Boston, 1954), p. 262.

Table 2.5 Apprenticeship contracts registered with the Giustizia Vecchia

Year	Total contracts (number)	Average age (years)	Average duration (years)	Average age after term (years)
1591	902	14.1	5.1	19.2
1606	1,009	14.8	4.9	19.8
1632	1,793	15.6	4.6	20.2
1659	1,242	14.1	4.9	19.0
1681	759	13.9	5.0	18.9
1711	559	13.9	5.0	18.9

Sources: For 1591, 1632, 1681, A.S.V., *Giustizia Vecchia, ser.* 14, *Accordi dei Garzoni,* b. 113, 119, 124. For 1606, 1659, and 1711 I have relied on Pancotto's *Le condizioni,* p. 35, reproduced in Beltrami, *Storia,* p. 200. Pancotto also supplies the following data on total contracts:

Year	Total contracts	Year	Total contracts
1592	1,447	1646	842
1597	1,078	1656	1,057
1598	1,402	1658	1,044
1621	1,120	1662	1,673
1626	1,240	1663	1,150
1643	1,080	1664	1,540
1645	1,022	1670	1,180

Note: Several factors render these data unsuitable for use as anything but a general index of apprenticeship. The total number of apprenticeship contracts registered with the Giustizia Vecchia accounts for only a part of the total number of entrants into the labor force in any given year. For one thing, not all the guilds were subject to the overseerage of the Giustizia Vecchia and so did not list apprenticeship agreements with that office. Woolworkers and arsenalotti were managed by other agencies, for example. And many workers never joined a guild or entered into formal contract for learning a trade.

Secondly, apprenticeship was not the only way to enter a guild. Most permitted a master's son to become a master himself by *privileggio,* bypassing the lower ranks. Of course, many chose this route. (A.S.V. *Inquisitori di Stato,* b. 785, fasc. *coroneri,* "Informazione." Numbers of "figli di capi maestri" in the guilds are recorded in the guild rolls of the Naval Personnel Administration, A.S.V., *Milizia da Mar,* nos. 538-557.)

tice was supposed to receive.[69] Yet a (silk) weaver could not begin to make cloth without at least one journeyman assistant and one apprentice to pull the cords. So even if there were a sufficiency of master weavers, there would still have to be an influx of apprentice workers into the craft to permit production.

This was exactly the problem that confronted the silk weavers in 1682. There were about 900 capi maestri in the guild, of whom about 200 had abandoned the craft because of *"impotenza"* and become brokers, boatmen, and small-time craftsmen. Others lent their name to whoever wanted to work extra looms. Even of the remaining 700 most were not working. The Senate permitted each master to oversee from one to six looms under his own roof and required at least two workers for each loom. It is estimated that there were 2,200 looms available to the 700 masters but 2,000 lavoranti and 1,500 garzoni would have been needed to operate them. There were actually only 500 lavoranti and 600 garzoni enrolled.[70] Little help could be expected from the families of the masters since very few of their sons had taken up silk weaving and their wives and daughters performed only minor jobs.

So the manufacture of silk cloth was really sustained by the journeymen and apprentices who did the routine work.[71] The spokesman of the guild demonstrated that there were sufficient looms and masters to permit, with the proper number of workmen, the *testori di seta* (silk weavers) to quadruple production from the actual 2,000-2,500 cloths every three months to 8,000-9,000.[72] This bit of optimism was natural enough considering that the 1680's were a boom period for Venetian silks. The rate at which the weavers were then producing silk cloths would never again be equalled.[73]

The control over the terms of apprenticeship was never fully exercised by the guilds as a means of restricting admission into the labor force. The supply of labor for the economy of Venice did not change

---

69. A.S.V., *Arte della Seta*, b. 106, "Informazione."

70. *Ibid.*, "Informazione." These figures are satisfactorily confirmed by the examination of silk weaving made by Michiel Foscarini in 1685 (A.S.V., *Cinque Savi*, n.s., b. 160, "Inquisition de Michiel Foscarini sopra il suffragio de testori di seta," Sept. 21, 1685). For that year Foscarini gives: maestri—1,086, owning 2,626 looms with 463 lavoranti. Milizia da Mar guild statistics for 1690 show 1,179 silk weavers of all ranks (below, table 3.1).

71. A.S.V., *Arte della Seta*, b. 120, fasc. 341, p. 3.

72. *Ibid.*, p. 3.

73. Sella, *Commerci*, p. 129, table 3.

very much throughout the seventeenth century. There was at no time a significant shortage of workers, and although the guilds—industrial guilds especially—complained of insufficient work to keep all members employed, neither was there at any time evidence of massive unemployment of such duration that the economy could not support the normal level of population and work force that prevailed through the century. The principal mechanism of adjustment to short-run disruptions was, as we have seen, migration to and from the mainland.

The other side of the coin in our investigation of the labor force is the unmeasurable factor of labor demand, which is basically determined by the market demand for the end product to whose manufacture labor contributes. The story of final product demand for Venetian, indeed for Italian goods in general, is well known.[74] With respect to industrial commodities and attendant commercial services, the economies of Venice and the other major peninsular cities were geared almost entirely to foreign consumption. In Venice, for example, of the nearly 11,000 wool cloths manufactured in 1656, all but 700 were exported.[75] Throughout the seventeenth century, as foreign competition increased and as Venice lost her primacy as the marketplace of the western world, the demand for her manufactures and the corresponding demand for industrial labor in Venice dropped steadily. With few exceptions, the industrial guilds recognized this erosion to be taking place and affecting their own employment prospects.

What was the reaction to falling demand for industrial labor? In the course of the century employment in waning industries diminished as unemployed industrial workers took on new jobs outside the manufacturing sector. The Venetian guild system was sufficiently flexible to accommodate this conversion without major dislocations. Another more active response was the attempt to reduce costs and thereby revitalize Venice's ability to compete in international markets. Here too the guilds were capable of bending with the wind. Certain masters undertook experiments aimed at such economies, but here adjustment did not succeed. Innovators were thwarted, not by the guilds, but by the state. Because of its obstinacy production costs remained so much higher than in other areas that the island's manu-

---

74. See, for example, Cipolla, "Economic Decline of Italy," esp. p. 133.
75. A.S.V., *Arte della Seta,* b. 120, fasc. 341, p. 2.

factures failed to achieve competitive pricing in almost all markets. From a commercial standpoint this was the critical problem of the century. It reflects the failure of the Venetian economy to accomplish the natural adjustment in costs and prices that should have occurred during the northern challenge. This failure cannot be imputed to the guilds, for they represented no obstacle to adjustment in the economy. Confronted with a set of serious problems—the fall-off in demand for industrial labor, the departure of many skilled workers from Venice, and the aging of the labor force—the guild system survived and provided the foundation for subsequent structural shifts in the organization of the economy.

3

The Composition of Employment: An Industrial Census for Early Modern Venice

The adjustments that Venice made after the termination of her long period of economic growth in the sixteenth century were most remarkable for their moderation. Venice accomplished a transition away from a manufacturing and export-centered economy without bringing down a catastrophe on its own head. No serious decline in total employment or in standard of living or real wage struck the city despite the disappearance of its old commercial and industrial monopolies. The Venetians managed to maintain their own well-being largely by moving away from jobs in failing industries into different occupations. These shifts in labor force structure took place gradually but steadily over the course of the seventeenth century, rather the result of young men going into a new set of professions than of other men changing occupations.

In an attempt to describe and account for the changes in the composition of employment over the course of the seventeenth century an employment census has been elaborated for the Venetian guilds, using information collected by the government magistracy known as the Milizia da Mar, the Naval Personnel Administration.

The Collegio da Milizia da Mar was created by the Senate in 1539 as an ad hoc commission to manage the financing and manning of a reserve fleet of one hundred light galleys to combat a growing Turkish menace in the Adriatic.[1] In 1542, following the conclusion of the Turkish war, the size of the Venetian reserve fleet was ordered doubled, with the standing contingent of light galleys remaining at one

---

1. Andrea da Mosto, *L'Archivio di Stato di Venezia, indice generale storico, descrittivo ed analitico* (2 vols., Rome, 1937) I, 199.

THE COMPOSITION OF EMPLOYMENT

hundred.[2] The Milizia da Mar remained permanently in charge of arming and staffing the fleet. Venetian war-galleys had traditionally been manned by free citizens of the Republic.[3] The guilds were now made responsible to the state for supplying able-bodied oarsmen in time of need and paying for their support while in service. From the time of its creation, one of the major jobs of the Collegio da Milizia da Mar was to apportion the obligation among the arti. This partition of the manning burden, known as the *caratada*, specified the number of men from each guild obliged to take up posts at the oars should the state so require.[4]

In the determination of the crew size and partition, the Senate decided first on the timing of reviews of the state of readiness, and subsequently on the number of galleys to be armed. They left the details of manning the oars to the Milizia da Mar. The Venetian light galleys of the period were triremes with about 26 benches on each side, three oars to the bench giving a working total of 156 oarsmen per vessel.[5] Typically, extra men were assigned as a safety margin. The Milizia usually figured on 160 men per galley and an extra thousand men for a fifty galley call-up. Once the total number of required oarsmen was determined, the Milizia da Mar circulated an order among the chief guild officers for a *descrittione* or guild census. Such guild membership data as survive constitute a comprehensive measure of employment in the Venetian economy as reflected in the pools of available galley crews.

Within a month each gastaldo was to present a *rollo* or guild membership list, organized by rank (master, journeyman, apprentice) and with the age of each member included. Notations in the guild lists were

2. Lane, *Navires,* p. 136; Romano, "Economic Aspects," p. 68. After the year 1633, the reserve fleet was returned to its former size, with fifty light galleys in readiness.

3. Lane, *Navires,* p. 6.

4. The Venetian word "carata" (Ital. *carato*) usually meant either a share of ownership in a vessel or a share of capital in a commercial venture. In the fleet's usage the "carata" of each guild was the number of men from that guild, the share of the total muster, assigned to galley service. The guilds were not by any means the sole contributors to the galley crews. Assessments of the various territories of Venice's mainland and littoral possessions were made as well, based upon the reports of the *rettori* to the Milizia da Mar. The five *Scuole Grandi* shared in the burden, and the Jewish communities of the Ghetto, while never obliged to contribute men, were taxed at muster time. See Pullan, *Rich and Poor,* pp. 145-156.

5. Lane, *Navires,* p. 9; Correr, *Cod. Donà dalle Rose,* b. 228, p. 231, "Nota che a Zurmar Galee n° 50 suttile de Banchi /26/ l'una a Galiotti n° 6/p Bancho li vol Galiotti N° 7800."

permitted, to denote enrolled members who were ineligible or unfit for service because of poverty, departure from the city, or double enrollment. The clerk of the Milizia da Mar then proceeded to calculate the number of men of each rank able to serve, that is between the ages of 18 and 45 and not otherwise disqualified, and this was noted on the back of each guild's rollo.[6] The clerks then determined the proportion of available men to the number of men required by the call-up and applied that proportion to each of the guilds in order to calculate its share of the total burden. The initial list of guilds and their shares was conditional and subject to appeal by those that felt their carata unduly heavy or believed themselves somehow unable to supply their number of men. In spite of the fact that there was no official licence or recognition for the procedure, the majority of arti filed appeals, and in infrequent cases the Milizia da Mar acceded to their pleas. After the final levy list was drawn up, the individual guild rolls were locked away in a box with two keys, one for the Milizia da Mar, the other for the Provveditori all'Armar. When the time came to man the fleet, the rolls were reopened before the assembled gastaldi and the individual guild members who would be assigned to the oars were chosen.[7]

---

6. A typical notation appears in the roll of the cloth-shearers (A.S.V., *Milizia da Mar,* no. 542, fasc. *cimadori*) in the following form:

	totale	habili	inhabili
Maestri	107	49	58
Lavoranti	55	40	15
Garzoni	8	8	-
Totale	170	97	73

The notations are sometimes more complex, frequently listing in addition to ineligible members the *bombardieri,* guildsmen who have been specially trained as cannoneers and were thus not subject to the levy as oarsmen. There were 300 bombardieri in 1571; in 1619 there was a recruitment drive to boost the number to 500 (A.S.V., *Archivio alle Arti, fabbri,* b. 128, Aug. 24, 1619, "Parte de Consiglio de Pregadi [Senate] in materia de Bombardieri").

7. The details of Milizia da Mar procedures outlined above are taken from descriptions that were part of communications between the Senate and the Milizia da Mar during years in which the fleet was under administrative review, principally: A.S.V., *Milizia da Mar,* no. 240, p. 16, June 20, 1539; no. 251, Senate order of Nov. 25, 1595; and A.S.V., *Senato, mar,* filza 1290, Nov. 25, 1595, "Scrittura da Presidenti del Collegio della Milizia da Mar," July 15, 1595. After the mid-sixteenth century guildsmen from Venice and from the mainland territories were called to serve only in the event of a major fleet build-up to supplement the standing crews of prisoners (*condannati*). In this capacity the additional crewmen were known as *zontaroli* ("zonta" = added). See Nani-Mocenigo, *Storia della marina,* pp. 39-42.

There is no doubt that at one time those who were selected for galley service left the city to man the oars in person when the fleet was armed, but this became less and less common by the late sixteenth and seventeenth centuries. Provisions for substitutions were built into the Senate's fleet orders:

It would also be an ideal proposition, that everyone who is chosen to go to serve in the galley were to go personally, but that cannot be executed because of many eligibles who are very rich and of high estate (*civil conditione*). Therefore, restricting ourselves to considering those who appear to us as honest, we will release anyone who can put another in his place, so long as the substitute is not himself required to serve.[8]

The immediate and predictable result was that those guilds who could so afford sent hired substitutes to the oars. In fact, there was an active market for unattached persons to serve guilds as crewmen, and brokerage for providing such men was common. Buying an oarsman was not cheap. In the years of the War of Crete (1645-1669) it cost between 1100 and 1700 lire for a guild to post a replacement in the galleys, most of that sum going for an advance on the salary of the *galeotto* and for payment to the broker who delivered him. A remaining 100-200 lire went for outfitting the recruit and for payments to ship's personnel.[9]

It is difficult to judge the prevalence of this practice but it may be said with certainty that it could not have been universal, for the price was doubtless too high for all to pay. A notation in the guild records of the fabbri indicates that there were between fifteen and twenty master ironworkers serving personally in the Adriatic fleet during the early years of the War of Crete.[10]

Associated with the levy of galley crewmen were a series of taxes

---

8. A.S.V., *Senato, mar,* filza 1290, July 15, 1595, section 8.
9. On the cost of posting *galeotti,* see A.S.V., *Arte della Seta,* b. 120, fasc. 349, for records of disbursements in connection with supplying crewmen in the name of *toschani* (silk merchants). A letter from the Silk Office to the Milizia da Mar of April 1658 enclosed in this fascicle complains that 449 ducats, 20 grossi had been given to a broker to find the eight crewmen that the guild merchants were obliged to supply, but he delivered only two. The Silk Office requested that the Milizia da Mar office force the broker to find and deliver the remaining six men. Other materials concerning substitute crewmen may be found in A.S.V., *Milizia da Mar,* nos. 414 and 726.
10. A.S.V., *Archivio delle Arti, fabbri,* b. 129, *Scrittura* of May 12, 1660, p. 6.

and forced deposits to hire crewmen and pay their salaries while in service. In the sixteenth century these taxes were "extraordinary," that is to say non-periodic: they were levied when the need arose. But the sudden demands played such havoc with guild finances that in 1639 this method was replaced by a regular tax, paid in time both of peace and of war, with receipts placed in escrow for use when the need arose. Known as the *tansa insensibile* because of the presumed gentleness of its collection, this tax was assigned to the guild in the same proportion as the carata of crewmen. Internally, the guilds partitioned the tax burden in a number of ways—usually among all members of their organization on the basis of ability to pay. Certain other arti, woolworkers for example, contributed a flat percentage of each piecework fee. Still others had each master pay a fixed amount for each piece of equipment in use. Clothweavers and trimmings makers payed on the number of working looms, silk throwers on each throwing mill, and stocking knitters on each working frame.[11] These and similar defense taxes made up a significant part of fixed and variable costs of production.[12]

It seems almost certain that by the second half of the seventeenth century collection of the tansa insensibile and related taxes became an almost complete substitute for the actual conscription of crews from the arti themselves. It is difficult to be sure what the state of the transition was because official documents invariably avoid recognition of the practice of commutation. The tradition of the guildsmen serving the Republic as crewmen was so strong and so well respected that conscription procedures remained as they had been in the past long after their importance became secondary to taxation. Divisions of crewing obligations were expressed in terms of men, not money, until well into the eighteenth century despite the fact that by this time few if any guild members ever took oar to hand.

So powerful was the will of the state to preserve this tradition that when small monetary contributions to maintain naval strength were called for during the War of Crete, even these were partitioned in terms of men rather than money. In the years 1647 and 1657 the amounts were small enough that, at 130 ducats per (fictional) man,

---

11. A.S.V., *Milizia da Mar,* no. 550, fasc. *sagomadori da oglio.*

12. For information on the tansa insensibile and associated taxes see *Bilanci generali della Repubblica di Venezia,* I (Venice, 1912), introd. pp. clxi-clxvii, 249-250, 541-547.

fractions were required to distribute the burden fairly. Instead of simply expressing the shares in ducats and grossi, the fictitious galeotti were fractionalized into quarters, carats, and grains! As the monetary equivalent of a crewman was figured at the rate of 130 ducats, one *quarto* equalled D 32 d 12 and one *carato* was D 5 d 10½ (1 *huomo* = 4 *quarti* = 24 *carati*). Only after the division was made in this fashion was the actual monetary amount specified.[13]

There were numerous instances of levies during the sixteenth and seventeenth centuries but not every one warranted a new census. Censuses were taken only when the Senate presumed that the structure of guild membership had changed enough to cause inequities if a call-up were made based upon old proportions. The Senate ordered new guild census examinations in the years 1539, 1595, 1603, 1610, 1612, 1618, 1638, 1660, 1672, 1690, and several times more in the eighteenth century.[14]

There are three principal types of guild census records: (1) Carata (levy) lists indicate each guild's share of the conscription burden for a given year. (2) Census summaries enumerate total membership for each guild, plus breakdowns into able-bodied men and ineligibles. Levy lists appear sometimes as adjuncts to those summaries. (3) Guild rolls, which individually list names and ages, were usually organized by guild rank and submitted by each of the arti to the Milizia da Mar when a census was ordered. These rolls survive only for the years 1660, 1672, 1690-1695, and fragmentarily for eighteenth-century census years.

The Derivation of the Census

The three principal types of these census records—the carata lists, census summaries, and guild rolls—require some minor manipulation to render them compatible with each other and to permit comparisons between observation years. In essence, the task is to create a uniform census from diverse bodies of data.

The nine caratade or partitions of the crewing burden among the guilds (table 3.2) do not permit absolute comparisons with one another

---

13. A.S.V., *Milizia da Mar,* no. 720, Sept. 7, 1647, and no. 721, Aug. 14, 1657. The fleet did not institute proceedings for new manpower surveys; both levies were based on the proportions of the caratada of 1638.

14. A.S.V., *Milizia da Mar,* no. 240, *registro decreti.* See the note on sources in the Bibliography for the location and contents of guild census records used in this chapter.

because of call-ups of differing sizes and a varying share of the total burden supplied by non-guild sources (territorial possessions and the scuole grande). However, the percentage liability of each guild to the total burden for each observation year is an accurate measure of the proportion of employment in each of the guilds.

For those years when census summaries and individual guild rolls survive (1595, 1603, 1660, 1672, 1690), a documentary listing of actual employment can be formulated. Along with the total membership of each guild the breakdown into "eligible" and "ineligible" (or "fit" and "unfit") is given as it appears in the guild documents. Eligibles generally are members between the ages of 18 and 45. Unfortunately, the lacunae in the records of actual employment are large. For the years 1595 and 1660 the information is practically complete thanks to the completeness of the census summaries. The census summary for 1603 is only a fragment. Information for the years 1672, 1690, and 1705 comes from individual guild rolls, and data is often missing. In its present state the census information does not lend itself to year-by-year comparisons.

For those years in which both the caratade and *some* actual membership statistics exist, an efficient method for estimating membership in all the guilds may be evolved: essentially to reverse the process by which the Milizia da Mar derived a guild's burden from its actual membership. Having determined what proportion of the able-bodied men in the labor force were needed to fill the galley benches, the Milizia da Mar then applied that proportion to each individual guild enrollment to arrive at its just share. For example, we may suppose that there were 10,000 able-bodied men in the labor force and that galley crews totalling 2,000 men were required. The proportion would be one in five. Ergo, a guild containing 50 able-bodied men would be assigned a carata of 10, a guild of 1500 able-bodied members a carata of 300, and so forth. The sum of the individual burdens would be equal to 2,000. Since our object is to figure out what a guild's total membership would be, knowing only its share of the crewing burden, we can proceed in the following manner:

(1) For each observation year where the levy (carata) and some membership data are known (these are 1595, 1603, 1660, 1672, 1690), we can calculate the equation that expresses the relationship of levy to able-bodied men for all guilds where both variables are known.

(2) For those same observation years we can also find the equation

THE COMPOSITION OF EMPLOYMENT

that expresses the relationship of able-bodied men to total membership where both are known.[15]

(3) Now for each of the other years, using the levy of all guilds
where actual membership information is missing, by applying the first
estimating equation we can derive the projected number of
able-bodied men. Following this, the total membership of these guilds
may be similarly projected from the number of able-bodied men by
employing the second estimating equation.[16]

(4) Finally, subtracting the number of able-bodied men from total
membership in each guild gives the number of ineligibles ("inhabili"
or "cattivi" in Milizia da Mar parlance). As a final task, in those
instances where guild rolls report only actual total membership, but
no breakdown by eligibility, we can apply the second estimator to the
actual membership statistic and derive the probable numbers of able-
bodied and ineligible men.

A synthesis of these procedures has produced an accurate census of
employment for the five observation years across the seventeenth century (table 3.1).

The table of guild obligations to supply crewmen, the levy lists
(table 3.2), is valuable as an analysis of employment in relative terms

---

15. In both instances the best estimator is a linear regression equation. See A. M.
Mood and F. A. Graybill, *Introduction to the Theory of Statistics* (New York, 1963),
pp. 328-330.

16. Coefficients of determination (R^2) for the estimating equations are uniformly
high:

	1595	1603	1660	1672	1690
"Carata to eligible men"	.9976	.7536	.8334	.7555	.7858
"Eligibles to total members"	.9858	.9971	.9618	.9707	.9753

The lower order of accuracy (higher unexplained variation) for the estimator of
eligible men from the carata statistics stems from two causes inherent in fleet procedure.
The proportion that the Milizia da Mar applied to the eligible membership of each guild
to derive the share could not be applied with great accuracy to the numerous small
guilds. Therefore those guilds with small carata shares show a high percentage of error
in estimation, although the absolute numbers are small. Secondly, the Milizia da Mar
made a practice of receiving appeals and making occasional adjustments in the share of
the burden of providing crewmen in special cases, for guilds which could not afford to
deliver their proportional quota. While such concessions were uncommon, distortions
they cause in the proportion of carata to eligible men account for unexplained variations
and somewhat diminish the efficiency of the estimator.

because of its extended range (1539-1690) and greater number of observation years. Its accuracy can be improved by replacing the breakdowns of carate for 1595, 1603, 1660, 1672, and 1690 with the percentage figures of actual membership from table 3.1. The result is a final list of employment in percentage terms which, when reduced to a classification of thirty-six basic occupational groupings, gives the broadest structural picture of employment in seventeenth-century Venice (table 3.3).[17]

OTHER SOURCES—THE CENSUS OF HOUSEHOLDS The exclusive use of guild-related sources for investigating employment has its potential dangers. For one, the records of the Milizia da Mar were compiled for the purpose of raising taxes, and tax declarations must always be handled suspiciously. The temptation for guilds to underestimate their membership must have been great although the state took strong measures to prevent cheating. Further, as previously mentioned, a sizable component of the city work force was not organized into guilds, and many guilds were even outside the jurisdiction of the Fleet Office. To assess the magnitude of these potential failings more fully, the guild census might be compared with the census of households taken in 1642 (among other years) by the parish priests and known as the *anagrafi dei piovani*. While the two bodies of data are not fully compatible one with the other, no serious discrepancies emerge from the comparison. The names of crafts and occupations are more conventionalized in the guild lists and, aside from those omissions noted above, no major source of employment fell outside the scope of the guild census. There were about 110 "organized" crafts in seventeenth-century Venice, and in the census of the priests I have counted no more than 30 additional occupations, most of them insignificant by numerical standards.

In certain ways the anagrafi dei piovani are less useful than the guild
(*text continued on page 78*)

17. The employment census that derives from the Milizia da Mar examinations of guild membership includes about two-thirds of the whole work force of the city (see above, table 2.2). Reviewing the omissions, we have: (1) arsenal workers, both in the major guilds and unaffiliated day-laborers; (2) merchant seamen; (3) wool merchants; (4) cap and hatmakers; (5) *suppialume,* a guild of glass-bead makers; (6) lawyers, physicians, notaries, teachers; (7) unincorporated "street professions"; (8) unincorporated day-laborers; (9) the unemployed who were not guild members; (10) lumber merchants; (11) trained cannoneers; (12) some fishermen (those outside the S. Nicolo community); (13) servants; (14) female workers outside the guilds.

Table 3.1 Total guild membership, by years

Guild	1595			1603			1660			1672			1690			1705		
	Tot.	Good	Bad	Tot.	Good	Bad	Tot.	Good	Bad	Tot.	Good	Bad	Tot.	Good	Bad	Tot.	Good	Bad
Acquaroli	56	43	13	71	62	9	56	40	16	78	42	36	41	18	23	-	-	-
Acquaviteri	-	-	-	117	100	17	143	108	35	162	113	49	150	91	59	125	-	-
Barbieri	282	213	69	324	312	12	458	315	143	511	337	174	657	354	303	740	-	-
Barileri	104	92	12	126	114	12	71	48	23	68	34	34	54	31	23	-	-	-
Bastasi	46	32	14	30	21	9	59	52	7	42	28	14	55	33	22	-	-	-
Battioro allemani	52	50	2	41	33	8	81	59	22	109	59	50	79	39	40	-	-	-
Battioro stagnoli	45	37	8	41	33	8	151	94	57	80	53	27	96	49	47	97	-	-
Battioro con scuola	41	28	13	74	62	12	133	77	56	132	70	62	149	70	79	251	-	-
Bechieri	71	49	22	93	79	14	110	83	27	93	66	27	83	40	43	89	-	-
Biavaroli	57	49	8	63	49	14	124	64	60	134	65	69	138	72	66	-	-	-
Boccaleri	91	69	22	100	83	17	43	28	15	33	24	9	42	27	15	38	-	-
Bombaseri	79	53	26	81	66	15	87	45	42	111	64	47	126	59	67	-	-	-
Bossoleri	84	62	22	69	55	14	72	46	26	99	58	41	139	80	59	140	-	-
Botteri	171	140	31	133	115	18	222	147	75	229	149	80	231	123	108	-	-	-
Burchielli	693	554	139	493	406	87	388	305	83	287	118	169	258	138	120	-	-	-
Calcineri	45	39	6	32	23	9	26	20	6	30	17	13	35	22	13	-	-	-
Caleghieri	727	624	103	901	800	101	968	580	388	769	505	264	1179	647	532	-	-	-
Casaroli	84	60	24	87	79	8	83	39	44	144	86	58	155	81	74	-	-	-
Casseleri	136	105	31	128	110	18	131	72	59	120	58	62	90	45	45	113	-	-
Centureri	49	35	14	58	48	10	8	4	4	9	6	3	-	-	-	-	-	-
Cerchieri	10	6	4	4	3	1	-	-	-	-	-	-	-	-	-	-	-	-
Cesteri	58	46	12	82	70	12	69	31	38	56	36	20	48	22	26	35	-	-

Chiodaroli	52	42	10	66	55	11	17	12	5	23	12	11	22	6	16	19	-	-
Cimadori	323	262	61	255	223	32	174	123	51	170	97	73	90	45	45	-	-	-
Cimolini	801	634	167	655	588	67	429	272	157	329	219	110	162	85	77	102	-	-
Conzacurami	128	109	19	133	114	19	124	78	46	79	59	20	69	63	6	105	14	13
Cordovani	44	32	12	71	60	11	50	32	18	58	38	20	122	63	59	27	-	-
Corieri	62	40	22	-	-	-	58	42	16	65	33	32	55	33	22	-	-	-
Coroneri	52	40	12	69	58	11	67	39	28	86	45	41	62	36	26	-	-	-
Crivelladori	97	80	17	95	81	14	59	49	10	66	29	37	33	17	16	-	-	-
Depentori	432	351	81	277	242	35	367	229	138	323	206	117	314	189	125	-	-	-
Drappieri	541	441	100	503	443	60	617	397	220	620	406	214	620	406	374	303	-	-
Fabbri	503	393	110	319	280	39	420	228	192	464	261	203	686	374	312	100	75	25
Far calze di seta	-	-	-	-	-	-	-	-	-	-	-	-	94	47	47	-	-	-
Fenestreri	84	69	15	106	91	15	79	46	33	74	44	30	101	57	44	-	-	-
Filacanevi	146	121	25	103	88	15	170	106	64	377	260	117	149	78	71	-	-	-
Filatoi	249	193	56	276	148	128	79	48	31	90	47	43	61	30	31	99	-	-
Forneri	189	164	25	173	150	23	263	209	54	285	201	84	271	146	125	-	-	-
Fruttaroli	438	343	95	298	261	37	544	213	331	482	189	293	1035	473	562	-	-	-
Galineri	93	75	18	103	88	15	92	57	35	100	50	50	133	69	64	-	-	-
Garbelladori	29	19	10	53	43	10	30	16	14	45	20	25	30	18	12	-	-	-
Gastaldia S. Nicolo	227	173	54	143	124	19	338	287	51	157	95	62	176	93	83	-	-	-
Gua cortelli	44	31	13	50	41	9	39	23	16	50	27	23	46	22	24	48	-	-

(cont.)

Table 3.1 Total guild membership, by years (cont.)

Guild	1595			1603			1660			1672			1690			1705		
	Tot.	Good	Bad	Tot.	Good	Bad	Tot.	Good	Bad	Tot.	Good	Bad	Tot.	Good	Bad	Tot.	Good	Bad
Ingucchiadori	-	-	-	79	67	12	75	26	49	63	35	28	47	22	25	-	-	-
Intagiadori	73	58	15	90	77	13	77	50	27	122	87	35	68	33	35	113	-	-
Laneri	1222	1117	105	1036	916	120	699	453	246	707	441	266	222	118	104	269	-	-
Lasagneri	-	-	-	-	-	-	23	12	11	31	16	15	31	13	18	34	15	19
Lavoranti al purgo	19	15	4	13	9	4	10	8	2	11	4	7	11	4	7	-	-	-
Libreri da stampa	108	93	15	111	96	15	196	119	77	228	145	83	275	148	127	-	-	-
Libreri di carta	42	32	10	66	55	11	64	36	28	73	45	28	87	44	43	59	-	-
Ligadori di fontego	10	5	5	8	6	2	6	1	5	32	11	21	10	6	4	-	-	-
Linaroli	142	118	24	143	124	19	133	80	53	111	65	46	77	38	39	87	48	39
Luganegheri	209	181	28	197	171	26	310	204	106	306	195	111	447	243	204	291	-	-
Mandoleri	12	12	0	20	15	5	38	23	15	84	46	38	58	21	37	-	-	-
Manganeri	35	28	7	63	53	10	19	7	12	19	12	7	28	11	17	29	14	15
Marangoni di casa	340	311	29	338	297	41	516	310	206	455	295	160	596	350	246	-	-	-
Marzeri	567	464	103	596	526	70	1243	705	538	1301	783	518	1747	961	786	-	-	-
Mercanti di malvasia	99	79	20	103	88	15	78	39	39	80	43	37	50	23	27	49	-	-
Mercanti da vin	98	77	21	133	114	19	40	25	15	52	23	29	53	25	28	-	-	-
Mureri	316	258	58	330	289	41	290	187	103	248	156	92	626	341	285	-	-	-
Oresi	405	346	59	338	297	41	481	221	260	536	288	248	663	392	271	568	-	-
Ortolani	111	91	20	133	114	19	62	24	38	141	95	46	41	18	23	-	-	-
Osti	96	88	8	74	62	12	115	64	51	98	56	42	104	54	50	-	-	-

Panataroli	42	28	14	63	53	10	70	42	28	15	2	13	41	18	23	-	-
Passamaneri	-	-	-	-	-	-	119	79	40	111	72	39	133	69	64	169	-
Paternostreri	-	-	-	-	-	-	99	81	18	141	84	57	119	62	57	122	-
Peateri	220	175	45	218	190	28	228	154	74	243	153	90	447	243	204	-	-
Peliceri	21	19	2	50	41	9	9	5	4	6	4	2	-	-	-	-	-
Pesce, compravende	94	14	80	-	-	-	50	26	24	58	28	30	117	60	57	57	-
Pestrineri	36	34	2	58	48	10	41	23	18	15	8	7	10	4	6	13	-
Petteneri da tella	13	10	3	12	9	3	13	7	6	14	5	9	11	5	6	-	-
Petteneri da testa	84	67	17	101	86	15	104	65	39	96	56	40	99	50	49	-	-
Pistori	349	340	9	322	282	40	285	240	45	282	239	43	691	377	314	-	-
Portatori da vin	468	421	47	250	219	31	409	302	107	526	381	145	583	318	265	-	-
Sabbioneri	12	8	4	8	6	2	33	14	19	25	16	9	17	5	12	-	-
Sagomadori da oglio	22	14	8	58	48	10	21	15	6	21	10	11	30	12	18	-	-
Salumieri	-	-	-	117	100	17	123	42	81	238	103	135	253	135	118	256	-
Sanseri	243	98	145	143	124	19	213	103	110	237	148	89	263	141	122	-	-
Saponeri	111	91	20	103	88	15	121	36	85	116	57	59	90	45	45	-	-
Sartori	642	528	114	503	443	60	549	393	156	637	384	253	714	446	268	-	-
Scalchi e cuogi	60	43	17	77	65	12	63	25	38	33	14	19	53	26	27	199	-
Scaleteri	143	113	30	114	98	16	169	104	65	172	103	69	103	53	50	-	-
Scorzeri	115	82	33	170	148	22	59	44	15	174	106	68	38	17	21	-	-
Sonadori	61	33	28	71	60	11	172	116	56	91	67	24	35	21	14	-	-

(cont.)

THE COMPOSITION OF EMPLOYMENT

Table 3.1 Total guild membership, by years (cont.)

Guild	1595			1603			1660			1672			1690			1705		
	Tot.	Good	Bad	Tot.	Good	Bad	Tot.	Good	Bad	Tot.	Good	Bad	Tot.	Good	Bad	Tot.	Good	Bad
Spaderi	103	82	21	83	62	21	38	21	17	51	34	17	48	22	26	38	-	-
Spechieri	356	303	53	237	207	30	712	586	126	809	590	219	648	353	295	518	-	-
Spicieri	509	428	81	399	351	48	634	388	246	678	406	272	951	521	430	-	-	-
Squeraroli	148	118	30	159	138	21	188	129	59	226	160	66	170	114	56	-	-	-
Strazzaroli	140	102	38	143	124	19	123	82	41	141	74	67	235	85	150	211	-	-
Tagiapiera	224	169	55	213	185	28	222	141	81	285	204	81	436	237	199	222	-	-
Tamisi e crivelli	6	5	1	4	3	1	16	10	6	12	8	4	15	4	11	-	-	-
Tellaroli	104	89	15	130	112	18	114	64	50	135	78	57	88	44	44	94	-	-
Tentori	393	342	51	303	266	37	277	195	82	255	162	93	447	243	204	-	-	-
Terrazeri	54	37	17	77	65	12	86	58	28	126	61	65	175	92	83	-	-	-
Tesseri fustagno	82	75	7	103	88	15	208	124	84	200	124	76	156	81	75	-	-	-
Tesseri pani lana	856	714	142	703	621	82	518	357	161	443	271	172	224	119	105	163	-	-
Tesseri di tella	277	234	43	170	148	22	164	91	73	173	89	84	144	75	69	-	-	-
Testori seta	1541	1308	233	703	621	82	1117	700	417	1159	789	370	1179	647	532	1221	-	-
Toschani	273	222	51	271	237	34	344	220	124	356	228	128	529	288	241	-	-	-
Traghetti	1741	1226	515	1710	1524	186	1243	804	439	1243	804	439	1243	804	439	-	-	-
Varoteri	107	79	28	122	105	17	71	42	29	101	62	39	107	66	41	-	-	-
Vazineri	19	13	6	16	12	4	10	6	4	-	-	-	-	-	-	-	-	-
Verieri	30	24	6	53	43	10	39	22	17	45	20	25	30	18	12	-	-	-
Zacheri	8	6	2	4	3	1	3	1	2	-	-	-	-	-	-	-	-	-

Marangoni	431	359	72	464	408	56	–	–	–	–	–	–	–	–	–	–	–	–
Arsenale	786	641	145	815	719	96	–	–	–	–	–	–	–	–	–	–	–	–
Calafati	161	129	32	166	143	23	–	–	–	–	–	–	–	–	–	–	–	–
Remeri																		
Total	22504	18194	4310	20253	17570	2683	21051	13314	7737	21626	13371	8255	24049	13176	10873	(7213)	(166)	(111)

(cont.)

THE COMPOSITION OF EMPLOYMENT

Sources: Citations for Milizia da Mar materials are given in abbreviated notation; for example, A.S.V., *Milizia da Mar,* no. 540, *fascicolo bombaseri,* is here reduced to M540, *bombaseri.* Sources by year are:

1595: Correr, *Cod. Donà dalle Rose,* b. 228, pp. 227-231.

1603: M708. The fragment of the 1603 census summary appears on the cover of this fascicle.

1660: M540, *bombaseri.* Also individual guild rolls in M538-557.

1672, 1690, 1705: individual guild rolls, M538-557. Where no source citation appears for the years 1672, 1690, and 1705, the roll can be found in the folder bearing the name of the guild in question within these 19 numbers. Often several numbers are shelved together in one busta. For access, the index "Milizia da Mar" in the Archivio di Stato contains the alphabetical list of folders and the corresponding bundle number where the folder may be found.

Unless otherwise noted, membership statistics are transcribed from the notation of the Milizia da Mar clerk on the back of each roll. In instances where this notation is missing, I have determined totals by counting names on the roll and such cases are footnoted, "by count."

A note, "dated by ages," means that the guild roll in question bears no date and that I have determined the approximate date by finding individual names which appear on other rolls and subtracting ages.

Where *bombardieri* are listed in guild rolls, they have been omitted by me from the numbers of able-bodied men to render guild-roll data compatible with census summaries which never include *bombardieri.*

Notes: Citations are referenced to data by guild and year. Italics identify figures that have been projected from draft quotas. Material in the original document which was visible only with the aid of ultraviolet light is indicated as "u.v." "Habili" and "inhabili" are rendered as "good" and "bad" respectively.

Acquaviteri (1660): the census summary membership totals are confirmed by the individual guild roll, M538, *acqua di vita;* (1690, 1705): u.v.

Barbieri (1705): M552, *scortegadori da bovi.* The misplacement of this guild roll is amusing. Why should the roll of the barbers guild have been put in the folder for slaughterers?

Barileri (1672): u.v.

Bastasi:

	1595 Good	1595 Bad	1603 Good	1603 Bad	1660 Good	1660 Bad	1672 Total
Bastasi da doana da mar	15	7	13	6	19	5	24
Bastasi da doana da terra	11	7	8	3	30	-	18
Bastasi in fonteco	6	-	-	-	3	2	-
	32	14	21	9	52	7	42

Battioro con scuola (1690): dated by ages; (1705): document total is 301. 47 non-active members and 3 bombardieri are subtracted for the usable total of 251.

Bechieri (1660): the census summary membership totals are confirmed by the guild roll in M539, *bechieri;* (1690): guild ranks were abandoned by the butchers in 1690 as the craft became an "open profession" (*arte aperta*) with no guild restrictions (M539, *bechieri,* scrittura of May 30, 1690); (1705): M539, 66 *bechieri;* M552, 23 *scortegadori da bovi.*

Biavaroli (1660): census summary gives: Total 124, Good 54 (*sic*), Bad 60.

Bombaseri (1690): of the 126 bombaseri, 43 have double professions and have become tellaroli, stramazeri (mattress makers), cordaroli, and sanseri.

Botteri (1672): an additional 158 members have left the craft or the city ("che non si trova").

Burchielli: for 1595, 12 boatmen's organizations are listed: for 1603, six; for 1660 and 1672, three.

Casaroli (1660): census summary gives: Total 83, Good 39, Bad 34 (*sic*).

Centureri (1660): the 1660 census summary gives: Total 4 (*sic*), Good 4, Bad 4.

Cerchieri (1660): by 1660 the craft had been abandoned in Venice.

Cesteri (1672, 1690, 1705): u.v.

Chiodaroli (1660): the census summary totals are confirmed by the guild roll, M542, *chiovaroli;* (1672): table total includes 5 "poveri" omitted from the document total; (1690): by count.

Cimolini: M544, *garzotti;* M542, *cimadori*

	1595 Good	1595 Bad	1660 Good	1660 Bad	1672 Good	1672 Bad	1690 Total	1705 Total
cimolini	-	-	141	79	75	51	95	102
garzotti & revedini	-	-	131	78	144	59	67	-
	634	167	272	157	219	110	162	102

Cordovani (1672): M547, *mercanti cordovani;* (1705): M542, *conzacurami.*

Corieri:

	1595 Good	1595 Bad	1660 Good	1660 Bad
corieri da Roma	18	14	28	4
portalettere di Padova	20	6	14	12
portalettere di Vicenza	2	2	-	-
	40	22	42	16

(cont.)

THE COMPOSITION OF EMPLOYMENT

Coroneri (1690): u.v.
Crivelladori:

	1595 Good	Bad	1660 Good	Bad	1672 Good	Bad	1690 Good	Bad
crivelladori e pesadori di formento	56	9	27	6	22	12	17	16
mesuradori di formento	24	8	22	4	25	7	-	-
	80	17	49	10	47	19	17	16

Depentori (1690): M543, *depentori:*

		Total	Good	Bad
Depentori	maestri	27	12	15
	lavoranti	28	20	8
	garzoni	12	0	12
Miniadori	maestri	27	14	13
	lavoranti	27	13	14
	garzoni	-	-	-
Coridoro	maestri	29	10	19
	lavoranti	57	47	10
	garzoni	-	-	-
Doradori	maestri	39	17	22
	lavoranti	39	38	1
	garzoni	-	-	-
Desegnadori	maestri	21	13	8
	lavoranti	8	5	3
	garzoni	-	-	-
		314	189	125

Fabbri:

	1595 Total	Good	Bad	1660 Total	Good	Bad	1672 Total	Good	Bad
fabbri, caldereri & subguilds	448	380	108	393	211	182	442	249	193
stagneri & peltreri	15	13	2	27	17	10	22	12	10
fabbri totals	503	393	110	420	228	192	464	261	203
fabbri: maestri				128			115	70	45
lavoranti				41			38	34	4
garzoni				67			68	15	53

	1595			1660			1672		
	Total	Good	Bad	Total	Good	Bad	Total	Good	Bad
non-working maestri	-						19	13	6
stadieri [1672 figures include also lavezeri, bronzeri, strazaferi]:									
maestri	11						15	8	7
lavoranti	-						13	9	4
garzoni	5								
maestri without shops	-						32	15	17
caldereri: maestri	27						29	19	10
lavoranti	12						18	17	1
garzoni	5						18	2	16
non-working maestri	-						5	1	4
mercanti di ferro e merce: maestri	31						32	20	12
lavoranti	14						9	9	0
garzoni	15						8	2	6
non-working maestri	-						2	2	0
schiopeteri: maestri	7						11	9	2
lavoranti	4						7	1	6
garzoni	5						-	-	-
non-working maestri	-						3	3	0
strazaferi: maestri	11						[see stadieri]		
lavezeri: maestri	16								
lavoranti	0						[see stadieri]		
garzoni	4								

Source: 1672, 1690: M543, *fabbri;* 1705: by count.

Far calze di seta: (1690, 1705): M541, *calze di seta.*

Filatoi (1603): M389, *Risposta, Arte di Filatogi,* May 12, 1630; (1660): census summary gives: Total 81 (*sic*), Good 48, Bad 31; (1690, 1705): by count.

Forneri (1690): by count.

Fruttaroli (1672): u.v., includes *erbaroli* (green grocers) and *naranzeri* (citrus fruit sellers); (1690): by count.

Gastaldia S. Nicolo (1660): census summary gives: Total 343 (*sic*), Good 287, Bad 51.

Gua cortelli (1690, 1705): by count.

Ingucchiadori (1690): by count.

Intagiadori (1705): count.

Laneri (1690): by count. *Confratelli* number 222. Omitted from this total are 34 working children and 50 workers who have moved to the mainland;

(cont.)

68

THE COMPOSITION OF EMPLOYMENT

(1705): by count. Of the 269 members, 189 are Venetians and 80 are foreigners working in Venice and affiliated with the guild.

Lavoranti al purgo (1672): M541, *camera del purgo.*

Libreri da stampa (1660): the census summary membership totals are confirmed by the individual guild roll, M545, *libreri da stampa;* (1690): by count.

Libreri di carta (1660): census summary gives: Total 61 (*sic*), Good 36, Bad 28; (1672): M542, *carteri;* (1690): M545, *libreri;* (1705): M542, *carteri.*

Linaroli (1690): by count.

Luganegheri (1705): by count.

Mercanti di malvasia (1660): the census summary membership totals are confirmed by the individual guild roll, M547, *mercanti di malvasia;* (1690): by count.

Mureri (1672): u.v.; (1705): a fragmentary guild roll (M546, *mureri,* u.v.) lists 240 master masons, but other ranks are not given.

Osti (1690): by count.

Panataroli (1672): M551, *saponeri, rollo di pistori,* 1672.

Passamaneri (1690, 1705): by count.

Paternostreri: listed in census summaries and rolls as *cristalleri e paternostreri da vero;* (1690): M542, *cristalleri,* 94 paternostreri (glass bead makers), stationeri da vero (glass sellers); (1705): *ibid.*, by count.

Peliceri (1660): summary totals confirmed by guild roll, M548, *pelizzeri.*

Pesce, compravende (1690): M542, *compravende pesce,* by count.

Pestrineri (1690): by count. Guild roll of 1693 is used.

Petteneri da testa (1690): by count.

Pistori (1672): M551, *saponeri.*

Salumieri (1660): summary totals confirmed by guild roll, M550, *salumieri;* (1690), 1705): by count.

Sanseri:

	1595			1660		
	Total	Good	Bad	Total	Good	Bad
Sanseri in Fontego dei Tedeschi	55	15	40*	23	11	12
Sanseri in Rialto	188	83	105	190	92	98
	243	98	145	213	103	110

*Listed erroneously as 39 in M540, *bombaseri* summary. *Sanseri di cambii* (exchange brokers) pay 200 ducats per year instead of contributing men, and are thus not included.

Saponeri (1672): M550, *sagomadori d'oglio:* (1690): M551, *saponeri,* by count.

Sartori (1690): dated by ages, total by count.

Scalchi e cuogi (1705): by count.
Scaleteri (1690): total is for 1696.
Scorzeri (1690): total is for 1695.
Spaderi (1690, 1705): by count.
Spechieri (1672): over 200 additional members are listed as "fuori," i.e., left
the guild or the city.
Spicieri (1660): M555, *spetieri*

		1660			1672		
		Total	Good	Bad	Total	Good	Bad
Spetieri da grosso	maestri	168	102	66	175	99	76
	giovani	135	114	21	295	186	109
	garzoni	132	56	76			
Spetieri medicinali	maestri	86	48	38	85	51	34
	giovani	48	45	3	123	70	53
	garzoni	65	23	42			
		634	388	246	678	406	272

Squeraroli (1690): by count.
Strazzaroli (1705): by count.
Tamisi e crivelli (1690): by count.
Tellaroli (1690): dated by ages; total by count.
Terrazeri (1690): by count.
Tesseri fustagno (1672): M544, *fustagneri;* (1690): by count.
Varoteri (1690): by count; total is for 1693.
Verieri (1660): summary totals confirmed by guild roll, M542, *cristalleri e
paternostreri da vero, rollo di verrieri.*
Marangoni Arsenale (1595): Lane, *Navires,* App., p. 231. Totals are for the
year 1591; (1603): Romano, "Construction of Warships," *C & C,* p. 75.
Romano has projected the numbers of shipwrights and oarmakers from
1591 proportions.
     Since arsenal workers were not subject to the draft of crewmen, the sub-
totals for "good" and "bad" are invalid except in reflecting the universal
proportions of age and fitness within these guilds. Since information on
Arsenal personnel is not known for later observation years, tables 3.3 and
3.9 are calculated on the basis of 104 guilds, omitting the three guilds of
the Arsenal.
Calafati: *see* Marangoni Arsenale.
Remeri: *see* Marangoni Arsenale.

THE COMPOSITION OF EMPLOYMENT

Table 3.2. Levy lists

Guild	1539	1595	1603	1610	1612	1638	1660	1672	1690
Acquaroli	12	14	19	20	19	19	19	16	15
Acquaviteri	0	0	30	30	0	16	25	34	35
Barbieri	40	68	60	70	60	90	95	100	102
Barileri	5	29	36	36	30	30	25	25	27
Bastasi	7	9	10	10	10	11	12	10	11
Battioro allemani	2	15	15	15	10	18	18	22	22
Battioro stagnoli	6	12	12	12	12	20	40	32	32
Battioro con scuola	3	8	14	20	16	20	20	30	30
Bechieri	40	15	21	36	25	35	40	44	44
Biavaroli	6	15	16	24	18	20	25	30	33
Boccaleri	24	21	24	36	24	24	15	12	12
Bombaseri	20	15	22	30	26	26	24	26	26
Bossoleri	8	19	4	16	14	14	10	10	10
Botteri	15	44	30	44	34	50	50	50	50
Burchielli	205	175	259	331	52	54	58	58	55
Calcineri	6	13	10	13	13	15	10	10	10
Calegheri	140	198	220	250	225	225	225	225	225
Casaroli	35	19	25	36	30	40	36	36	36
Casseleri	24	33	38	40	33	32	25	25	24
Centureri	6	11	8	12	0	10	0	0	0
Cerchieri	8	2	1	0	0	0	0	0	0
Cesteri	10	14	17	20	17	17	17	17	14
Chiodaroli	3	13	11	12	8	10	6	5	4

THE COMPOSITION OF EMPLOYMENT

Cimadori	40	82	82	90	86	80	60	54	0
Cimolini	100	200	236	206	140	181	176	158	0
Conzacurami	12	34	36	40	30	32	30	26	27
Cordovani	8	9	13	25	25	20	30	30	30
Corieri	0	0	0	0	0	10	16	12	11
Coroneri	16	12	12	20	11	13	20	20	21
Crivelladori	20	24	22	27	25	36	36	36	38
Depentori	37	110	90	110	75	85	80	90	68
Drappieri	70	140	175	180	180	200	185	180	0
Fabbri	89	128	106	126	116	124	126	132	134
Far calze di seta	0	0	0	0	0	0	0	0	0
Fenestreri	16	21	26	30	28	30	26	28	28
Filacanevi	20	36	25	40	30	35	40	35	35
Filatoi	20	60	50	60	52	52	30	28	26
Forneri	30	52	51	60	52	54	60	65	67
Fruttaroli	70	107	98	130	100	130	130	138	167
Galineri	10	23	25	40	28	32	32	32	32
Garbelladori	12	5	6	10	6	6	6	6	6
Gastaldia S. Nicolo	62	54	40	50	40	44	40	40	40
Gua cortelli	2	9	5	5	4	8	8	8	10
Ingucchiadori	0	0	16	20	18	20	12	12	12
Intagiadori	4	18	20	18	15	17	16	20	20

(cont.)

Table 3.2 Levy lists (cont.)

Guild	1539	1595	1603	1610	1612	1638	1660	1672	1690
Laneri	175	383	375	383	350	350	300	270	0
Lasagneri	0	0	0	0	0	0	4	4	6
Lavoranti al purgo	4	5	5	5	5	6	4	3	3
Libreri da stampa	28	29	28	28	26	30	30	30	32
Libreri di carta	5	9	11	11	11	14	14	16	17
Ligadori di fonteco	2	2	2	2	2	2	3	2	2
Linaroli	24	38	40	48	42	42	40	40	40
Luganegheri	30	58	60	70	60	75	80	85	90
Mandoleri	10	4	5	10	7	9	16	18	16
Manganeri	12	8	10	16	10	14	12	10	10
Marangoni di casa	50	98	113	130	115	130	130	130	126
Marzeri	147	141	210	210	210	250	350	350	330
Mercanti di malvasia	10	26	25	30	25	30	30	30	31
Mercanti da vin	25	24	36	60	40	40	40	40	40
Mureri	50	81	110	130	112	130	130	125	123
Oresi	60	109	113	120	116	124	134	140	140
Ortolani	6	29	36	36	18	20	15	15	15
Osti	25	28	14	18	14	18	25	25	27
Panataroli	10	8	10	12	12	14	15	15	15
Passamaneri	0	0	0	0	22	20	20	20	18

Paternostreri	0	0	0	40	0	40	40	35	35
Peateri	30	56	68	80	70	90	90	90	90
Peliceri	10	5	5	5	5	2	2	2	0
Pesce, compra-vende	35	4	0	0	0	7	7	10	10
Pestrineri	2	10	8	8	8	8	6	6	7
Petteneri da tella	2	3	3	3	1	2	3	2	2
Petteneri da testa	12	21	24	24	20	30	30	30	30
Pistori	30	108	107	110	110	120	125	130	135
Portatori da vin	25	132	80	140	100	110	110	115	115
Sabbioneri	5	2	2	2	2	4	4	4	4
Sagomadori da oglio	8	4	8	12	10	10	12	12	13
Salumieri	0	0	30	30	24	28	28	30	30
Sanseri	30	30	40	40	40	42	66	64	56
Saponeri	10	29	25	30	30	40	40	40	40
Sartori	40	167	175	180	150	160	160	160	158
Scalchi e cuogi	19	14	15	30	16	20	10	6	7
Scaleteri	6	36	29	36	30	40	30	32	32
Scorzeri	30	25	50	60	50	52	55	45	46
Sonadori	10	10	13	13	13	16	5	5	7
Spaderi	13	25	14	20	20	18	10	8	10
Spechieri	10	96	75	96	80	140	140	130	127
Spicieri	50	136	136	136	136	156	170	180	183
Squeraroli	25	38	46	46	20	36	40	46	47

(cont.)

Table 3.2 Levy lists (cont.)

Guild	1539	1595	1603	1610	1612	1638	1660	1672	1690
Strazzaroli	20	32	40	50	45	50	62	62	67
Tagiapiera	40	54	66	80	80	85	80	85	88
Tamisi e crivelli	3	2	1	2	2	4	4	3	3
Tellaroli	20	28	35	40	35	40	40	60	65
Tentori	60	109	100	110	80	100	90	90	90
Terrazeri	5	12	15	15	13	13	13	13	13
Tesseri fustagno	32	23	25	30	30	35	35	35	36
Tesseri pani lana	100	226	250	250	210	230	180	162	0
Tesseri di tella	18	74	50	60	48	56	56	54	50
Testori seta	100	414	250	250	200	270	250	225	225
Toschani	35	70	88	90	90	110	100	100	105
Traghetti	487	368	632	690	0	380	380	0	0
Varoteri	30	26	32	36	36	35	30	30	31
Vazineri	4	4	4	4	0	0	0	0	0
Verieri	12	7	6	8	8	8	6	6	6
Zacheri	0	1	1	2	0	0	0	0	0
Total	3304	5367	5787	6577	4746	5910	5855	5442	4633

Sources: Citations for Milizia da Mar materials are given in abbreviated notation; for example, A.S.V., *Milizia da Mar*, no. 540, *fascicolo bombaseri*, is here reduced to M540, *bombaseri*.

Sources by year are:

1539: M705.

1595: Correr, *Cod. Donà dalle Rose*, b. 228, pp. 227–231, also M707.

1603 and 1610: M707.

1612 and 1638: M540, *bombaseri*.

1660: A.S.V., *Senato, terra, filza* 883, January 1673, *m.v.*, also A.S.V., *Archivio delle Arti, fabbri*, b. 110, *Registro termination e sententie*, pp. 106–107.

1672: *ibid.*, also M273.

1690: *ibid*

Notes: Citations are referenced to data by guild and year. If no source citation accompanies a datum, then the figure appears in the table exactly as in the documentary listing.

Bastasi (1539): totals are sums of the three separate guilds, e.g., for 1539:

Bastasi da doana da mar	3
Bastasi da doana da terra	2
Bastasi in fonteco dei tedeschi	2
	7

Bechieri (1660): as of 1660 *bechieri* include *scortegadori da bovi* (A.S.V., *Senato, terra,* filza 687, Jan. 24, 1660, *m.v.*) Formerly the slaughterers were exempt from supplying crewmen (A.S.V., *Senato, mar,* filza 1290, Nov. 25, 1595).

Burchielli (1539): the number of separate boatmen's organizations in the levy lists decreases from 12 in 1539 to 3 in 1660.

Cerchieri (1610): by the seventeenth century coopers bought their barrelhoops from the mainland and the craft died out in Venice (A.S.V., *Giustizia Vecchia,* ser. 15, b. 131).

Cimolini: the Naval Personnel Administration grouped three subguilds together: preliminary shearers (cimolini), teaselers (garzotti), and burlers (revedini).

Corieri (1638): the sum of obligations of three guilds: *corieri di Roma, portalettere di Padova,* and *portalettere di Vicenza.*

Crivelladori: I have grouped together two guilds, the *crivelladori e pesadori di formento* and the *mesuradori di formento.*

Drappieri (1690): not given.

Fabbri:	1539	1595	1603	1610	1612	1638	1660	1672	1690
fabbri e caldereri	70	124	100	120	110	120	120	126	127
stagneri e peltreri	7	4	6	6	6	4	6	6	7
coltreri	12								

Far calze di seta: there are no levy listings for the stocking-knitters guild which orginated in the 1680's.

Paternostreri: appears in lists as *cristalleri e paternostreri da vero;* (1612): not given.

Sanseri: I have combined the two guilds of *sanseri in Rialto* and *sanseri di Fonteco dei Tedeschi.* Other small brokers' groups—exchange brokers, grain brokers, and brokers in the Ghetto—are not present in levy lists.

Spaderi: appears in carata lists as *spaderi e coltreri.*

Traghetti (1612, 1672, 1690): not given; (1638 and 1660): A.S.V., *Senato, terra,* filza 687, March, 1661.

Vazineri (1612): incorporated into *spaderi e coltreri.*

Zacheri (1612): incorporated into *spaderi e coltreri.*

Table 3.3. Distribution of employment among occupation groups, by percentage

Group	1539	1595	1603	1610	1612	1638	1660	1672	1690
Art & music	1.42	2.33	1.85	1.87	1.62	1.71	2.56	1.91	1.45
Baking	2.30	3.42	3.57	3.31	3.75	3.86	3.74	3.49	4.60
Barbering	1.21	1.33	1.72	1.06	1.10	1.52	2.18	2.36	2.73
Boatmen	21.85	12.56	12.87	16.74	14.94	8.87	8.83	8.20	8.10
Books & paper	1.00	0.71	0.94	0.59	0.68	0.74	1.23	1.39	1.50
Brokerage	0.91	1.15	0.76	0.61	0.74	0.71	1.01	1.10	1.09
Butchering	1.21	0.34	0.49	0.55	0.46	0.59	0.52	0.43	0.34
Carpentry	1.51	1.61	1.80	1.98	2.12	2.20	2.45	2.10	2.48
Chemicals	0.18	0.21	0.22	0.18	0.22	0.34	0.72	0.37	0.40
Cloth merchants[a]	9.56	8.07	9.17	9.09	10.72	11.30	12.06	12.18	13.25
Cooperage, pottery	2.60	2.70	3.05	2.67	2.54	2.59	2.55	2.34	1.93
Couriers	0.0	0.29	0.0	0.0	0.0	0.17	0.28	0.30	0.23
Distilling	0.0	0.0	0.62	0.46	0.0	0.27	0.68	0.75	0.62
Fishing	2.94	1.52	0.76	0.76	0.74	0.86	1.84	0.99	1.22
Food-selling	4.93	4.65	5.38	5.47	5.06	5.79	6.25	7.12	8.99
Glass & mirrors	0.67	1.83	1.54	2.19	1.62	3.18	4.04	4.60	3.31
Grain dealers	0.79	0.73	0.84	0.78	0.79	0.95	0.87	0.92	0.71
Hotel & kitchen service	1.33	0.74	0.80	0.73	0.55	0.64	0.84	0.61	0.65
Jewelry	1.82	1.92	1.80	1.82	2.13	2.10	2.28	2.48	2.76
Knitting	0.0	0.0	0.42	0.30	0.33	0.34	0.36	0.29	0.59
Leather & furs	2.91	2.19	3.21	2.70	2.69	2.55	1.52	1.97	1.40
Lime & sand	0.33	0.27	0.21	0.23	0.28	0.32	0.28	0.25	0.22
Masonry, stonework	2.87	2.81	3.30	3.42	3.77	3.86	2.84	3.05	5.14
Metalwork	3.94	4.13	3.74	3.36	3.48	3.79	4.07	4.29	4.71

Oil & soap	0.54	0.63	0.86	0.64	0.74	0.85	0.67	0.63	0.50
Porters & stevedores	1.39	2.74	1.91	2.61	2.41	2.40	2.52	3.13	2.86
Rope	0.60	0.69	0.55	0.61	0.55	0.59	0.81	1.74	0.62
Ship & boatbuilding	0.76	0.70	0.84	0.70	0.37	0.61	0.89	1.04	0.71
Shoemaking & cobbling	4.24	3.44	4.79	3.80	4.14	3.81	4.60	3.56	4.90
Spices	1.88	2.55	2.40	2.22	2.61	2.74	3.15	3.34	4.08
Tailoring	1.21	3.04	2.67	2.74	2.76	2.71	2.61	2.95	2.97
Textile workersb	13.14	15.31	14.94	14.17	14.68	14.60	9.24	8.58	5.87
Turning & woodcarving	0.85	0.99	1.21	0.82	0.74	0.74	1.03	1.42	1.12
Weaving	7.57	13.04	8.93	8.97	8.98	10.00	9.53	9.13	7.08
Windows	0.48	0.40	0.56	0.46	0.51	0.51	0.38	0.34	0.42
Wine merchants	1.06	0.93	1.25	1.37	1.20	1.18	0.56	0.61	0.43
Total	100.01	100.00	100.00	99.99	100.01	100.00	100.01	100.00	100.00

Source: tables 3.1 and 3.2.
aIncluding mercers and drapers
bExcluding merchants and weavers

THE COMPOSITION OF EMPLOYMENT

censuses of the Milizia da Mar for analyzing employment. By far the major deficiency is that only the occupation of household heads is recorded in the anagrafi; no account is taken of brothers and sons living under the headship of a more senior worker. Thus, if the five sons of a carpenter were all carpenters, we do not know it; likewise if sons were to have deserted the professional calling of their father while living in his domicile the anagrafi would give no such indication.

Another problem is that the numerous statutory middle class, the *cittadini*, are rarely identified in the household census by occupation. This group, which was of particular importance in commerce, government service, and the professions, was about 7 to 10 percent of the population of Venice during this century. Finally, the census of the priests was taken only three times in the 1600's and the records are not at present complete for any one observation year.[18]

On the other hand, one great advantage for scholarship that the house-by-house, parish-by-parish anagrafi provide is a spatial portrait of occupational distribution throughout the city. The impression one receives is of a city sharply subdivided into distinct, local economic regions. This comes as no great surprise for an early modern city and yet, considering that in the seventeenth century, as today, no point in the city was more remote from any other than an hour's walk, it is noteworthy that most people lived within the immediate neighborhood of their work centers. To illuminate this point, let us have a closer look at the 1642 censuses of Castello and Dorsoduro, the two most maritime quarters of the city. Both regions covered large areas—Dorsoduro, including the Giudecca, was the biggest sestiere and Castello was third in terms of area behind Cannaregio (which was still something of a garden-spot). In 1642 Castello and Dorsoduro were alike in two important respects. Each held within its confines one of the poorer popular parishes of the city (S. Pietro di Castello and S. Nicolo dei Mendigoli in Dorsoduro) and each relied more on the sea for the livelihood of its populace than other districts. Castello, in which about 23,000 persons lived in 5,000 households, was the site of

18. Beltrami, *Storia,* p. 72. Beltrami, the first to use the anagrafi dei piovani as a systematic source of demographic data, adduces evidence from a census of S. Polo in 1642 which would form a complete run of six sestieri for that year. Now, twenty years after the publication of Beltrami's book, I have been unable to find the S. Polo census and consequently no complete census of the city at one time is accounted for in my findings. For the location of extant household census records see the note on sources in the bibliography.

the Arsenal and the center of the seafaring community. Dorsoduro, with 20,616 individuals in 4,174 households, was the center of the community of fishermen. In Dorsoduro better than one of ten households was headed by a fisherman. Of these 565 households, 381 were in the parish of S. Nicolo, 140 on the Giudecca Island, and only 44 others located elsewhere in the district. The S. Nicolo community was organized under a *gastaldo* and subject to galley taxes like a guild. It was, correspondingly, a privileged community from at least a ceremonial standpoint, for the gastaldo would by tradition treat with the doge as an equal one day a year, embracing him in comradeship as a sign of lower-class support for the aristocratic government.

After fishing, the next occupation in order of importance in Dorsoduro was woolworking which occupied a total of 354 families including raw wool processors, weavers, shearers, and finishers. The center of the wool industry was in nearby S. Croce on the canal known as the Rio Marin, and the vast majority of the city's woolworkers lived in and around this area, overflowing into Dorsoduro. Across the Grand Canal, in all of Castello woolworkers headed a total of only 26 families!

The silk industry was more dispersed than woolen manufacture for there was less need for central facilities. Still, silk had to be boiled and thrown, and Dorsoduro was something of a silkmaking center with over 200 households engaged in this craft. Interestingly, many of these silkworkers were single women, whose occupation was listed only as "fa seda." Noteworthy also is the fact that in Dorsoduro, as in all the rest of the city, fully 10 percent of the households were headed by widows.

Other major occupations in Dorsoduro were servants (211 households) and boatmen (181 *barcaroli,* 41 *peateri* households). Two hundred fifty families were headed by individuals for whom no profession was listed on the census forms. Fifty families in the district (304 individuals), most of them on the Giudecca, drew their livelihood from the tanneries, and many of the city's market-gardeners (*ortolani*) lived and worked on the Guidecca as well. Of the myriad occupations that were not peculiar to one district but common to each and every neighborhood in Venice, Dorsoduro had its normal measure: shoemakers, porters, masons, bakers, various shopkeepers and local provisioners—each accounted for a small but significant proportion of the local labor force.

THE COMPOSITION OF EMPLOYMENT

Castello was in many ways similar to Dorsoduro, even down to the activity of the poor quarter. There is no record of an equivalent in Castello to the "Doge of the Nicoletti" but community spirit ran high enough to power teams of *castellani* in various regattas and in the pugilistic free-for-alls on the *ponte dei pugni*. Yet the household census shows that Castello was very different from Dorsoduro in terms of employment. There were practically no clothworkers, few leatherworkers, and only seventeen families of fishermen in the entire district. Castello was dominated by the port and the Arsenal. Over two hundred families in the district were headed by professional sailors. Although the proportion of widows to the total population was no higher in this quarter than elsewhere, it can be presumed that many Castello widows were the wives of seamen who sailed from the city and did not return.

The shipbuilding industry was the mainstay of the local economy of Castello; more than one family in ten was headed by an Arsenal worker. There were 395 carpenters' households, 265 families of caulkers, and 73 of oarmakers.[19] Nowhere in the city was the localization of craft and dwelling more evident than here. In 1641 workers in the state shipyard belonging to the major crafts (carpenter, caulker, oarmaker) numbered about 1,200.[20] There were at the time 730 households in Castello headed by major craft workers so that, even if each of these families supplied no more than one worker, 60 percent of the Arsenal work force is accounted for in Castello. In reality the figure must be closer to 80 or 90 percent, for the sons of many master craftsmen must have served the Arsenal under their fathers' tutelage. The average size of families headed by Arsenal workers in Castello was about 4.5 persons. Most of the sawyers, Arsenal foremen, and shipmasters also lived in the port district. Aside from the seamen and shipwrights no other occupational group bulked large enough to be deemed characteristic of the district. There were many porters and servants for work on the *molo* and in the inns of the region, but the remaining households represented every walk of life in Venice from nobleman to fish-peddler.

Actually the largest group in Castello was no group at all. The census lists over 900 families with whom no craft was associated. They are

19. The census-taking priests did not trouble to distinguish between house carpenters and shipwrights, but it is fair to assume that the vast majority of carpenters in Castello worked for the shipyard.

20. Romano, "Economic Aspects," p. 71.

recorded as *persone da sole,* or simply by a surname, or often by place of origin if they were recent or transient arrivals in the city. The average family size of this miscellaneous body of households was 3.4, significantly below the district average of 4.2, and the average number of juveniles in these families (1.2) was radically less than the norm (about 2 per family). The tempting assumption is that these are exclusively poor households which, without the steady livelihood of a professional calling, were forced to limit family size. But this idea must be rejected, for the "profession-unknown group" is too heterogeneous to generalize. In fact, for every hundred families in this group there were in their employ about 18 domestic servants—a much higher ratio than most of the crafts enjoyed. Only 32 maids and manservants were to be found employed among all the 730 Arsenal workers' families. While the profession-unknown group cannot properly be classified as "the poor," it is probable that industrial day-laborers belonging to no guild formed the majority of the unclassified group in the anagrafi dei piovani. It stands to reason that there were many unclassified workers in Castello because both the Fleet and the Arsenal made heavy use of non-guild wageworkers who were hired for temporary employment.

For just this kind of information the anagrafi prove to be most useful. They provide a feel for the city economy and the location of its various concentrations of living and working centers, and they offer demographic data about family composition that is of considerable value *sui generis.* But they cannot serve to check directly on the guild censuses, for three reasons: the observation years are not close enough to the observation years of the Milizia da Mar censuses—differing results may be attributed either to discrepancies in the census materials or to changes that took place in employment composition over time. Second, lacking an observation year in which all six districts are represented means that the occupational distribution will be askew; the concentration of certain occupations in localities exacerbates this problem. Finally, as we have said, a census of occupations by household heads rather than by individual workers necessarily omits much. The household census of the priests is of interest for the economic history of the city of Venice, but it is grist best suited to the demographer's mill.

The General Characteristics of the Labor Force

The guilds which were subject to the census of personnel conducted

THE COMPOSITION OF EMPLOYMENT

by the Milizia da Mar represented about two-thirds of the eligible work force of Venice. Over the course of the seventeenth century certain trends stand out in high relief as common to most of these guilds. With respect to their size, the age and quality of their membership, and the nature of rank within, this major segment of the labor force reveals common strengths and common weaknesses which were the critical determinants of Venice's economic welfare during her fight to adjust to new commercial circumstances.

It is notable that although there were massive shifts from one sector of the economy to another, the size distribution of the guilds remained more or less constant over the century (table 3.4). This is an important indication of a stabile yet flexible system of economic organization which at once accommodated intersectoral shifts and inhibited over-concentration.

Table 3.4. Size distribution of Venetian guilds

Membership	1595	1603	1660	1672	1690
Over 1,000	3	2	3	2	4
500-999	10	8	9	9	12
250-499	14	16	14	14	10
100-249	24	33	27	31	26
50-99	25	29	27	24	22
Less than 50	24	13	22	19	24
Observations	100	101	102	99	98

Source: table 3.1.

AGE AND QUALITY   In contrast to the lack of change in the distribution of guild membership during the century, drastic alterations occurred in the personnel within the guilds. The decline in the number and proportion of workers in the most productive ages, between 18 and 45, is apparent in table 3.1. In 1595 and 1603 able-bodied men of this age group comprise 81 and 87 percent respectively of total guild membership. By 1660 this proportion is reduced to 63 percent and by 1672, 62 percent. In 1690 only one out of two guild members (54%) was within the prime age group. The decline in the proportion of 18-to-45 year-olds occurs almost universally, without reference to the

THE COMPOSITION OF EMPLOYMENT

occupational fortunes of the guild.[21] Industrial guilds were quite as subject to this decline as were the boatmen, merchants, construction workers, or foodsellers, and even those engaged in occupations which thrived during the years of economic crisis—the mirror-makers, spice dealers, and goldsmiths, for example. By and large, the guilds that originated in the seventeenth century suffered the same depletion of 18-to-45 year-old workers as the older guilds.[22]

Aging was the cause of the fall-off of manpower in the maximum productivity age group. There was an apparent aging trend for the population as a whole in the latter half of the century, especially in comparison to the years 1630-1660 when, after the plague, young immigrants refilled the city. This migrational "clump" skewed the age distribution of the population throughout the century—first toward youth in the 1630's and 1640's and then progressively toward aging as the large immigrant group grew old together (table 3.5).

The aging trend in the labor force is notably and understandably more pronounced than that of the population in general. Since we

---

21. These average proportions are derived from membership figures before missing values were added, this because the imputed values themselves are based upon the proportions of eligibles to total membership as they emerge from the documentary statistics. In fact, the slopes of the regression lines give an accurate portrayal of the declining proportion of able-bodied men.

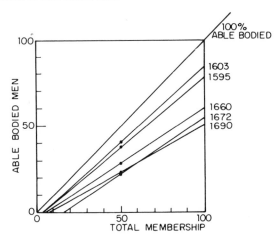

22. An exception was the silk stocking makers guild which first incorporated in the 1680's and whose membership in 1705 was three-quarters eligible.

THE COMPOSITION OF EMPLOYMENT

Table 3.5. Age composition of the Venetian population (by percentage)

Age group	1601-10	1631-40	1661-70	1691-1700
0-17	36.0	39.5	37.2	32.3
18-49	44.5	40.8	42.2	46.3
50+	19.5	19.7	19.6	21.4

Source: Beltrami, Storia, p. 91. For comparison, the age distribution of the population of England and Wales for 1695 was: 0-19 years, 47.8%; 20-49 years, 35.6%; 50+ years, 16.5%. Expectation of life at birth was 32 years (Peter Laslett, The World We Have Lost [New York, 1965], p. 103).

may readily suppose that the majority of migrants in the immediate post-plague period were labor-force entrants, it follows that the dispersion around the mean age of workers was reduced and that as the century wore on and this dominant cohort grew older, the mean age of the work force increased apace. Table 3.6 shows the pervasiveness of this trend in the second half of the century.

Judging from the severity of the drop in numbers of able-bodied men for the first half of the century, it is a safe guess that if age statistics for the guilds were available for the years 1600-1660, the increase in average age would stand out by contrast even more strikingly than it does in the 1660-1705 period.

The long War of Crete during the middle of the century almost surely accelerated the aging of the work force by removing those same able-bodied men listed on the guild rolls, although we have no means to estimate the magnitude of this effect. Over its quarter-century course the war cost many Venetian lives, especially during the campaigns of the fifties and the final siege of Candia at the end. We know that as early as 1647, after the government became concerned with the prospect of the city becoming depopulated of draft-age men, the old conscription method was formally abandoned; official procedures were prescribed for hiring mercenary (even foreign) crews and using sentenced criminals at the oars.[23] From that point the enrollment

23. Nani-Mocenigo, Storia della marina, p. 40. Late in the sixteenth century, guild members were allowed to send substitutes for galley service on an individual basis, but with the establishment of the tansa insensibile in 1639 procurement through official channels became the standard procedure for arming the galleys.

Table 3.6. Average ages of members for eighteen selected guilds, 1660-1705

Guild	Masters				Journeymen				Apprentices				All ranks combined			
	1660	1672	1690	1705	1660	1672	1690	1705	1660	1672	1690	1705	1660	1672	1690	1705
Battioro stagnoli	-	36.8	44.9	44.9	-	27.5	24.7	28.5	-	16.3	15.5	17.1	-	28.5	29.7	33.8
Battioro con scuola	-	46.7	46.6	40.8	-	-	38.3	31.2	-	-	13.6	14.7	-	-	37.8	35.2
Bechieri	42.7	37.7	46.3	46.0	33.3	37.8	-	-	18.9	25.8	-	-	36.6	35.5	-	-
Cesteri	-	45.0	52.1	50.2	-	32.1	31.5	41.3	-	15.6	16.0	13.6	-	35.7	41.2	40.3
Chiodaroli	45.2	48.4	58.2	58.9	43.0	36.3	49.4	47.0	24.5	24.0	-	-	42.5	41.5	53.8	50.2
Conzacurami	-	46.5	51.7	48.9	-	32.4	-	39.0	-	20.0	-	14.5	-	43.7	51.7	46.9
Filatoi	-	43.7	44.8	41.6	-	31.9	39.4	-	-	15.9	16.8	-	-	32.8	40.8	41.6
Laneri	-	-	-	-	-	-	-	-	-	-	-	-	-	29.6	45.6	38.8
Linaroli	-	37.9	40.3	38.3	-	31.5	35.8	28.9	-	15.5	15.2	16.6	-	28.5	33.4	29.9
Mercanti di malvasia	43.5	43.8	47.8	49.1	30.1	28.7	30.8	27.9	14.6	15.9	16.9	19.8	33.4	32.7	38.1	40.2
Oresi	-	39.2	41.5	45.5	-	27.2	28.3	39.1	-	14.7	20.6	29.5	-	28.4	37.5	42.0
Passamaneri	-	36.4	43.9	49.3	-	27.7	28.3	25.6	-	15.3	15.3	15.9	-	29.3	36.3	37.3
Salumieri	42.9	36.8	41.0	40.7	-	24.1	29.4	-	16.0	15.2	16.4	-	37.0	29.0	32.9	40.7
Saponeri	-	40.7	41.5	-	-	23.5	27.2	-	-	16.5	16.7	-	-	31.1	33.4	-
Spaderi	-	43.9	41.6	48.6	-	29.3	27.4	41.9	-	17.4	16.8	-	-	33.9	34.1	46.1
Tellaroli	-	37.2	41.6	49.4	-	23.2	26.0	27.1	-	14.9	15.8	-	-	28.3	31.6	39.6
Tesseri lana	-	43.9	50.0	48.0	-	27.3	23.5	23.0	-	19.0	-	13.5	-	38.6	42.9	43.6
Testori seta	-	41.1	-	44.3	-	31.3	-	35.8	-	18.0	-	12.5	-	36.8	-	38.2

Source: A.S.V., Milizia da Mar, b. 538-557.

THE COMPOSITION OF EMPLOYMENT

of guildsmen becomes largely an administrative fiction. Still, some workers did serve their guilds in the benches of galleys and as cannoneers, and many more guild members must have seen service as the hirelings of wealthier counterparts who could afford to send others in their place. The notable drop in the number of able-bodied gondoliers of the city's *traghetti* by the year 1660 (table 3.1) might be due to such practices.

The average ages as listed in table 3.6 for the eighteen guilds give clear evidence of the aging problem. Only the goldthread makers (battioro con scuola) show a decrease in mean age in the latter part of the century. For all others, the mean age rose between 1672 and 1705. Although all ranks show increases in age, the effect is most uniform and severe among the masters.

The aging effect dominated most occupations regardless of their relative state of prosperity. Among the goldsmiths and jewelers (oresi) for example, whose numbers rose and whose fortunes flourished throughout the century, the average age of members continued to increase. The age of the average master jeweler was 39 years in 1672 and 46 in 1705. More dramatically, the age of the average journeyman jumped from 27 to 39 over the same span. It is true however that in superannuated professions which had lost their attraction to potential recruits the aging proceeded much more rapidly. Over the last third of the century the mean age of swordsmiths increased by 12 years. Likewise for the various wool guilds (laneri, cimadori, chiodaroli, tesseri di panni di lana) the average increased considerably faster than for most others, and by the eighteenth century when output was less than 2,500 cloths per year, the mean age of woolworkers was among the highest of all Venetian workers.

RANK   Guild regulations and customs about ranking were designed to protect continuity of practice, employment, and skills. Apprentices to the profession would receive instruction while working for individual masters and, upon completion of a statutory term, could graduate to the rank of journeyman. Journeymen, while still typically associated with the shop of a single master, were free agents not under long-term contracts. Accession to the highest rank of master was permitted by the guild only after proof that the journeyman was capable of maintaining the standards of the craft and transmitting them to his trainees. Only then could he open an enterprise or a shop in his own name.

The continuity built into this system could not always be perpetuated. When the supply of labor was inadequate or when recruitment to the guild failed, gaps developed in the progression of workers through the ranks. In many industries this could debilitate the production process because masters (whose status was usually more that of "production manager" than "workman") needed other hands to perform the basic operations of the craft.[24] Such problems occurred frequently in Venetian industrial guilds during the latter part of the seventeenth century.[25] An analysis of guild membership categorized by rank (table 3.7) holds several surprises in store. Contrary to what might be supposed, masters are typically the largest group. For the half-century spanned by the observation years, masters on the average comprise roughly half the membership of a guild. Lavoranti account for only a fourth to a third, and apprentices only a fourth to a sixth. Even so, the rank structures did not remain constant over time. The percentage of masters to total guild membership increased steadily during the second half of the century. The proportion of lavoranti shows no clear trend, while the share of apprentices steadily diminished. This clearly indicates the inability of the guilds, on the average, to obtain new members in sufficient numbers to offset aging in the labor force. In 1660 masters accounted on the average for 49 percent of total membership, in 1705 for 58 percent. Correspondingly the proportion of apprentices dropped from 25 percent in 1660 to 14 percent in 1705.

The phenomenon of aging within the guilds was common to most occupations, but in those professions which became unattractive as a result of their declining economic fortunes, the proportion of masters increased more sharply than in other occupations. While most guilds experienced some rise in the relative number of masters as a natural corollary to aging, the effect was less pronounced in occupations which remained profitable. These variations may be observed in detail by

---

24. See above, chap. 2, pp. 44, 46.

25. Apprehension about internal changes in the guilds was frequently expressed before the Giustizia Vecchia along with requests for changes in guild statutes; see A.S.V., *Giustizia Vecchia, Collegio alle Arti,* b. 223.

Table 3.7. Distribution of members among the guild ranks

Guild	1660			1672			1690			1705		
	Mas	Lav	Gar	Mas	Lav	Gar	Mas	Lav	Gar	Mas	Lav	Gar
Acquaroli	56	0	0	-	-	-	-	-	-	-	-	-
Acquaviteri	86	57	0	123	13	26	118	32	0	84	28	13
Barbieri	226	117	115	254	132	125	354	187	136	400	184	156
Barileri	53	6	12	46	3	19	38	10	6	-	-	-
Bastasi	57	12	0	42	0	0	-	-	-	-	-	-
Battioro allemani	40	25	16	55	19	35	-	-	-	-	-	-
Battioro stagnoli	-	-	-	42	10	28	42	14	40	49	23	25
Battioro con scuola	53	46	34	44	48	40	69	54	26	142	73	36
Bechieri	34	76	0	58	17	18	50	33	0	89	0	0
Biavaroli	74	0	50	81	15	38	-	-	-	-	-	-
Boccaleri	9	24	10	11	20	2	9	26	7	12	26	0
Bombaseri	36	13	38	-	-	-	62	34	30	-	-	-
Bossoleri	35	14	23	67	15	17	81	39	19	89	22	29
Botteri	164	12	46	168	61	0	-	-	-	-	-	-
Burchielli	105	213	70	-	-	-	-	-	-	-	-	-
Calcineri	26	0	0	30	0	0	35	0	0	25	25	0
Calegheri	278	424	266	-	-	-	-	-	-	-	-	-
Casaroli	49	0	34	-	-	-	-	-	-	-	-	-
Casseleri	55	36	40	61	29	30	-	-	-	79	31	3
Centureri	4	1	3	9	0	0	-	-	-	-	-	-
Cerchieri	-	-	-	-	-	-	-	-	-	-	-	-
Cesteri	23	16	10	26	22	8	27	18	3	16	12	7

Chiodaroli	6	9	2	11	11	1	22	16	6	9	10	0
Cimadori	106	66	2	107	55	8	-	-	-	-	-	-
Cimolini	362	0	67	329	0	0	162	0	0	102	0	0
Conzacurami	76	18	30	63	7	9	74	25	12	88	15	2
Cordovani	30	7	13	42	3	13	-	-	-	19	5	3
Corieri	58	0	0	-	-	-	-	-	-	-	-	-
Coroneri	32	13	22	46	12	28	48	9	5	-	-	-
Crivelladori	59	0	0	66	0	0	33	0	0	-	-	-
Depentori	219	93	41	-	-	-	143	159	12	-	-	-
Drappieri	-	-	-	-	-	-	-	-	-	-	-	-
Fabbri	221	81	118	272	90	102	-	-	-	266	0	0
Far calze di seta	-	-	-	-	-	-	-	-	-	25	47	28
Fenestreri	42	13	24	47	15	12	28	25	41	-	-	-
Filacanevi	125	0	45	291	86	0	61	30	10	-	-	-
Filatoi	28	35	16	33	24	23	34	16	11	36	41	22
Forneri	66	122	75	65	160	60	78	113	80	-	-	-
Fruttaroli	322	53	169	331	61	90	706	163	166	-	-	-
Galineri	59	12	21	56	14	30	-	-	-	-	-	-
Garbelladori	30	0	0	-	-	-	-	-	-	-	-	-
Gastaldia S. Nicolo	94	224	20	-	-	-	-	-	-	-	-	-
Gua cortelli	39	0	0	50	0	0	39	3	4	36	9	3

(cont.)

Table 3.7. Distribution of members among the guild ranks (cont.)

Guild	1660			1672			1690			1705		
	Mas	Lav	Gar	Mas	Lav	Gar	Mas	Lav	Gar	Mas	Lav	Gar
Ingucchiadori	36	0	39	40	4	19	36	4	7	-	-	-
Intagiadori	43	16	18	49	45	28	-	-	-	70	25	18
Laneri	699	0	0	707	0	0	222	0	0	269	0	0
Lasagneri	8	7	8	10	7	14	31	0	0	15	10	9
Lavoranti al purgo	10	0	0	11	0	0	-	-	-	-	-	-
Libreri da stampa	75	70	51	64	117	47	66	167	42	-	-	-
Libreri di carta	32	11	18	43	13	17	54	13	22	38	21	0
Ligadori di fonteco	6	0	0	-	-	-	-	-	-	-	-	-
Linaroli	45	45	43	40	33	38	37	23	17	39	22	26
Luganegheri	148	116	46	-	-	-	-	-	-	195	96	0
Mandoleri	15	9	14	-	-	-	28	13	17	-	-	-
Manganeri	6	2	11	6	5	8	16	6	6	12	10	7
Marangoni di casa	393	0	123	-	-	-	596	0	0	-	-	-
Marzeri	743	144	356	641	660	0	-	-	-	-	-	-
Mercanti di malvasia	41	16	21	36	23	21	26	17	7	29	12	8
Mercanti da vin	40	0	0	52	0	0	53	0	0	-	0	-
Mureri	260	0	30	237	11	0	-	-	-	240	0	0
Oresi	129	131	221	253	87	196	436	75	152	210	208	150
Ortolani	62	0	0	70	0	71	-	-	-	-	-	-

Osti	21	57	37	20	78	0	15	59	30	-	-	-
Panataroli	-	-	-	15	0	0	-	-	-	-	-	-
Passamaneri	58	25	36	62	19	30	80	36	17	94	36	39
Paternostreri	51	24	24	-	-	-	83	11	0	108	14	0
Peateri	218	0	10	237	0	6	-	-	-	-	-	-
Peliceri	3	6	0	6	0	0	-	-	-	-	-	-
Pesce, compra-vende	50	0	0	-	-	-	117	0	0	-	-	-
Pestrineri	-	-	-	8	7	0	10	0	0	13	0	0
Petteneri da tella	6	4	3	12	0	2	0	0	1	-	-	-
Petteneri da testa	57	21	26	51	27	18	56	32	11	-	-	-
Pistori	30	255	0	45	237	0	-	-	-	-	-	-
Portatori da vin	409	0	0	526	0	0	-	-	-	-	-	-
Sabbioneri	16	3	14	25	0	0	-	-	-	-	-	-
Sagomadori da oglio	21	0	0	21	0	0	-	-	-	-	-	-
Salumieri	94	29	0	132	29	77	144	34	75	157	37	62
Sanseri	213	0	0	-	-	-	-	-	-	-	-	-
Saponeri	72	0	49	69	8	39	51	17	22	-	-	-
Sartori	222	117	210	340	147	150	385	129	200	199	0	0
Scalchi e cuogi	63	0	0	33	0	0	53	0	0	-	0	0
Scaleteri	42	58	69	33	84	55	103	0	0	-	-	-

(cont.)

Table 3.7. Distribution of members among the guild ranks (cont.)

Guild	1660			1672			1690			1705		
	Mas	Lav	Gar	Mas	Lav	Gar	Mas	Lav	Gar	Mas	Lav	Gar
Scorzeri	17	35	7	91	0	0	38	0	0	-	-	-
Sonadori	172	0	0	91	0	0	-	-	-	-	-	-
Spaderi	13	13	12	25	14	12	24	16	8	22	16	0
Spechieri	324	215	173	392	267	150	-	-	-	392	120	6
Spicieri	254	183	197	260	418	0	-	-	-	-	-	-
Squeraroli	90	69	29	81	103	42	80	69	21	-	-	-
Strazzaroli	101	0	22	63	78	0	183	16	36	131	80	0
Tagiapiera	24	143	55	25	218	42	-	-	-	23	173	26
Tamisi e crivelli	9	5	2	8	3	1	10	2	3	-	-	-
Tellaroli	74	4	35	71	28	36	45	19	24	29	25	40
Tentori	108	123	46	88	127	40	-	-	-	-	-	-
Terrazeri	39	47	0	56	45	25	95	51	29	-	-	-
Tesseri fustagno	92	52	64	103	50	47	116	30	10	-	-	-
Tesseri pani lana	307	199	12	323	153	5	167	57	0	137	24	2
Tesseri di tella	61	64	39	62	70	41	52	69	23	-	-	-
Testori seta	475	368	274	733	426	0	-	-	-	823	367	31
Toschani	-	-	-	-	-	-	-	-	-	-	-	-
Traghetti	-	-	-	-	-	-	-	-	-	-	-	-
Varoteri	35	14	22	60	9	32	42	28	37	-	-	-
Vazineri	6	1	3	-	-	-	-	-	-	-	-	-
Verieri	32	0	7	-	-	-	23	0	2	-	-	-
Zacheri	3	0	0	-	-	-	-	-	-	-	-	-

Marangoni arsenale	–	–	–	–	–	–	–	–	–	–	–	–
Calafati	–	–	–	–	–	–	–	–	–	–	–	–
Remeri	–	–	–	–	–	–	–	–	–	–	–	–
Observations	10110	4539	3908	9352	4592	2071	5886	1999	1433	4811	1847	751

Sources: 1660: A.S.V., *Milizia da Mar*, no. 540, fasc. *bombaseri*; 1660-1705: *ibid.*, no. 538-557.

Note: Because indications of rank in the guild rolls are often incomplete, and occasionally not given at all, and because the rolls categorize non-working masters, sons of masters, and bombardiers outside the ranks, the sum of masters, journeymen, and apprentices for any guild in table 3.7 ("mas," "lav," "gar," respectively) frequently does not correspond to total membership as reported by table 3.1.

THE COMPOSITION OF EMPLOYMENT

comparing the different weavers' guilds which, despite the similarity of their crafts, met with a variety of fortunes (table 3.8).

The woolcloth weavers were among the hardest hit by the fall-off in demand for Venetian products. Output of wool cloths at mid-century, already much reduced from earlier levels, was about seven to nine thousand cloths per year. In the early years of the eighteenth century it was barely more than two thousand.[26] The number of wool weavers was depleted through deaths and mass departures by more than two-thirds between 1660 and 1705, with a concomitant elevation in the

Table 3.8. Weavers' employment and proportion of masters

Weavers' Guild	Number of weavers			
	1660	1672	1690	1705
Wool cloth	518	443	224	163
Fustian	208	200	156	-
Cheap cloths	164	173	144	-
Silk cloth	1,117	1,159	1,179	1,221

Weavers' Guild	Percent of the labor force			
	1660	1672	1690	1705
Wool cloth	2.46	2.05	0.93	-
Fustian	0.99	0.92	0.65	-
Cheap cloths	0.78	0.80	0.60	-
Silk cloth	5.30	5.36	4.90	-

Weavers' Guild	Masters' share of guild membership (percent)			
	1660	1672	1690	1705
Wool cloth	59.3	67.3	74.6	84.1
Fustian	44.2	51.5	74.4	-
Cheap cloths	37.2	35.8	36.1	-
Silk cloth	42.5	63.2	-	67.4

Source: table 3.1.

---

26. Domenico Sella, "The Rise and Fall of the Venetian Woollen Industry," *C & C*, p. 110.

proportion of masters. Depressed aggregate demand caused contraction in most, if not all industries, but those whose fortunes were not exclusively bound up in export manufacturing were hurt less directly and with less impact. Such was the case in the non-woolen branches of the textiles sector. The fustian weavers diminished slightly in number and in labor force share and the proportion of masters in the guild grew rapidly. The weavers of cheap cloths (*tesseri di tella*) also fell off in number and labor force share, but in this case the proportions of the ranks within the guild remained almost constant through the half-century.

The silk industry saw its share of troubles during the seventeenth century, for it too depended largely on export for the sale of its product. However, by altering the characteristics of the product and of traditional methods of selling, the industry managed to maintain a stable value of output and to make actual gains in total employment over the century. Despite a short period of difficulty in securing recruits in the 1680's the profession continued to be sufficiently attractive that the proportion of apprentices and journeymen did not fade away as it did in the woolweavers guild.[27]

The selective deterioration of guilds in other industries which failed to sustain output under seventeenth-century market conditions was the natural consequence of the aging and recruitment problems afflicting the labor force.

The combination of commercial and demographic difficulties of the seventeenth century had distinct effects upon the quality of the labor force. The working population grew older; the proportion of workers in the years of their maximum productivity decreased; and entry of new workers into the guilds dropped selectively, intensifying incapacity where it already existed. These interrelated phenomena reinforced the inclemencies of the international market. It is an admissible hypothesis that the decay within the labor force affected the sources of Venetian productivity in the industrial sector so adversely that what might have been merely a cyclical depression became an auto-generating industrial decline.

---

27. See above, chap. 2, text and notes 45 and 70.

THE COMPOSITION OF EMPLOYMENT

Allocation of Labor

While the level of total employment did not fall in Venice during the seventeenth century, the economy responded to the diminished aggregate demand, both foreign and domestic, with adjustments in the structure of employment. Workers transferred out of failing industries into more stable occupations, and new entrants were not recruited for the declining guilds. Industrial output, of course, suffered. But the overall output of goods and services in all sectors could not have fallen off to any significant degree without affecting adversely the number of people the economy could support, or the amount of that support—the real wage; and in that there was no reduction, nor in the size of the work force or of the total population.[28]

The census of 107 guilds can be condensed under 36 basic occupational categories for purposes of observing the changes in the employment structure (table 3.3). Here it is more evident which occupations, having lost their attractiveness, declined as a share of the total labor force, and which occupations replaced them and grew. The most serious losses were among boatmen, leatherworkers and furriers, textile workers, wine merchants, and butchers. Major growing occupations were foodsellers, bakers, spicers, construction workers, printers, tailors, retailers, jewelers, and glass and mirror-makers.

Dividing the membership of the guilds into the three basic economic sectors—food (mainly processing and selling), manufacturing, and services—reveals that manufacturing accounts for 55 to 59 percent of total employment over most of the seventeenth century but that by 1690 it falls to a low of 50.68 percent (table 3.9). A division by subsectors pinpoints decline in industrial manufacturing and non-food service employment and growth in foods, retail and trade, and construction.

It is noteworthy that the apportionment of labor to the manufacturing sector was the same at the end of the seventeenth century, after Venice's day as an industrial power had passed, as it had been in 1539 prior to her great industrial spurt. Peak periods of manufacturing employment (vis-à-vis total employment in 1595-1603, 1612-1638, and

---

28. See below, chap. 4, pp. 131-132.

Table 3.9. Percentage distribution of labor among economic sectors

Category	1539	1595	1603	1610	1612	1638	1660	1672	1690
Broad sectors									
Food	14.59	14.05	14.23	14.70	14.13	15.36	15.97	16.31	18.97
Manufacturing	49.82	58.15	57.75	54.65	55.23	58.82	54.86	54.81	50.68
Services	35.60	27.80	28.02	30.64	30.65	25.82	29.17	28.88	30.35
Total	100.01	100.00	100.00	99.99	100.01	100.00	100.01	100.00	100.00
Subsectors									
Food	14.59	14.05	14.23	14.70	14.13	15.36	15.97	16.31	18.97
Industry	31.59	39.97	36.92	35.82	35.69	39.24	35.50	36.33	28.89
Craft	14.71	14.54	16.66	14.43	14.85	14.64	14.83	14.38	15.76
Construction	3.52	3.64	4.17	4.40	4.69	4.94	4.53	4.10	6.03
Non-food services	26.60	18.99	19.29	22.03	20.24	14.86	16.31	15.77	15.46
Retail and trade	9.00	8.81	8.72	8.61	10.41	10.96	12.86	13.11	14.89
Total	100.01	100.00	100.00	99.99	100.01	100.00	100.01	100.00	100.00
Export-related employment									
Export-related	33.93	44.25	40.65	39.30	41.04	43.98	39.11	39.42	33.42
Non-export	66.08	55.75	59.34	60.69	58.96	56.02	60.89	60.58	66.58
Total	100.01	100.00	100.00	99.99	100.01	100.00	100.01	100.00	100.00

Sources: tables 3.1 and 3.2.

THE COMPOSITION OF EMPLOYMENT

1672) correspond approximately to peak output years for wool-cloth production, the best available proxy for industrial output as a whole.[29] In the years between and shortly after the plagues (1570's-1630's) the manufacturing share of the labor force was at its highest, paralleling the quick recoveries of wool output to secular levels. This speed of recovery of the labor force belies once and for all the notion that short-run discontinuities in labor supply were responsible for the long-run failure of Venetian industry to compete.[30]

Shifts away from manufacturing among the city labor force were concentrated in the areas of retailing, construction, and food processing, while other service professions—tailoring, arts and music, and transportation—showed little growth either in labor share or in absolute numbers. Individual guilds showing the largest growth in employment were barbers, gold-beaters and chemists, grain sellers, fruit sellers, printers and bookshop owners, pork butchers, carpenters and masons, drygoods retailers, dried-fish sellers, mirrormakers, spice dealers and sugar refiners, and pavers.[31] Food services showed particularly large gains. The number of shops increased during the seventeenth and eighteenth centuries; the number of food shops in the city doubled between 1661 and 1773.[32] The increased concentration of employment, in food services particularly, is difficult to explain. It can only be surmised that such occupations afforded more security than the selling of goods or services of higher income elasticity. The appealing suggestion that Venice's growing preeminence as a host city for tourism, revelling, and *dolce far niente* caused a boom in hostelry and catering services is hardly supported by the employment census: membership of the inn-keepers and cooks and butlers guilds remained small and static.

---

29. See Sella, "Rise and Fall," p. 109.

30. The thesis that occasional labor shortages were at least in part responsible for industrial failure crops up in Pullan, *C & C,* introd. p. 13, and "Wage-Earners," p. 169, as well as in Cipolla, "The Economic Decline of Italy," p. 140.

31. Growth in the mirrormakers and printers guilds is a surprising exception to the glum industrial employment picture, especially considering that both industries were subject to the fiercest foreign competition. The monopolies in mirrormaking and printing, which were once exclusively Venice's, were broken in the seventeenth century by French glass manufactories and Dutch and German printshops. Yet Venice did not entirely lose her grip on the international market, and employment in both guilds grew through the century.

32. Beltrami, *Storia,* pp. 50, 214.

MANUFACTURING   Of the more than half of the Venetian labor force employed in the manufacturing sector, most were engaged in production processes which, in a premodern sense, could rightfully be called "industrial": there was in these processes a degree of division of labor and specialization along with some use of capital equipment. Clothmaking traditionally led other manufactures in the degree of specialization of labor, use of machinery (looms, throwing mills, etc.), and large-scale establishments (drying shops, dyeworks, etc.). Textile workers made up the majority of the industrially organized work force. Other manufactures in which the technology of production required industrial characteristics were, for example, chemical industries like distilling, paintmaking, sugar refining, soapmaking, and dyeing—all prominent Venetian industries. The processing of hides and the manufacture of leather articles was a highly specialized industry represented by no less than five different guilds in Venice. Perhaps the most industrialized activities of all were shipbuilding,[33] glassmaking and mirrormaking—industries in which production most closely resembled modern manufacturing, with large production units and significant economies of scale, a highly specialized division of labor, and relatively extensive capital inputs. These too were Venetian specialties. Still and all, textile manufacture typically accounted for about one half of all non-handicraft workers in the manufacturing sector, with all other industrial activities employing the remaining half. The employment census indicates that textile workers represented an even larger share of the total industrial labor force, but since the census omits arsenal workers and one of the glassmakers guilds (*suppialume*) it gives an undervaluation for non-textile industrial labor.

Handicraft manufacturing occupations were numerous and varied in Venice. Their share of the labor force, which amounted to about one-sixth of the total work force early in the century, seemed largely unaffected by shifts in the composition of employment. Craft occupations were not attractive alternatives for those who abandoned the industrial labor pool.

---

33. The private shipyards (*squeri*) had some industrial traits, but the state arsenal was unique in the early modern world for its grand scale of production and its sophisticated organization of labor.

THE COMPOSITION OF EMPLOYMENT

THE MANUFACTURE AND SALE OF CLOTHS   The importance of the clothmaking industries from the standpoint of employment has been already noted, as this industry was preeminent in the Venetian economic order. Clothmakers, cloth vendors, and workers in associated crafts made up fully one-third of the incorporated work force. Making and selling cloth, as the Venetians fully understood, had widespread linkages with other industries: chemicals for dyestuffs; wood and metal working for looms, frames, mills, shops, and other capital equipment; and transportation.[34] Adjustments in textile employment were critical to the economy of Venice, despite the diversity of industries in the city. The economy hinged on cloth manufacture because so many consumers' livelihoods were linked to it. If the textile industries of Venice had failed altogether during the seventeenth century, complete economic collapse would surely have followed. This never came to pass. Overall employment in textiles diminished somewhat during the century but departures from the industry were neither precipitate nor drastic.

Of all textile manufactures woolen cloth was the most important in terms of both employment and output. With the steep decline in foreign demand for Venetian woolens the percentage of total employment in the industry fell from over 15 percent in 1595 to about 3 percent by 1690, and simultaneously the output of wool cloths fell from 21,000 to 2,000 (figure 3). The collapse of the wool market was the greatest single blow to the Venetian economy during the seventeenth century.

Silkmaking fared better than wool as the industry adapted better to equally vigorous competition from new foreign silk-cloth producers. During the seventeenth century silk-thread spinning—and the guild of *filatoi*—virtually died out in Venice, undercut by the cheaper and more efficient terraferma mills. Gold-thread making on the other hand grew appreciably because of new emphasis on fine and expensive cloth-of-gold, and this rise is mirrored in the increasing membership of the guild of *battioro con scuola* (*tiraoro*). While the actual number of silk cloths produced in Venice diminished over the century, the

---

34. Recognition of this interrelatedness caused the silk guild to assert that an infinite number of people derived their incomes from the silkmaker's craft (above, chap. 2, note 30).

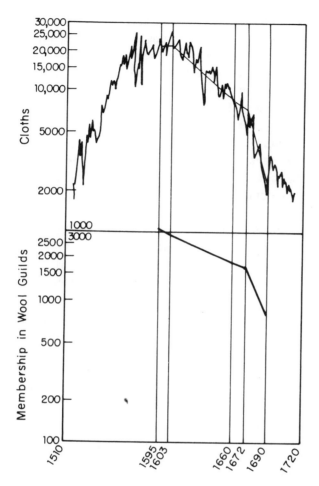

3. Output and employment in the woolen industry
Source: Sella, "Rise and Fall," p. 108; table 3.10.

value of output probably remained more or less constant because of
the shift to finer qualities. This changeover helped keep the industry
alive and in competition with the new French cloths in new markets—Turkey and Germany rather than France and England.[35] A

---

35. Sella, *Commerci,* p. 86.

THE COMPOSITION OF EMPLOYMENT

second adaptation that permitted the survival of silkweaving was the partial elimination of the putting-out silk merchant; thus at diminished cost weavers could use part of their time and some of their looms for manufacturing cloth privately for local sale. While the practice had been permitted since the mid-sixteenth century, private enterprise increased only during the second half of the seventeenth century. In keeping with the general prosperity of the industry, the number of silk merchants actually rose during this period but their share in the production process and in sales became smaller. In 1638 and 1659, 11 percent of the active looms were being worked by the weavers for their own private account but by 1689 that figure had jumped to 36 percent.[36]

In other branches of the textile industry—cottons, canvas and lesser fabrics, trimmings, knitted goods, dyeing, and retailing—total employment grew consistently through the seventeenth century (table 3.10), raising the textile sector share of total employment from 11 percent in 1595 to over 16 percent in 1690. Most of this growth is attributable to the increased numbers of cloth retailers, particularly the mercers guild (*marzeri*) whose numbers tripled over the century.

EXPORT-RELATED EMPLOYMENT   International markets tightened for Venetian goods and output in export-related industries declined during the seventeenth century. Eventually the relative security of participation in domestic markets outweighed the lure of higher profits that accrue to riskier foreign commerce.

The effects of a declining export sector are manifold and far-reaching. A compelling, organic view of a city or regional economy maintains that an economic unit lives on its exports.

The economic base type of analysis distinguished between basic (primary) industry and service (nonbasic or residential) industry. This distinction is in keeping with a premise that . . . states that the reason for the existence and growth of a region . . . lies in the goods and services it produces locally but sells beyond its borders. These "basic" activities not only provide the means of payment for raw materials, food, and manufactured products which the region cannot produce

---

36. A.S.V., *Arte della Seta,* b. 120, fasc. 343 *extra* 20; *ibid.,* b. 103, fasc. 101, pp. 13-18.

Table 3.10. Total membership in textile guilds

Guild	Membership				
	1595	1603	1660	1672	1690
Woolen industry guilds					
Chiodaroli	52	66	17	23	22
Cimadori	323	255	174	170	90
Cimolini	801	655	429	329	162
Laneri	1,222	1,036	699	707	222
Lavoranti alla Camera del Purgo	19	13	10	11	11
Manganeri	35	63	19	19	28
Petteneri da tella	13	12	13	14	11
Tesseri di panni lana	856	703	518	443	224
Woolen industry total	3,341	2,803	1,879	1,716	770
Silk industry guilds					
Battioro con scuola	41	74	133	132	149
Filatoi	249	276	79	90	61
Testori seda	1,541	703	1,117	1,159	1,179
Toscani	273	271	344	356	529
Silk industry total	2,104	1,324	1,673	1,637	1,888
Other textile industry guilds					
Bombaseri	79	81	87	111	126
Drappieri	541	503	617	620	620
Far calze di seta	-	-	-	-	94
Ingucchiadori	-	79	75	63	47
Linaroli	142	143	133	111	77
Marzeri	567	596	1,243	1,301	1,747
Passamaneri	-	-	119	111	133
Strazzaroli	140	143	123	141	235
Tellaroli	104	130	114	135	88
Tentori	393	303	277	255	447
Tesseri fustagno	82	103	208	200	156
Tesseri di tella	277	170	164	173	144
Other textile industry total	2,325	2,251	3,160	3,321	3,914
Total	7,770	6,378	6,712	6,674	6,572

Source: table 3.1.

THE COMPOSITION OF EMPLOYMENT

itself but also support the "service" activities, which are principally local in productive scope and market areas.[37]

"The economic primacy of exports" is especially apt for Venice, an island community whose reliance on the export ("basic") sector for food and raw material imports and domestic activities ("service") was near absolute. Her dependence was mitigated only by the city's capacity to tax her outlying dominions. With this in mind it becomes clear that any change in the value of output of export commodities and services or (ceteris paribus) any change in employment allocated to the basic sector will have a disproportionately great effect—a multiplier effect— on the capacity of the economy to support the city.

The erosion of the basic exporting sector of the Venetian economy in terms of percentage total employment was considerable, especially in the latter half of the seventeenth century. In 1690 the economic structure of the city with respect to export-related employment was virtually identical to the structure in 1539, before the industrial spurt began. Across the seventeenth century export-related employment declined by almost a quarter, most drastically in the two final decades documented (table 3.9). It would be an oversimplification to blame the wool guilds alone, although the decline in the share of total employment of the woolen industry matches the decline in the export sector,[38] for there were cases of rising employment in export-related occupations such as spice-trading and mirrormaking. Falling employment in other export industries—principally soapmaking, leather-working, and glassmaking—together with the textile employment situation account for the decline in export employment.

Considering the newness and intensity of the foreign competition with which Venice was assaulted, and the severity of protectionism abroad which further isolated Venice from her old customers, the city's showing in the maintenance of export employment levels is not altogether bad. Doubtless economic growth for the city came to an end when the export sector, once totalling almost one half of all

---

37. Walter Isard, *Methods of Regional Analysis: An Introduction to Regional Science* (Cambridge, Mass., 1960), p. 190.

38. The woolworkers' share of total employment in 1595 was 13.2 percent, in 1690 3.2 percent. Between those two years employment in the export sector diminished by 10.83 percent of total employment (table 3.9).

employment, was reduced to one-third of the labor force, but surely things could have been worse. Had Venice's ability to sell abroad collapsed entirely employment levels in both export and domestic market sectors could hardly have remained at the century's equilibrium level as they did.

The port of Venice did not collapse with the economic troubles of the seventeenth century but its character changed from that of the fulcrum of world trade to that of a regional service port.[39] Even in her new capacity Venice thrived, but that is not the only reason for sustained employment in the export sector. The new regional trade was largely in agricultural goods and raw materials which passed through the port untransformed; the city economy contributed little or no added value to these commodities. Employment in the export sector remained at a viable, if reduced, level because, despite the vicissitudes of the century, Venice continued to sell manufactured products abroad although at a level far below that of the days of her world primacy as a commercial center. The city's wares traveled (of necessity) to the new markets of Europe. There developed in Venice the specialty manufactures of the luxury goods trade whose market had always been the most international and the least liable to exclusion by tariff barriers. Sugar refining, silk manufacturing, leather tooling, jewelry making, furniture making, and all types of glass and mirror manufactures became the staple industries of Venetian international commerce in the late seventeenth century and their manufactures found their way to England, France, and Germany despite all obstacles. Characteristic of the production process for luxury articles was higher than normal labor intensity—a feature which was a boon to the otherwise somewhat sluggish economy in that a high level of employment per unit of output was realized.[40]

Emphasis on the production of luxury goods was, in fact, the solution to the shrinking market demand for the general run of Venetian manufactures. By sustaining a modicum of export trade in

39. Gino Luzzatto, "Le vicende del Porto di Venezia dal primo medio evo allo scoppio della guerra 1914-1918," in his *Studi di storia economica Veneziana* (Padua, 1954), pp. 1-36.
40. See above, chap. 2, text and note 46.

THE COMPOSITION OF EMPLOYMENT

this manner a collapse in total employment was prevented.[41]

This analysis of the changes that took place in the structure of Venetian employment during the course of the seventeenth century reveals no drastic movements. Nevertheless it is clear that much change, both voluntary and imposed, occurred and that certain branches of the economy plainly succumbed. The decimation of the woolen industry, the contraction of the manufacturing sector and of employment in export-related occupations were recognizable defeats for Venice. They were part of the de-industrialization of the city that left the eighteenth-century Venetian economy bearing close structural similarity to the economy of the early sixteenth century, before Venice's real growth period of manufacturing ever began. In almost all instances, the composition of employment in 1690 resembles more closely the composition in the year 1539 than in any intervening observation year. Sectoral structure reveals a diminution of manufacturing and a rise of services to the point where, in terms of their shares of total employment, both were approximately at 1539 levels.[42]

Employment in export-related occupations follcwed the same pattern—an early seventeenth-century peak followed by progressive return to the exact proportions of employment distribution of 1539. Since Venetian industries manufactured largely for sale abroad, retrograde movement of the labor force share in manufacturing and export occupations are in essence one and the same phenomenon. The partial failure of the city's export sales accounts for the regression of the employment structure to that of centuries past.

---

41. The luxury trade had been a Venetian forte for centuries, and early Venetian manufactures attained a reputation for high quality, which the government protected with tenacity. But luxury goods manufacture became a real Venetian specialty only in the late seventeenth and eighteenth centuries when recent reductions in long-distance transport costs first made it feasible for Europeans elsewhere to transport relatively inexpensive non-luxury goods over long distances. In the age of the galley only the costliest commodities were worth trading on an international scale; in the age of the flyboat, less than lavish goods traveled the sea-routes for the first time.

42. It should be noted in passing that while maturing industrial economies of the present day also show employment shifts away from manufacturing into the service sector, the critical difference is that these shifts occur as other factors—capital, principally—are substituted for industrial labor. Therefore, proportional reductions in manufacturing employment are not coincident with falling industrial output as was the case in early modern Venice. On the sectoral distribution of employment in modern economies, see Simon Kuznets, *Modern Economic Growth; Rate, Structure, and Spread* (New Haven, 1966), pp. 106-111.

4

Technology, Capital, and Costs

Although Venetian manufacturing was destined to fail during the seventeenth century, there was no place in early modern Europe where industry was more advanced and diverse than in Venice. One need only compare the technical state of Venetian industry in the sixteenth and seventeenth centuries with the descriptions of the manufacturing arts and sciences in *L'Encyclopédie, ou dictionnaire raisonné des sciences, des arts et des metiers* (1751-1765).[1] With few exceptions, almost all the manufactures catalogued in the *Encyclopédie* were active enterprises in Venice in the two centuries preceding the French compendium's publication. They ranged from the major crafts of the metalworkers, textile manufacturers, and glassmakers to the less lofty crafts of the coopers, potters, basketmakers, ropemakers, jewelers, and leather gilders. Even the rosary-beadmakers, the *paternostreri,* have their counterpart in the *Encyclopédie*: the craft of "bondieuserie."

Venice certainly did not lose her industrial leadership because she was a technological laggard. In fact, against her will, the city was the leading exporter of new techniques in early modern Europe. So far as technology is concerned not much had changed between the time of Venice's preeminence in industry and the mid-eighteenth century. Power-driven machinery had made no new inroads into manufacturing processes. As in the thirteenth century the main sources of power were man, draft animals, and water. Judging from contemporary illustrations the quality of machined parts had improved, but design

---

1. I have used *A Diderot Pictorial Encyclopedia of Trades and Industry; Manufacturing and the Technical Arts in Plates Selected from* L'Encyclopédie, ou Dictionnaire Raisonné des Arts et des Métiers *of Denis Diderot,* ed. Charles Coulston Gillispie (New York, 1959).

TECHNOLOGY, CAPITAL, AND COSTS

of basic equipment remained largely unchanged since the time of Zonca's *Nova theatro di machini et edificii* (1607).

The Diderot illustration of a Piedmont silk-throwing mill for example, aside from minor refinements, shows the same device pictured by Zonca in 1607. This machine, one of the most complex mechanisms of the early modern period, had antecedents in the throwing mills of medieval Lucca and Bologna.[2] The Bolognese version became widely adopted in the Veneto during the seventeenth century, making obsolete the handwork of the Venetian guild of silk-throwers.[3] The Piedmont mill was first introduced into France in 1670 and into England not before 1718. In Italy it was still in use at the close of the nineteenth century.[4] The history of the silk-throwing mill is a good example of the slowness of the rate of diffusion of pre-modern technology in spite of an impressive rate of progress in physical and engineering science.

In other branches of manufacturing the story is much the same. The only other important instance of mechanization of handicraft manufacture in seventeenth-century Venice was in stocking knitting. Silk-stocking knitting "in the English fashion" was brought to Venice in 1671 and the guild called *Far calze di seta* was incorporated soon thereafter. In the 1680's stocking looms were being constructed by Venetian *fabbri* and a decade later there were between ten and thirty masters working at the craft.[5]

During the sixteenth century and before, many of the technical

---

2. Florence Edler de Roover, "Lucchese Silks," *Ciba Review,* 80 (1950), 2917; Usher, *History of Mechanical Inventions,* p. 276.

3. A.S.V., *Milizia da Mar,* no. 722, scrittura *filatoggi,* Aug. 17, 1660: "La causa principale del nostro esterminio procede dalle poche sede, che al presente in questa Città si lavorano, originata dall' erettione di tanti molini in Terra Firma, che hanno levato tutto il lavoro à nostri, capitando le Sede in questa Città lavorate, onde primo venivano greze." On the introduction of the Bolognese mill in the Veneto, see Sella, "Industrial Production," p. 241.

4. Usher, *History of Mechanical Inventions,* p. 276.

5. A.S.V., *Cinque Savi,* n.s., b. 11; *ibid.,* insert of Sept. 16, 1704; *ibid.,* May 1, 1690. This notation says there are 10 masters of the craft. The guild roll of 1690 (A.S.V., *Milizia da Mar,* no. 541, fasc. *calze di seta*) also lists 10 independent masters, but in addition indicates that there were 11 master merchants and 7 other masters in the employ of the 10 shopowners, giving a total of 28 stocking-makers of master rank. Silk-stocking making became a thriving new industry in Venice. In 1705 the number of masters was 25 and total employees numbered about 100—the same as in the decade of the craft's inception. But by 1727 the number of masters alone had swelled to over 70, and over 250 frames were in use.

methods of Venetian industry were unknown elsewhere in Europe. However, beginning in the 1500's master craftsmen began to leave the island, lured by remunerations that were tantamount to bribery,[6] to set up Venetian-style industries in foreign parts. Regardless of all the prohibitions and threats levelled by the government the emigration of craftsmen continued, and in this fashion Venice unwillingly shared with the rest of Europe her techniques of cloth-of-gold weaving, soap-making, printing, dyeing, glassblowing, and mirrormaking.

The manufacture of gold cloth in Lyons, the French silkmaking center, was introduced by master weavers from Venice.[7]

The glories of the early Venetian press were the type fonts created for the artistic cinquecento printers. By the early seventeenth century type was being smuggled out of the city under the guise of "worked lead."[8]

Venetian soapmakers exported their talent for producing the purest and finest of luxury soaps to new centers of production in Italy.

The renegade masters of Murano installed themselves virtually everywhere. Antwerp, Liège, Brussels, Amsterdam, Osnabrück, Copenhagen, Nuremberg, Kiel, Dessau, Berlin, Vienna, Lubljana, Nevers, Orléans, Paris, Nantes, Barcelona, Toledo, and cities in England, Scotland, Sweden, and the New World all became sites of furnaces for the manufacture of "Venetian style glassware," staffed by the former lagoon islanders.[9]

Venice's unique role in the early modern era as exporter of technique to European industry further suggests that, during her prime, Venice's industrial practices were "state of the art."

----

6. One renegade Murano glassmaker in England was under contract to William Mansfelt, holder of a royal glass monopoly. He was paid the equivalent of 20 ducats per week—five to ten times his probable earnings in Venice! At a time when English money wages were about half those of Venetian workers, he earned as much in a day as the average Venetian master builder earned in a week (see table 4.7). On the transplanted glassmaker, see *Cal. S. P. Ven.*, vol. 24, no. 418, Mar. 26, 1638.

7. *Ibid.*, vol. 23, no. 209, Nov. 4, 1633.

8. "E sotto tutte le pene predette [prison, the galley, exile, and loss of goods] . . . , ne meno condur fuori alcun materiale, o instrumento pertinente alla Stampa, *come Carattere da Stampa, sotto nome di Piombo lavorato,* o altrimenti; Torcoli, Inchiostro, o vernice liquida, e Madri, con le quali si gettano i Caratteri [that is, typecasting matrices] e ogni altra cosa, come e detto pertinente alla Stampa, . . . " (*Ordine dei Reformatori del Studio di Padova,* Mar. 10, 1603, in *Parti Veneziani,* no. 21, p. 71. Italics are mine.)

9. Gasparetto, *Il Vetro di Murano,* pp. 101-113.

TECHNOLOGY, CAPITAL, AND COSTS

But what was the state of the art in Europe generally? Was there any real technological progress in manufacturing, or were modern European (and Venetian) industries just late-model medieval handicrafts?

Modern writers prefer to emphasize positive developments in science and engineering in the preindustrial period. This emphasis is intended to reverse and deny the once common view that technological progress was altogether lacking in the Middle Ages and abiding thereafter only in a few unconnected personal triumphs such as those of Leonardo and Galileo.[10] Currently there is general recognition of a continuity of technological advance in premodern Europe, which is not to be quarrelled with; but something is lost in the telling, for the emphasis on technical advances has somewhat obscured the more general problem of change in actual production processes (adoption and diffusion). Leaving aside for the present the advances of theoretical sciences—for "technology owed little directly to science before the nineteenth century"[11]—the best manufacturing practices changed very little between the water-power revolution of the Middle Ages and the steam-power revolution of the nineteenth century.[12] Experimentation in machine design and inventions of new equipment and processes occurred continuously, but their adoption was rare and diffusion into industry was slow.

The European method of textile-making—perhaps the most important of all industries—was absolutely static for five centuries. The silk-throwing mill, in use in the fourteenth century in Italy, took four centuries to reach England and remained basically unchanged and unsurpassed for five hundred years. Every step in the manufacture of a bolt of wool cloth, the sequence of the processes and their execution from washing the fleece to pressing the finished article was identically the same in fourteenth-century Tuscany as in eighteenth-century Venice. In fact, it took a wool weaver in seventeenth-century Venice as long or longer than his fourteenth-century Tuscan counterpart to

---

10. A. R. Hall begins chapter 2 ("Scientific Method and the Progress of Techniques") of the fourth volume of the *Cambridge Economic History of Europe* with a statement of the positive view of premodern technology and a renunciation of the old notion of static science and technology.

11. *Ibid.,* p. 99.

12. On water power, see Lynn White, Jr., *Medieval Technology and Social Change* (Oxford, 1962), pp. 80-85, and E. M. Carus-Wilson, "An Industrial Revolution of the Thirteenth Century," *Economic History Review,* 11 (1941), 39-60.

create a cloth of equal length. In Prato in 1396 a weaver usually completed a cloth in about two weeks.[13] Cloths of similar lengths required between seventeen and thirty-six days in early modern Venice (table 4.3).

The extraction of silver by amalgamation with mercury was practiced in the 1500's by Spanish colonists in Central America, and although the process was described in print, it was not employed in European metallurgy until two centuries later.[14]

The two best trade manuals published in Venice—Giovanni Ventura Rosetti's *Plictho* (1540), on dyeing, and Antonio Neri's *L'Arte vetraria* (1612), on glassmaking—both went through a multitude of editions and translations over the course of a century and a half without so much as a change in wording.[15]

Of course not all production processes remained unchanged in the early modern period. Certain inventions and changes in technique met with immediate acceptance and rapid diffusion throughout the continent. Movable-type printing was no isolated inventor's whimsy. Within fifty years of its inception printing was a major Euro-

---

13. Raymond de Roover, "Labour Conditions in Florence around 1400: Theory, Policy, and Reality," *Florentine Studies; Politics and Society in Renaissance Florence,* ed. Nicolai Rubinstein (London, 1968), p. 303. The two-week estimate for the completion of a cloth is an approximation. Federigo Melis, *Aspetti della vita economica medievale; Studi nell'Archivio Datini di Prato* (Siena, 1962), p. 628, shows that the weaving phase, from receipt of warp yarn to return of fabric, often took many weeks. Both the Tuscan and Venetian cloths measured 50-55 *braccia* in length; both Florentine and Venetian braccia being equal to about six-tenths of a yard (De Roover, "Labour Conditions," p. 303; Sella, *Commerci,* pp. 101-119).

14. *Cambridge Economic History,* IV, 100.

15. I have received warnings from many quarters about attaching too much significance to the evidence of the trade manuals. The very purpose of their publication is unclear, for it is unlikely that they were actually used for learning a trade. The apprenticeship system encouraged transmission of skills by word of mouth, and best practice methods were unlikely to leak into public print. It has also been suggested to me that much of the stuff of technical change is not the material that trade manuals treat. Recombinations of inputs, changes in organization, and minor but cumulative improvements in formulas, tools, and methods—which may ultimately be of great importance to raising the quantity or quality of output—will never show up in general treatises.

Even in the light of these caveats I find it significant that general descriptions of production processes retained validity sufficient to warrant publication for so many years. Even if trade manuals do not embody best practice methods, neither are they published to immortalize techniques which are deemed antique. It is certainly notable, for example, that Neri's glassmaker's handbook of 1612 was newly published in France in 1752, translated by no less a person than Baron d'Holbach. Neri's 140 year-old methods may not have been "best practice" at that time, but clearly they were not outmoded either. Why then would the translation have been published at all?

pean industry. The stocking frame made hand knitting obsolete within a hundred years, and the invention of casting or rolling plate glass revolutionized that industry in a still shorter time. These examples, however, were exceptions not because they were inventions, for there was plenty of inventing going on, but because they were so rapidly accepted and introduced into actual production processes. For the most part the scientific and technical advances of the early modern period did not find their way into the established modes of manufacturing.

Industrial Experimentation in Venice

Far from being the enemies of industrial change,[16] the Venetian guilds themselves often proposed new projects for trial. It was, after all, the livelihood of guild members that was threatened by Venice's marketing failures and it is to be expected that the guilds would endeavor to change this trend by altering their products or reducing costs to make them more competitive. There was little threat of the introduction of labor-saving or labor-eliminating devices. It was not machinery but foreign competition that put men out of work, so the guildsmen were at times the staunchest supporters of new projects that stood a chance of succeeding in international markets.

The regulatory agencies whose function it was to maintain the long-standing reputation for high quality of Venetian manufactures were sometimes the agents of conservatism. The state itself, fearful of licensing wholesale "sullying" or *contraffazione,*[17] was much more prone than the guilds to stifle or delay attempts to introduce new techniques or products. Actually the government could not be accused of excess in its watch over industrial experimentation. It did sanction experiments and usually judged results by administering proofs or trials. The difficulty was that market circumstances called for cost-re-

16. Carlo Cipolla, dealing with the early modern Italian economy at large, places much of the blame for stagnation on the guilds as obstructors of innovation ("Economic Decline of Italy," p. 138).

17. Literally, "counterfeiting" or "falsification," the word was used to mean "despoiling the reputation," not necessarily with imitative intent. For example, a maker of a cheap grade of wool cloth without official sanction might be a *contraffatore,* not because his product was a forgery of fine cloth—it could be a distinguishably different product—but because the very existence of a cheap Venetian cloth, unless it was clearly identified as an inferior product, could damage the city's reputation for quality.

ducing innovations even at the risk of debasing product quality. Most new projects succeeded in this cost-cutting but the mentality of the government could not accept the sacrifice of quality standards even if it was dictated by economic good sense.

The most common examples of obstruction to cost and quality reduction were in the dyeing industry. Dyeing in the cloth was an expensive part of woolen manufacture, accounting for roughly from 8 percent to as much as 36 percent of total production cost. Dyeing costs were greatest for fine cloths on which use of only rare dyestuffs was permitted. At the top of the list were the scarlets, tinted according to the secret Venetian method of mordantizing the dyestuff, *grana di scarlatto,* with alum and tartar.[18] The *grana* or kermes, an animal dyestuff, was fabulously expensive. When Venetian textiles were threatened by cheaper foreign cloths it was in the best interests of all parties to reduce the dyeing costs. Over the course of the seventeenth century many master dyers experimented with substitute methods for dyeing in scarlet without the expense of kermes. Similarly, silk dyers tried to develop ways of avoiding the use of *cremese,* a related dye, for dyeing silk crimson.[19] Early attempts in silk involved the substitution of formulations of *oriana* (orchil, a purple vegetable dyestuff). This was partially successful and was permitted for silks only if a small proportion of the old, expensive crimson was added to the mixture. But the Silk Office came to object to this procedure claiming that the combination caused a different color to be produced. Oriana dyeing was forbidden.[20]

The oriana incident was hardly an isolated case. In the late sixteenth and early seventeenth centuries when Mexican cochineal met with easy adoption and much success as a less expensive alternative to kermes throughout Europe, Venice remained diffident. The old laws obliging

---

18. Franco Brunello, *L'Arte della tintura nella storia dell'umanità* (Vicenza, 1968), p. 141.

19. A.S.V., *Arte della Seta,* b. 99.

20. *Ibid.,* b. 100, fasc. 59, June 26, 1651. The cause of the prohibition may have been the failure of one experiment. In the years when experiments with orchil were taking place, one Iseppo Uberti proposed to the Provveditori di Comun that he be given a 50-year patent on a secret orchil process that would reduce dyeing costs by two-thirds over dyeing with crimson, and diminish the final cost of the cloth by 10 grossi per braccio. This was in 1636. When his method was put to the test (apparently by treatment with alum to try drawing out the color), Uberti's cloth failed while a true crimson cloth passed proof, and a swift denunciation was issued. Soon after, a ban on all dyeing with oriana was issued (A.S.V., *Cinque Savi,* b. 477, vol. II, no. 15).

TECHNOLOGY, CAPITAL, AND COSTS

producers of high grade woolens to dye red exclusively with kermes were adamantly enforced. Meanwhile, the Flemish imported tons of cochineal from Mexico via Spain for dyeing woolens destined for sale in the Mediterranean. Later the English developed "Bow dyeing" and the French "Gobelin scarlet" based upon the new dyestuff, while Venetians were constrained from using these techniques because of the limitless faith of the government in the virtues of retaining high-quality traditional methods.[21]

Numerous other proposals for reducing the cost of dyeing were introduced. Earlier, in 1611, a substitute scarlet for woolens was tried, using archimia in place of grana.[22] A time-saving technique was proposed to cut down on the five or six hours of boiling cloths in the dyeing caldrons.[23] There was even a try at cultivating a new dyestuff in the Veneto.[24] But despite all efforts at devising new methods the Senate regulations for the dyeing of wool and for silk-cloth manufacture remained virtually unchanged over the course of the seventeenth century.

Perhaps the most important class of experimental projects in the Venetian textile industries were the attempts at reproducing the types of wool and silk cloths with which competitor countries had successfully supplanted traditional Venetian products in world markets. These experiments were not so much true innovation as they were active commercial combat. Unfortunately, the attempts came too late for Venice to share in the commercial successes of her English and Dutch rivals. Wool weavers petitioned for permission to introduce cheaper varieties of cloth to Venetian manufacturing throughout most of the seventeenth century, in spite of the fact that their daily earnings per cloth were lower when they wove cheaper fabrics.[25] Still, cheap cloth projects were licensed only in the last quarter of the century.[26] The finished product, made mostly with inexpensive short staple wool bought either locally or from Spain, was lighter and less rich than the

---

21. Brunello, *L'Arte della tintura,* pp. 203-205.
22. *Parti Veneziani, Provveditori di Comun,* Apr. 17, 1611.
23. A.S.V., *Provveditori di Comun,* b. 54, July 31, 1676.
24. A.S.V., *Cinque Savi,* n.s., b. 170, fasc. 218, Apr. 7, 1701.
25. A.S.V., *Milizia da Mar,* b. 556, fasc. *tesseri di pani di lana,* 1677. Daily net earnings for weaving cheaper varieties of cloth were about 12.5-14 soldi per cloth for each master. Finer fabrics brought in 15-16 soldi per cloth per day. See table 4.3.
26. Characteristics and production figures for these cheap cloths are given by Sella (*Commerci,* App. E, pp. 117-122).

panni alti of Venice. Expensive dyeing was prohibited.[27]

Techniques for making cheaper cloths were brought to Venice by foreigners. The first of these, in 1673, was one Santo Gallitiolini (or Galicioli) who was granted a patent for making *londrine*. He had apparently brought with him a new method of pressing cloth. His enterprise failed, and in 1676 when the Cinque Savi were considering a new and similar project they related that Gallitiolini was just making old-style cloth with small changes in design, calling it "al'olandese" just to please potential Turkish buyers. The Turks apparently were not pleased by his price of about 20 lire per brazzo. He made only 367 cloths in three years and "the Turks always [left] them in the warehouses."[28] The Cinque Savi permitted the new contender, Giovanni Bucherij, a Dutchman, to try his hand but he too failed.[29] A third hopeful, a Fleming named Pietro Comans, arrived in 1683 with fourteen workers to set up a holland-cloth shop but he claimed that vigorous opposition in Venice robbed him of his courage to work in the city so he went to the Trevisan countryside. Thirteen years later, after some success, he was granted the right (but not exclusive patent) to set up shop in Venice. The terms stipulated that he be allowed to work free of any molestation. Comans may have had some success. In 1695 only 28 *londrine* were made in the city, but by 1698 64 cloths were produced and shortly thereafter a minor resurgence of production occurred.[30] These developments still were years too late to loosen the English and Dutch grip on European cloth markets.

It is doubtful whether the new dyeing and weaving projects deserve to be called innovative. Typically they were imports of processes long established elsewhere and in almost every case they failed to take hold in Venice. Moreover, the general purpose of these projects was not to improve industrial efficiency, but rather to diminish costs by lowering

---

27. For regulations concerning *mezzetti*, the first sort of cheap cloth made in the city, A.S.V., *Cinque Savi,* b. 122, fasc. 80, pt. 3.

28. Sella, *Commerci,* p. 119, and A.S.V., *Cinque Savi,* b. 126, fasc. 59, Apr. 29, 1673; *ibid.,* fasc. 60, *scrittura* of Jan. 9, 1676, *m.v.; ibid.,* b. 125, fasc. 60, *scrittura* of Dec. 17, 1676.

29. Sella, *Commerci,* p. 120.

30. A.S.V., *Cinque Savi,* b. 125, fasc. 63. In 1679 the government abandoned the system of privileged patents for making these fabrics, and the weaving of londrine declined for a while. In the first six years of the eighteenth century production grew again as follows: (1700) 264; (1701) 370; (1702) 180; (1703) 283; (1704) 517; (1705) 664 (A.S.V., *Cinque Savi,* n.s., b. 126, fasc. "Marco Cesarotti").

By international standards, five or six hundred cloths were merely a drop in the bucket.

product quality. Yet they were the major industrial experiments of seventeenth-century Venetian manufacturing. Although earlier Venice was a world leader in the technology of production, she relinquished her role in the seventeenth century and was surpassed by emerging Atlantic producers. It was not, however, new technologies that defeated Venice. Despite the insignificant level of innovative activity, the technology of Venetian manufacturing was equal to that of any of her new competitors. It was the newcomers who had first caught up to Venetian technology in the seventeenth century with the aid of the less patriotic Venetian master craftsmen.

In the critical early years of the seventeenth century the mercantilist powers, particularly England, came to an abrupt and dramatic realization, a turning point in European marketing. Making fine stuff and "selling dear," they saw, was not the only way—not even the best way—for an export manufacturer to deal with foreign markets. A new feeling arose in England that cloths for export should be sold as inexpensively as possible.[31] Accompanying that feeling came the inevitable appreciation that even the most scrupulous industrialist must be willing to compromise high standards of quality to be able to produce and sell goods cheaply, especially as a new entrant into an established market. It was this change in marketing mentality put into practice, not any great feats of technical prowess, that won the Mediterranean market for the North Atlantic manufacturers.

On the other hand Venice, or more properly the Venetian government, was incapable of even conceptualizing the idea of low-quality manufacturing as a cost-reducing marketing device. Low quality was by reflex associated with the involuntary degradation of industrial art. It was this unwillingness to countenance purposeful relaxation of standards for cost economy that lay at the root of Venetian competitive failures in a mercantilist world.

Capital Equipment in Industry

The seventeenth century is sometimes said to have been a century of capital formation leading up to the start of industrialization in Europe.[32] Generally speaking, however, neither the technology nor

---

31. Supple, *Commercial Crisis and Change,* p. 147.
32. On capital formation in early modern Europe see: E. J. Hobsbawm, "The Crisis of the Seventeenth Century," in *Crisis in Europe, 1560-1660,* ed. Trevor Aston (Garden City, N. Y., 1967), pp. 40-43; Maurice Dobb, *Studies in the Development of Capitalism* (London, 1963), chaps. 4 and 5; and Nef, "Progress of Technology . . . in Great Britain, 1540-1640."

the absolute scale of production in European industry changed to any great degree, and accumulated funds of capital were not directed to construction of equipment. Such was almost certainly the case in Europe generally, and particularly in Venice. It was at one time argued that even in the Middle Ages and Renaissance production was basically capitalistic, involving "gigantic plants" and "large-scale enterprises." This is now known not to have been the case.[33] Scale of production was uniformly small.[34] Capital costs were inconsequential in comparison to payments to other inputs (raw materials and labor). "Little or nothing was invested in equipment."[35]

Since early modern manufacturing in Europe achieved no significant alterations in the technology of production, one might expect that the composition of inputs remained more or less the same as in earlier days. This in fact was the case. Capital equipment, although not an altogether insignificant factor of production, was most definitely a secondary element in terms of productivity and production costs.

Records dealing with capital equipment usage are hard to come by since the government, the source of most surviving archival records, was less interested in the physical content of shops than in the labor force or in taxable production. But the inventories made upon the death of a shop owner and registered with the judiciary can provide some examples of the value of equipment in various enterprises, even though such records cannot possibly offer a comprehensive picture of the use of capital.[36]

---

33. The argument and phrases are from Alfred Doren, in reference to the Florentine woolen industry; quoted and refuted by Raymond de Roover, "Labour Conditions," pp. 296-297.

34. There were of course exceptions, of which the most notable in Venice was the extraordinary shipbuilding complex, the Arsenal. More commonplace instances of enterprise on a large scale were cooperative rope factories, mines, glass furnaces, and cloth-tentering shops, in which the physical requirements of certain structures (ropewalks, stretching frames, furnaces) determined shop size.

35. De Roover, "Labour Conditions," p. 298; Melis, *Aspetti,* tables 27 (facing p. 554) and 29 (p. 561).

36. A.S.V., *Giudici Petizion,* b. 337-489. This is an archive of inventories of personal possessions and shops made upon owners' deaths to assist in the distribution of estates. Most inventories, although itemized in detail, do not include estimates of value. Inventories range from very small estates to immensely rich ones. See Appendix III for the texts of two such documents.

The inventories are arranged in the archive only by date. Making good use of the documents would be a nearly impossible task were it not for the detailed indices prepared by Dr. Maria Francesca Tiepolo and generously made available to me by her.

TECHNOLOGY, CAPITAL, AND COSTS

What we learn from shop inventories is that in most cases the value of equipment rarely approached the total value of raw materials on hand and inventories of final products. More impressive still is the observation that when home and shop inventories appear together, the total value in an owner's place of business is rarely more than half that of his personal effects: paintings, furniture, clothing, etc. In a typical case, the equipment of a *squero* or private boatyard was estimated at 437 lire 14 soldi in 1692. The late owner had household possessions valued at over 1,842 lire—more than four times the value of his boatyard.[37] The kitchens of many large homes were valued at more than this particular boatyard.

In terms of the physical equipment itself, the inventories show how rudimentary the application of capital really was. Metalworkers' shops rarely contained more than one forge and anvil, assorted hammers, tongs, cutters, and other tools.[38] Frequently the value of unused metals and finished manufactures such as locks, caldrons, and simple machinery exceed the estimated value of capital equipment. There is an undeterminable degree of bias toward undervaluation of capital in many of these comparisons, for the value of a piece of capital equipment was heavily discounted for its condition; i.e., how "used" it was. New raw materials and inventoried products are usually estimated at full value. In an eighteenth-century example, a list of type fonts with weight and cast value (value of the type less the cost of the metal) shows unused type is valued at up to five times the cost of an equal weight of old type.[39]

Even taking into consideration undervaluations of equipment, inventories plainly reveal that, as in centuries past, a very small proportion of the funds of an enterprise were invested in equipment. For the most part company funds (*cavedal, capitale*) meant circulating

---

37. A.S.V., *Giudici Petizion,* b. 392/57, no. 21, Aug. 21, 1972, inventory of Antonio del Favro, *squerarol.* This squero, judging by its contents, was not really a shipyard, just a small boatbuilder's shop.

38. *Ibid.,* b. 346/11, no. 85, Jan. 12, 1616, *m. v.,* inventory of Antonio Guerra, *favro; ibid.,* b. 350/15, no. 99, Dec. 30, 1627, inventory of Ghirardo Zanardelo, *favro; ibid.,* no. 40, Sept. 26, 1626, inventory of Iseppo Gatoni, *calderer; ibid.,* b. 353/18, no. 42, Sept. 9, 1631, inventory of Antonio Cumbi, *favro.*

39. *Ibid.,* b. 482/147, no. 36, Oct. 3, 1786, inventory of Giovan Paolo Baglioni, *librer e stampator.* A font of *testin di colonia* characters weighing 537 pounds, unused, was valued at 1000 lire not including the value of the typemetal; 1147 pounds of the same type, used, were worth only 150 lire, and 833 pounds of that type, listed as old, a mere 80 lire.

capital which was used to buy raw materials or which was maintained as deposits or credit balances with subcontracting firms. Often it included inventoried stores of manufactures.[40] Equipment was rarely a significant component of a company's net worth.

Perhaps the most interesting view of industrial characteristics supplied by the study of shop inventories is for the printing industry. There was a wide range of shop sizes and scales of production within the industry. There were shops valued at many thousands of ducats, while a bookshop owner could be a publisher "on the side" for a very small investment. The cost of a press was extremely low; used ones were usually valued at under 100 ducats, frequently less than half that figure. One could operate with only one press or upwards of ten.[41] Pietro Pinelli, publisher of all goverment-printed notices and documents, maintained only four presses in his shop.[42] Aside from the presses very little in the way of equipment was needed. Most shops had a few iron frames for composing pages, a small vat or two for inks, and wooden furniture such as benches, work-tables, and type-cases. The largest element of capital costs in a Venetian printshop was the type, of which the cost of the typemetal itself was a small share. Value added in casting was about two-thirds of the total value of new type.[43] The metal was almost infinitely reusable. When type became worn, it was melted down and recast from matrices bearing the impress of hand-crafted punches. Only a few of the very largest print-shops maintained *gettarie* complete with punches, molds and matrices, crucibles and other typefounding apparatus; smaller establish-

---

40. De Roover observed this to be the case for Florentine industry in the fifteenth century ("Labour Conditions," p. 298). For Venice, indications of the use to which business funds were put are best found in private partnership contracts which were usually renegotiated periodically. In a transaction of 1664 (March 10), a shop and company for making and selling silk cloth were given over to a business partner with a capital of 19,500 ducats "in silk, inventories of finished and semifinished cloths, credits, and a small amount of cash" (A.S.V., *Ospitali e luoghi pii diversi, Eredità Gozzi*, b. 556).

41. The shops of Nicolo Ciera (A.S.V., *Guidici Petizion*, b. 403/68, no. 24, Nov. 10, 1706) and Antonio Tivani (*ibid.*, b. 416/81, no. 35, Oct. 16, 1719) had only one press (*torcolo*) apiece. The large Baglioni printshop had eleven presses.

42. *Ibid.*, b. 411/81, no. 55, Feb. 23, 1719, *m. v.*, inventory of Pietro Pinelli.

43. In the Baglioni inventory (see note 39, above) 32 cases of type of varying weights are listed, each accompanied by an estimate of the cost of manufacture, e.g., "[lbs.] 981 carattere Canon Corale stimato di fattura Lire 270." The "stimo di fattura" is a misnomer since the estate appraisers discounted this figure for depreciation, based on the condition of the type. The cost of the reusable metal was only about one-third the total value of undepreciated type.

ments apparently hired the services of independent typefounders.[44]

The most complete inventory of a seventeenth-century printshop is that of the stamparia of Bortolo Bruni made in 1673. This shop was of intermediate size, valued at a little over 1,500 ducats, exclusive of a large inventory of books. It had four presses: two valued at 80 ducats, one at 50 and one at 40 ducats. Aside from the extensive supply of type, there is little other equipment. The breakdown of assets as estimated by the assessors is typical of the distribution of value in a print-shop:

	Value (ducats)	Percentage
Inventory (books)	514 *d* 4	26
Type	1,122 *d* 18	55
Presses	250	12
Other equipment, furniture	137	7
Total	2,023 *d* 22	100%

Excluding inventory and the cost of type, less than 400 ducats is embodied in equipment—this for an intermediate-size establishment.[45] There are complete printshops on record with a total worth of as little as 140 ducats.[46] Clearly the printing industry is an exemplary case of the seventeenth-century industrial condition—low capital use and low capital cost.

In other industries the pattern of capital equipment usage is much the same. A gold-thread spinner's shop, for example, was valued at

44. The Baglioni press maintained a foundry valued at over 12,000 lire. Typefounders (*gettatori da stampa, fonditori*) as well as compositors were part of the guild of libreri da stampa, but they maintained internal separation from the printers and booksellers within the guild. In 1595 while the guild was subject to obligations for supplying galley crewmen, compositors as a group were declared exempt by the Senate (A.S.V., *Senato, mar,* filza 1290, Nov. 25, 1595, "Arti che non sono tansate per Galeotti").

45. Text in App. 3.

46. The stamperia of Antonio Tivani (note 41, above), consisted of the following articles:

1 press with bronze screw and plates estimated at	D.	45
3 fonts of type: 1 *garamonica* (Garamond) with cursive, 1 *garamonica magno* with cursive, 1 *caratere di filosofia* with some cursive; various miniature plates for frontispieces: total weight of type, lbs. 790 @ 11 ducats per 100	D.	86 g 13
typecases, forms, tools, estimated at	D.	8 g 17
	D.	140 g 6

about 519 ducats in 1645.[47] Of that amount 360 ducats was invested in twelve spinning wheels for gold thread and the rest in small hand tools and shop furnishings. The total value of the smith's estate was some 1,412 ducats of which the major share (63%) was household furnishings.

Another inventory of interest is that of a silk dyer, made upon his death in 1658. From a technological standpoint dyeing is rather a curious craft, for although it required little equipment other than a few big pots and a fire, the high degree of skill it demanded and its importance in textile production mark it as a major industry. The inventory of the dyer Giacomo Pesanti lists equipment of one major caldron and three vats plus an assortment of about thirty small vessels: casks, barrels, tubs, etc. The most expensive single piece of equipment was a bronze mortar with two pestles worth 155 lire (25 ducats). The rest of the shop implements consisted mainly of andirons, stirrers, scales, sieves, and cutting implements. All these materials accounted for only 23 percent of the estimated value of the shop. The remaining 77 percent consisted entirely of stores of dyestuffs—indigo, brazilwood, orchil and *bonicel*. Once again the craftsman's shop in its entirety represented a minor portion of his complete estate. In the case of Pesanti, the estate was valued at 8,227 lire, 7 soldi (1,327 ducats). The shop, equipment, and dyestuffs were valued at 3,287 lire (530 ducats 4 grossi), or about 40 percent of the total estate.[48]

Scale

Inventories give some indication of what were typical shop sizes but they cannot be relied upon completely. Enterprises catalogued as part of the estate of one individual are likely to be solely owned by the named party. Such one-owner operations would usually be the smallest ones. Larger enterprises tended to be operated in corporation or in partnership, and their disposition upon the death of a partner is predictably not recorded as part of an estate. Nevertheless, we can see that for the individually owned shop production was designed for operations involving one, possibly two, masters plus assistant labor

---

47. A.S.V., *Giudici Petizion*, b. 361/26, no. 39, Oct. 24, 1645, inventory of Alessandro Gropis, *tiraoro*.
48. Text in App. III.

except in infrequent cases where the scale was larger (such as the print-shop with eleven presses).

Among the documents offering better evidence of the limited scale of production are the rolls of the wool-weavers guild. They were organized by shop, listing first the master-owner, other masters, if any, who worked for him, then *lavoranti* and *garzoni*.[49] The largest listed shop in the last quarter of the seventeenth century employed seven men. The rolls of 1693 and 1705 each list only one shop of four or more workers; the rest are exclusively of one to three men. This measure, I believe, also tends to slight undervaluation because it omits unincorporated day laborers who were in all likelihood hired during seasonal production peaks. It also omits family members who may have helped. Still, an average shop size of two to three "official" or permanent workers is typical for the century.

The guild of tanners in 1595 spoke of 404 persons whose livelihood came from the craft of leather tanning ("che vivono di acconciar corami")—including masters, journeymen, apprentices, and their families. In fact, excluding families, there were 128 guildsmen, working in 42 shops throughout the city.[50] This gives an average of about three permanent workers per shop.

The records of the soapmaking industry reveal a somewhat larger scale of production than is typical for the century (table 4.1). Although in the course of a century of declining production the number of soapworks and caldrons dropped radically, the physical scale of soapworks did not change. Typically a soapworks maintained three soapboiling caldrons.[51] Each caldron when working at capacity could convert 90,000 pounds of oil into 270,000 pounds of soap per year.[52] It is difficult to tell how many workers ran a savonaria under optimum

49. A.S.V., *Milizia da Mar,* no. 556, fasc. *tesseri di panni di lana,* rolls of 1672, 1693, and 1705.

50. A.S.V., *Cinque Savi,* n. s., b. 132, fasc. 207, Aug. 5, 1595.

51. Judging from table 4.1 this average remained constant over time. An inventory of a soapworks made in 1610/11 lists "tri caldiori nelli fornelli di savonaria" (A.S.V., *Giudici Petizion,* b. 344/9, no. 48, Feb. 28, 1610, *m. v.,* inventory of Marco Rubi, *mercante di pani di lana*). The owner, apparently a wool merchant who invested in a soapworks managed by another party, also maintained a woolshop and dyeing ovens.

52. A.S.V., *Cinque Savi,* n.s., b. 145, fasc. 1, no. 9. The proportion given is: 80 *caldiere* consume 600 *migliara* of oil per month (1 migliaro = 1,000 lbs.). In *ibid.,* fasc. 1, no. 1, it is noted that 1 migliaro of oil is needed to make three of soap. Sella's formula (see table 4.2) is more precise.

Table 4.1. Shop size in the soap industry

Date	Number of shops	Number of caldrons	Number of workers
1595	-	-	111
1603	-	40	103
1625	30	90-100	-
1660	-	25	121
1672	-	-	116
1692	6-7	16-18	90
1710	7-8	21-25	-

Sources: For shops and caldrons, A.S.V., *Cinque Savi,* n.s., b. 145, fasc. 1 and 49; Sella, *Commerci,* p. 133. For workers, see above, table 3.1.

conditions because guild membership over the century did not decline significantly while the number of operational soapworks and active caldrons did. Therefore we can only presume that the end-of-century average of thirteen to fifteen men per shop, five workers per caldron, represents a condition of extreme underemployment. This presumption would not be permissible were it not for the fact that in the early part of the century when annual production was many times higher, the ratio of workers to caldrons was much lower.[53] Underemployment of men *and* equipment prevailed by the end of the 1600's in an export-oriented industry such as soapmaking. At the beginning of the century soapmaking facilities in the city were being stretched and nominal capacity was being exceeded. But by 1660 (if not before) physical plant was shrinking, and by the end of the century even those facilities that remained could not be kept fully active. With only half the number of caldrons that had existed in 1600, Venice produced less than a quarter of the soap that she had a hundred years before (table 4.2). But the scale and style of production remained more or less uniform over the years.

Often the guilds or the government exercised a limiting hand on the scale of enterprises. This was done with the intention of preventing

53. Early in the century yearly production from about 40 caldrons was 13 million pounds. At that time the average number of workers per caldron was 2.6 (tables 4.1 and 4.2).

TECHNOLOGY, CAPITAL, AND COSTS

Table 4.2 Capacity and output of soapworks

	c. 1600	c. 1700
Number of caldrons	40	20
Annual input capacity (*migliara* of oil)[a]	3,600	1,800
Projected annual output at capacity (pounds of soap)[b]	11,401,200	5,700,60•
Actual annual output[c]	13,000,000	3,100,00•

Sources: for c.1600, Sella, *Commerci,* p. 132-133; for c.1700, A.S.V., *Cinque Savi,* b.145, fasc. 1, no. 4, which gives annual quantities of oil to the soapworks.
[a]90,000 pounds of oil (90 migliara) per caldron per year.
[b]3,167 pounds of soap per migliaro of oil (Sella, *Commerci,* p. 133).
[c]The average for the years 1696-1705 is 976.1 migliara which would yield 3,091,308.7 po•
of soap. A document in the same fascicle reveals that average annual exports of soap ove•
same period was 2,570,670 pounds.

unfair advantages that might accrue to large producers from economies of scale, or to protect the quality of manufactures by insuring that
masters would not entrust too much of the manufacturing process to
subordinates. The first legislation of this nature appears as early as
1491 when a government regulation first prohibits master silk weavers
from maintaining more than six looms under one roof.[54] This rule was
restated in each subsequent set of regulations and never relaxed,
though partially circumvented in 1622. Certain weavers had petitioned
for special dispensation for families in which both father and son, or
several brothers, were all master weavers and could save rent and other
fixed costs by living and working together.[55] Permission was granted
in the case of a man and his brother or son living under the same roof,
each being a master over eighteen years old, that each could operate
six looms in the same house or shop.

The intention of the original law was to prohibit scarce weaving
jobs from going all to a few large producers, because, as the regulation stated, some weavers make as much silk cloth as they wish and
others are without work. The problem persisted. A restatement of the

54. For details and restatements of this law: A.S.V., *Arte della Seta,* b. 11, fasc.
leggi; A.S.V., *Cinque Savi,* b. 477 (*setificio* 1309-1771); Correr, *Mariegola Testori,*
passim.
55. A.S.V., *Cinque Savi,* b. 56, Nov. 2, 1622. The original petition was dated May
16, 1622.

six-loom rule in 1559 complained that although the law was enacted so that all of the guild could participate in the manufacture, it had been violated by some greedy masters who continued to operate twenty or twenty-five looms.[56] Eventually the law became entirely effective and the limit of the shop size of silkweaving remained permanently in force.

For woolweavers a similar law prohibiting the maintenance of more than two operational ("in piedi") looms at one time was promulgated in 1669 by order of the Provveditori di Comun. It never appeared in the Senate wool regulations of subsequent years, and the extent to which it was ever enforced is unknown.[57]

Venice, in retrospect, does not seem to have been subject to the strong mistrust of monopoly that held such sway in other medieval and early modern industrial centers.[58] Her early leadership in establishing a system of privileged patents and copyrights is ample testimony to the Republic's willingness to permit some restraint of trade in order to encourage innovation and efficiency.[59] It is therefore surprising that there were so few instances of attempts at combination for production efficiency or to command monopoly buying or selling power. I have found records of only two such attempts—both of minor consequence and of short duration.

With the demise of the guild and craft of barrel-hoop making in Venice by the early 1600's the city's coopers were forced to rely upon the supply of hoops brought in by barge from forges in Padua and Treviso. Because of increasing prices and a scarcity of supply, the guild, acting as a buying combine, purchased all hoops for the craft and sold them to members at a fixed price[60]—an arrangement which lasted for fifteen years (1636-1651). In 1681 the guild of *botteri* also formed a "fontego" for buying mainland hoops.[61]

---

56. A.S.V., *Arte della Seta*, b. 1, fasc. *leggi*, Nov. 11, 1559.

57. A.S.V., *Provveditori di Comun*, b. 54, Aug. 23, 1669.

58. On the medieval view of monopoly and attendant policies in Florence, see de Roover, "Labour Conditions," pp. 286-296. It was only in the seventeenth century that the appeal of high efficiency led European governments to begin sanctioning monopolies.

59. On Venetian patents, G. Mandich, "Le privative industriali venziane, 1450-1550," *Rivista di diritto commerciale*, 34 (1936), 1-39.

60. A.S.V., *Giustizia Vecchia*, ser. xv, b. 131, *barileri*, Apr. 13, 1636.

61. *Ibid.*, b. 133, filza 107, *botteri*, June 29, 1681.

TECHNOLOGY, CAPITAL, AND COSTS

In the early part of the eighteenth century, in connection with a new silk-cloth project for the manufacture of "florentine-style draperies," the subguild of silk-dyers proposed the formation of a universal silk-dyers' company combining all the independent members. The proposal, which was agreed to by the Senate, provided that one central dyeworks be erected on the mainland near a river and that there be ten shops or outlets in Venice where merchants could consign and receive goods.[62] After about three years of operation this arrangement came under heavy attack from silk merchants who denounced it as a monopoly in restraint of free trade, and although the company survived the monopoly was broken.[63]

In other industries, enlarging the established scale of production either by individual expansion or by combination seems never to have been attempted.

It is difficult to evaluate the effect of scale-limiting regulations and anti-combination actions. Did they discourage innovation in business organization? Would it have been best for the textile sector to permit agglomeration? Would the industry have concentrated into the hands of a few "weaving barons"? In all likelihood efficiency would have been higher had concentration been allowed to proceed unchecked, and with lower costs Venetian textiles might have had a better chance on the international market, with attendant benefits accruing to the entire economy. On the other hand, it is far from certain that Venice could have coped with the implications of agglomeration for income distribution. The result surely would have been the displacement of thousands of textile workers and the premature end of the independent master. Venice's great accomplishment during the period of her economic troubles was successfully to avoid widespread unemployment and labor difficulties in the face of reduced demand. There is no telling the effect that industrial concentration might have had on the sensitive balance of employment during the seventeenth century.

Production Costs

An examination of factor payments in the textile industry shows once again that labor was the predominant input for Venetian

---

62. A.S.V., *Arte della Seta,* b. 100, fasc. 60, Sept. 28, 1711, pp. 1-5.
63. *Ibid.,* pp. 21-23.

industry in the early modern period. In the business accounting of the period, payments to capital were considered merely a component of labor expenses and represented only a small percentage of total costs. Costs of production are almost invariably described solely as the sum of raw materials costs plus piecerates to the different sets of workers involved in the article's manufacture. A document of 1677, which subdivides weavers' fees into their component parts, affords a good picture of production costs in the weaving stage (table 4.3). We can readily see that out of fees actual payments for labor equal two-thirds of the total. Expenses—that is raw materials other than yarn—and auxiliary labor services account for 15 to 25 percent of the total fee. Pure capital payments—upkeep and depreciation of the loom—make up the remaining 10 to 20 percent. The principal master weaver received from 11 1/3 to 29 1/2 lire depending upon the quality of the cloth and the time it took to complete the weaving. This worked out to daily earnings of 14 to 16 soldi for each cloth in operation.

To discover more about cost structure in the woolen industry we can again compare production figures for seventeenth-century Venice with those for Tuscany in earlier centuries. The costs of the various production processes in wool cloth manufacturing can be adduced for fourteenth-century Prato, sixteenth-century Florence, Venice in the early seventeenth and early eighteenth centuries, and terraferma products in the 1700's (table 4.4). Since the organization of the table has short-cut descriptions of the steps in the individual production processes, it is important to note at the outset that for all instances—spanning four centuries—virtually no change took place in the twenty to thirty individual production steps which are here compressed into five. Some steps varied depending more upon the quality of the fabric than upon the period or place of its manufacture. A second shearing was sometimes omitted. Special grades of Venetian cloth were made exclusively from carded wool. But for the most part, techniques were all the same.[64] The relative distribution of

---

64. While absolute costs are expected to vary with the quality of the product, all groups of workers raised their rates when working with higher quality materials, so a degree of proportionality limits the effect of quality on the relative cost structure. For the purposes of the present discussion, "production costs" omits the costs of raw wool and refers only to what Melis terms "transformation costs," i.e., transformation from fleece to fabric.

Table 4.3. An analysis of wool-cloth weaving costs (in *soldi*)

Grade of cloth	Equipment, supplies, outside services[a]	Loom upkeep, depreciation	Wages Master's	Partner's	Total payment to weaver	Cost analysis (by percentage) Labor	Capital	Materials	Total days required	Master's daily earnings (*soldi*)
Low grade										
panno di 60 (any wool)	152	75	226.5	226.5	680	67	11	22	17	14
olandino, passini 9	176	71	246.5	246.5	740	67	9	24	20	12.5
olandino, passini 15	262	238	500	500	1,500	67	16	17	35	14
Medium grade										
panno di 60 sotto parangon	182	104	287	287	860	67	12	21	20	14
panno di 70 sotto parangon	196	121	316.5	316.5	950	67	13	20	24	13
saglia di 60 sotto parangon	248	219	466.5	466.5	1,400	67	15	18	30	15
saglia di 70 sotto parangon	272	218	490	490	1,470	67	15	18	30	16
High grade										
panno di 70 di parangon	206	161	376.5	376.5	1,120	67	14	19	25	15
saglia di 70 di parangon	282	308	590	590	1,770	67	17	16	36	16

Source: A.S.V., *Milizia da Mar*, no. 556, fasc. *tesseri di panni di lana*, 1677.
[a]includes combs, spools, cord, spooling, sizing the loom, oil, and delivery charges.

Table 4.4. Components of cost in Italian wool-cloth manufacture, 14th-18th centuries (by percentage of total cost)

Process	Prato 1300's	Florence 1500's	Venice 1612	Treviso 1713	Venice 1700's	Venice 1716	Venice 1716	Padua 1737
Preliminary processes	25.51	15.42	22.10	31.53	22.37	20.92	19.37	30.21
Spinning	21.22	30.16	36.60	_a	15.56	24.26	9.93	32.15
Weaving	12.94	18.21	18.59	23.03	20.07	13.88	11.86	9.31
Finishing processes	15.83	6.26	20.01	15.10	25.81	21.93	12.71	11.59
Dyeing	15.46	16.44	.89b	6.02b	8.35	14.67	36.82	-
Brokerage, rent, fees	9.04	13.51	1.78	24.29	6.93	4.33	10.12	17.55

Sources: Prato, 1300's: Melis, *Aspetti della vita economica, prospetto* xxvii (opposite p. 554). Florence, 1500's: *ibid., prospetto* xxix, p. 561, derived from material in Raymond de Roover, "A Florentine Firm of Cloth Manufacturers," *Speculum,* 16 (1941).

Venice, 1612: Bibl. Marc., *Ital.* VII, *Cod.* 1741 (9638), "Scrittura sulle fabbriche di panni," January 27, 1612, *m. v.* The grade of cloth is a "panno di 100," first quality broadcloth.

Treviso, 1713: A.S.V., *Cinque Savi,* n.s., b. 128, fasc. 9, pt. 1. The grade of cloth is "panno mischio," a cheap woolen.

Venice, 1700's: A.S.V., *Cinque Savi,* n. s., b. 139, fasc. *Camera del Purgo,* "Notta di spese per fabricar pezza una saglia d'Parangon." The document bears no date but piecerates indicate the first decades of the eighteenth century. The grade of cloth, "saglia di parangon," is first quality serge.

Venice, 1716: A.S.V. *Cinque Savi,* n. s., b. 121, fasc. "Prohibitioni Panni Forastieri," pt. 3. The grade of cloth, "panno ad uso d'olanda," was a light worsted, the Venetian equivalent of the Dutch and English "New Draperies."

Venice, 1716: *ibid.* The grade of cloth, "padoanelle," was a cheap, low quality fabric.

Padua, 1737: A.S.V., *Provveditori di Comun,* b. 54. The grade of cloth is given as "panno di Padova (fino)."

Notes:
  aspinning costs included in preliminary processes.
  bdyed in the wool. All others are dyed in the cloth.

TECHNOLOGY, CAPITAL, AND COSTS

costs also shows little variation. No one operation diminished sufficiently as a percentage of total cost to indicate a change in technology.

Preliminary processes—sorting, shearing, cooking and washing of
wool, beating, carding and combing—show low variation. They were
essentially unskilled operations, and domestic labor was commonly
used. Spinning, also primarily a domestic craft, shows surprisingly
large variation as a percentage of total cost, although without respect
to either the period or the quality of the cloth. This variation is partially attributable to the use of selvage (reprocessed loom remnants).
While the preliminary processes were low-cost operations, spinning
was typically the most expensive of all the textile operations. Over the
centuries weaving costs were the most stable, amounting to a constant
10 to 20 percent of production costs. Dyeing too was fairly stable, the
variations reflecting the type of dye more than anything else. When
the inexpensive *padoanelle* cloth was dyed in scarlet, dyeing accounted
for one-third of total cost.

Of all the sub-processes the many finishing stages vary the most in
relative cost from example to example. Burling was fairly constant;
shearing cost more (proportionately) in Venice than it had in Tuscany
two centuries before. Tentering was always a minor expense; mechan-
ized fulling too was cheap. Teaseling, the raising of the nap with
thistles or wire teasels, was the most expensive finishing operation,
amounting in Venice to 4 to 8 percent of total cost.

The figures in the category of "brokerage, rent, fees" have little
comparative value, since variations represent largely differences in
accounting; inclusion of materials, rent, and taxes is not uniform for
all examples.

Dealing with Venice alone, and comparing clothmaking in 1612
with manufacture one century later, we see that preliminary processes,
weaving, and finishing are virtually unchanged as percentages of total
cost, while spinning has become less expensive. Dyeing costs are not
comparable, for the cloth of 1612 was dyed in the wool—a process
involving negligible expense. On the whole, then, the story that this
comparison tells is "no change" in cost structure in the early modern
Venetian woolen industry.

Wages

Payments to labor were the chief production costs in early modern manufacturing. Based upon fragmentary information it is possible to surmise that money wages in Venice rose throughout the century—rapidly from the 1590's through the years of recovery of the 1630's, then only slightly through the remainder of the century. Since there was only a mild increase in price over the seventeenth century, the approximate real wage must have been fairly constant—a conclusion that fits the pattern of stable population and employment, and stable economic output despite manufacturing declines.

Pullan's examination of builders' wage rates to the year 1630 (table 4.7) shows steadily increasing money wages through the second half of the sixteenth century followed by a still rapid rise in the first third of the seventeenth century.[65] There were short-term reversals as well as periods of abrupt increase which Pullan relates to short-term labor market conditions caused by war, plague, famine, and their aftermath. From 1606 to 1625 wage rates remained stable, rising again in the years just preceding the plague of 1630-1631. Over the long term money wages approximately doubled from mid-sixteenth century to 1630. Indications of wage levels past Pullan's period are difficult to come by and presently we are forced to rely for evidence upon the legislated piecerates of the woolen industry (table 4.5). While clearly lacking the responsiveness of unregulated wages, these mercedi were reviewed with sufficient frequency to permit adjustment to general economic conditions such as the price level.[66] Although they do not reflect short-run conditions such as a short-term labor shortage, which would not have been grounds for relitigating fees, the mercedi are in a sense the most accurate indicators of payments to labor, for most major industries used the piecework fee system rather than the market wage.

Woolworkers' fees rose in the period covered by Pullan's builders' wage series, although not by a factor of two as in the building trades. There was a period of actual reduction of legislated fees between 1584 and 1588 paralleling the decline in master builders' wages. In 1635 fees had risen to well above 1564 levels, and the trend continued for weaving and shearing; by 1716 fees in all processes had approximately doubled from 1588 levels.

---

65. Pullan, "Wage-Earners," pp. 173-174.
66. See above, chap. 2, pp. 16-19.

TECHNOLOGY, CAPITAL, AND COSTS

Table 4.5. Woolworkers' piecerates, 1564-1716 (in *soldi*)

Process	1564	1584-86	1588	1612	1635	1657	1675	1716
Beating:								
Spanish wool	5	6	5	5	6	-	6	-
English wool	3	4	3	-	6	-	6	-
Local wool	4	5	4	-	6	-	6	7
Carding:								
Spanish wool	3	3.5	3	3	3.5	-	3.5	-
English wool	3	3.5	3	-	3.5	-	3.5	-
Local wool	3	3.5	3	-	3.5	-	3.5	7
Combing:								
Spanish wool	6	-	6	7.5	9	-	9	-
English wool	4	6	5	-	9	-	9	-
Local wool	5	-	5	-	9	-	9	-
Weaving:								
Cloth of 100	-	-	1,141.5	1,189	-	-	-	-
Cloth of 80	-	-	570.5	-	-	-	-	-
Cloth of 70	-	-	565	-	-	725	950	1,700
Cloth of 60	-	-	519	-	-	659	680	-
Shearing:								
Cloth of 100	-	300	300	300	-	-	540	-
Cloth of 80	-	240	240	-	-	-	-	480
Cloth of 60	-	-	-	-	-	-	240	-
Stretching:								
all qualities	-	36.17	36.17	-	-	-	60	60

Sources: For 1564 and 1584-86, A.S.V., *Arte della seta,* b. 105, fasc. 130; for 1588, Bib Marc., *Parti Veneziani,* no. 95, "Regolatione dell' Arte della Lana"; for 1612, Bibl. Marc. *Ita* VII, *Cod.* 1741 (9638), "Scrittura sulle fabbriche di panni"; for 1635 and 1657, A.S.V, *Ar della seta,* b. 105, fasc. 130; for 1675, *ibid.,* and A.S.V. *Milizia da Mar,* no. 556, fasc. *tesseri panni di lana* (1677); for 1716, A.S.V., *Cinque Savi,* n.s., b. 121, fasc. "Prohibitione di pan forastieri fabriche in Venezia e Terraferma," pt. 3.

Other indications likewise suggest only moderate inflation: the price of grain at Udine and Chioggia shows virtual stability over most of the century;[67] house rents in Venice rose almost imperceptibly (table 4.6). These fragments of information suggest that wages and prices stayed in line with one another over a century of very mild inflation.

Excessive labor costs have been cited as one of the chief causes of Venice's inability to maintain a competitive advantage in world mar-

67. Braudel, "La vita economica di Venezia," p. 91.

Table 4.6. Average rents in the Corte San Rocco, 1631-1704

Decade	Average yearly rent (ducats)	Decade	Average yearly rent (ducats)
1631-40	14.7	1671-80	19.3
1641-50	16.1	1681-90	17.2
1651-60	15.4	1691-1700	17.2
1661-70	19.8	1701-04	15.5

Source: A.S.V., Scuola di S. Rocco, prima consegna, reg. 45-49.

Note: These are decade averages of contractual rentals for some apartments leased by the Scuola San Rocco continuously over most of the seventeenth century. All of the apartments were contained in four buildings composing the Court of S. Rocco in the Parrocchia of Angelo Raffaele. The Scuola San Rocco was one of the largest real estate owners in Venice and this group of houses was only a small portion of the institution's holdings. Although the Scuola was basically a charitable organization, renting houses was a major revenue source and no charity was involved in the leasing agreements. The "case" or apartments were occupied by almost every type of worker and tradesman in the city from jewelers, wool and spice merchants, to wool-beaters, arsenal workers, and boatmen. The apartments themselves vary in size and cost from a modest two-room on the ground floor to a twenty-two-room "casa grande."

Pictures and floor-plans of these apartments may be seen in A.S.V., Scuola di S. Rocco, 2da consegna, reg. 26, "Catastico universale di tutte le fabbriche e stabile in specialita della veranda Scuola di San Rocco," Anno 1770, pp. 30-35.

kets.[68] It is argued that the industrial guilds had monopoly power in factor markets and were able to maintain wages at a higher level than productivity would have justified.[69] There is no doubt that labor costs in Venice were higher than in competing newcomer countries. This gulf between domestic and foreign wages began in the second half of the sixteenth century when Venetian productivity was at an all-time high. It should be noted that no system is more rigorous in pegging productivity to factor payments than piecework, for whatever the regulated rates, if there was little or no output there was little or no payment.

68. Cipolla," Economic Decline of Italy," p. 139.
69. Ibid., p. 140.

TECHNOLOGY, CAPITAL, AND COSTS

The supposition that guilds were capable of monopoly truculence is mistaken, for workers' guilds, like merchants' guilds, could only make proposals to the state committees that governed the industry. After litigation, committee recommendations were in most cases reviewed and enacted by the Senate, a body unlikely to permit coercion. As Sella notes, most contemporary complaints regarding wages, especially about the guilds, reflect the position of the merchants and must be regarded as suspect.[70] For every complaint from the merchants about the unfair exactions of the workers, it is certain that there is a corresponding petition from the guilds beginning, "We famished and forgotten brothers . . ."

It is possible to evaluate the wage situation of Venice vis-à-vis her competitors by comparing Pullan's figures with those compiled by Phelps Brown and Hopkins for England (table 4.7).[71] To do this, the English builders' wages are converted at the current exchange rate from pence sterling to Venetian ducats and then into Venetian soldi. A monetary exchange ratio is thus stipulated which will express the wages of one country in the money of another. Such procedures are fraught with statistical danger. Without indexing with reference to prices money wages, even when expressed in a common currency, do not permit accurate comparison of real wages. Further complications are introduced if multiple translation of account monies into actual currency payments is required. Since, however, our present concern is with the wage as a factor payment, not with real income or standard-of-living, a simple money-wage comparison may be used so long as its shortcomings for other applications are acknowledged.

Exchange ratios for the period 1603-1637, taken from correspondence transcribed in the *Calendar of State Papers, Venetian,* vary between four and six ducats to the pound sterling; in thirteen quotations, only two fall outside that range.

The derived wage figures indicate that there was an approximate parity in earnings between English and Venetian builders' wages from the mid-sixteenth century to about 1580. From that point Venetian wages rose rapidly while English wages remained static, so that by

70. Sella, "Rise and Fall," p. 124.
71. E. H. Phelps Brown and Sheila V. Hopkins, "Seven Centuries of Building Wages," in *Essays in Economic History,* ed. E. M. Carus-Wilson (3 vols., New York, 1966), II, 168-178.

Table 4.7. English and Venetian builders' wages compared, 1550-1629

Decade	English wage		Venetian wage
	(pence)	(soldi)	(soldi)
Masters			
1550-59	8-10	17-31	29
1560-69	10	21-31	31
1570-79	10-12	21-37	36
1580-89	12	25-37	43
1590-99	12	25-37	49
1600-09	12	25-37	57
1610-19	12	25-37	63
1620-29	12	25-37	66
Laborers			
1550-59	6-8	12-25	20
1560-69	6-8	12-25	21
1570-79	8	17-25	23
1580-89	8	17-25	27
1590-99	8	17-25	35
1600-09	8	17-25	38
1610-19	8	17-25	40
1620-29	8-10	17-31	41

Sources: Pullan, "Wage-Earners," pp. 173-174; Phelps Brown and Hopkins "Seven Centuries of Building Wages," pp. 168-178.

Note: All monies are monies of account. The ducat used in exchange quotations is the bank ducat, permanently pegged to the lira of account at the rate of 1 ducat = 6 lire, 4 soldi. This bank ducat, or ducat of account, in no way corresponds to the gold ducat which was worth well over 10 lire by the seventeenth century (A.S.V., *Ospitali e Luoghi Pii Diverse,* b. 551, "Stampo di cechino et suo accrescimento di tempo in tempo"). One lire equals 20 soldi.

(cont.)

Sterling - Ducat exchange ratios				
Source: Calendar of State Papers . . . Venice:				
Vol.	No.	Date	Quotation	Ratio
2	841	2/12/1517	40d = 1 ducat	1:6
10	35	5/8/1603	34d = 1 ducat	1:7.06
11	950	6/16/1610	£1 = 4 ducats	1:4
12	150	2/23/1610	57d = 1 ducat	1:4.21
12	543	6/3/1612	£15,000 = 60,000 ducats	1:4
14	712	3/31/1617	£150 = 600 ducats	1:4
16	775	3/19/1621	10s = 2.5 ducats	1:5
16	779	3/19/1621	£500 = 2,000 ducats	1:4
17	466	5/23/1622	£44,000 = 176,000 ducats	1:4
18	51	6/9/1623	£200 = 1,000 ducats	1:5
18	569	9/6/1624	£35,000 = 150,000 ducats	1:4.29
20	24	11/16/1626	£70,000 = 200,000 ducats	1:2.86
22	438	6/21/1630	£11.25 = 45 ducats	1:4
22	529	10/11/1630	£6,000 = 32,000 ducats	1:5.16

Low estimate: £1 = 4 ducats or 24 lire, 16 soldi

High estimate: £1 = 6 ducats or 37 lire, 4 soldi

The estimated range of English wages in soldi is calculated by converting Phelps Brown and Hopkins' lower wage estimate into Venetian soldi using the low estimate of exchange and likewise applying the high estimate of exchange to the high estimate of the English builders' wage.

1629 Venetian rates had reached roughly double the English wage.[72] Payments to both masters and journeymen (craftsmen and laborers in Phelps Brown and Hopkins's terminology) show these movements to a roughly equal degree.

The first three decades of the seventeenth century were years of particular wage stability in England.[73] This was the period when England made her capture of international cloth markets, both Mediterranean and Atlantic. Her forte was inexpensive grades of wool cloth: kerseys and cheap broadcloth.[74] It was crucial to England's

72. The decades of rising wages in Venice correspond to a period of peak output in the woolen industry and to a period of price inflation for southern Europe.

73. Phelps Brown and Hopkins, "Seven Centuries of Building Wages," p. 172, fig. 2.

74. Sella, Commerci, pp. 60-61. On England's cloth exports to the Mediterranean see Davis, "England and the Mediterranean," pp. 118-120, and Supple, Commercial Crisis and Change, pp. 5, 6, 27-28.

success as a new competitor that economies were achieved not only by weaving lighter and coarser fabric but also by paying less to workers than did her competitors, and so effecting a further reduction in costs.

There are no surprises to be found in the history of capital, technology, and costs in early modern Venice. In fact it would be misleading to treat Venice as anything but typical of the European economy in general during the seventeenth century. The level of applied technology was much the same as in any other European manufacturing center. Production in many respects closely resembled medieval manufacturing, and yet Venice was Europe's chief exporter of new techniques in this era. Links with the near future are as obvious as those with the past; survivals to the present century are obscure but extant nonetheless. The scale of Venetian production seems minuscule by today's standards; yet, as Landes has shown, even at the turn of the twentieth century well over 90 percent of all French and German enterprises employed five or fewer persons.[75] A Venetian glassworks at the time of Antonio Neri (c. 1612) was essentially the same as the glass furnace pictured in the *Encyclopédie*. The Venetian furnace has hardly changed since, and in fact the eighteenth-century drawing could equally well portray, down to the smallest detail, a present-day Venetian enterprise like the renowned Venini factory. The city of Venice never favored itself as a site of revolution—political, industrial, or otherwise.

---

75. David S. Landes, "Social Attitudes, Entrepreneurship and Economic Development: A Comment," *Explorations in Entrepreneurial History,* ser. 1, 6 (1954), 253, 266-267.

Government Policy, Outside Influences, and Economic Decline

The paradox of early modern Venice—relative decline in commerce and industry with no absolute decline in overall income—was as much a product of policy-making as of simple market behavior. Outside influences which threatened the equilibrium of domestic welfare called forth not only the automatic reactions of the market, but also certain considered policy responses on the part of the state. The policies which resulted shaped the economic century as surely as did changing factor productivity or terms of trade. The foremost problems confronting Venice were: the demands of the state budget; the exploitation of the mainland to sustain city income; the War of Crete; and the control of competitive behavior in the face of the industrial rivalry of foreign powers and of the Venetian empire itself.

Problems of the State Budget and the Exploitation of Empire

Although the seventeenth century has never been christened with a generally accepted name, for the economic history of western Europe it is the "Age of Mercantilism." Economic nationalism was not invented between the sixteenth and eighteenth centuries but the codification of its practical laws and their universal acceptance into national polity took place during these years. In fact, well before the seventeenth century unconnected antecedents to formal mercantilism abounded in economic legislation in Europe.[1] Economic nationalism was already an active and pervasive reality in Venice during the Renaissance.

---

1. C. H. Wilson, "Trade, Society and the State," *Cambridge Economic History of Europe,* IV, chap. 8, p. 498.

GOVERNMENT POLICY, OUTSIDE INFLUENCES, AND DECLINE

The Venetian Senate was the body that formulated the economic policy of the Republic and maintained scrutiny over economic performance. Its committees were responsible for overseeing every aspect of production and distribution.[2] The strategy of the state fisc was to have revenues from foreign sources pay the bills for Venice. Venice's virtual monopoly in Mediterranean trade and industry enabled her to exert positive control over her economic destiny throughout much of the premodern period.

The foremost consideration was the maintenance of trade advantages, for not only did trade provide livelihood to a large segment of the population—particularly the aristocracy—but, in addition, the most important source of regular government revenues were the customs tariffs.[3] Only an economy whose trade situation was totally secure could rely so completely on indirect taxation of this sort. As long as Venice held a monopoly of the trade in Eastern products, and European market demand was inelastic, foreign purchasers were major contributors to the Venetian state budget through tariffs.[4] All other aspects of Venetian economic policy were protective adjuncts for maintaining the trade advantage and its fiscal benefits. Home industry was thought of as merely a supportive operation to the city's commercial enterprise. Venice's main industries (shipbuilding excepted) manufactured almost exclusively for export.[5] The government through Senate subcommittees regulated activity in major industries in order that no harm should come to the revenue-producing capacity of the city. The overall labor force was kept under the eye of the Senate by liaison between guilds and agencies like the Cinque Savi alla Mercanzia and the Giustizia Vecchia. It was no abstract concern for the perpetuation of craftsmanship that prompted this surveillance. Tariff revenues depended upon successful sales. More

---

2. Of about 100 Senate subcommittees, at least 45 were directly concerned with economic affairs (Da Mosto, *L'Archivio di Stato di Venezia, indice del testo*).

3. Luzzatto, *Storia,* pp. 113-114.

4. There were political as well as fiscal reasons why Venice would be expected to rely on indirect taxation. Generally, a ruling oligarchy avoids direct taxation on (its own) real property in favor of passing the burden to business or commerce. Venice, however, does not fit this pattern especially well since for most of her history the oligarchy was the mercantile community as well.

5. For example, of some 11,000 wool cloths manufactured in 1656, only 700 were consumed domestically (A.S.V., *Arte della Seta*, b. 120, fasc. 341, p. 2).

GOVERNMENT POLICY, OUTSIDE INFLUENCES, AND DECLINE

than a third of the total income of the state—perhaps fully one half of ordinary tax revenues—came from duties on commerce and industry in the late 1500's (table 5.1).

The fiscal reliance on foreign trade explains in large measure the ineffectual reactions of Venice to the pricing policies of the northern competition. The combined burden of import levies on raw materials, manufacturing taxes, assessments on the labor force, and export duties created so high a minimum-cost floor that individual merchants were powerless to effect significant cost reductions. Import duties alone were so staggering that smugglers ran great risks to bring all sorts of commodities, even bulky industrial raw materials, into the city, bypassing customs at night in small boats equipped with "devilish devices" to conceal the goods.[6]

The hopeless predicament of cloth pricing is typical of the problem confronting all export industry. Nearly one half the cost of a piece of wool cloth was tax burden. Of an average price of 79 ducats per cloth (during the years 1588-1630), fully 33 ducats (42%) went to public coffers—by far the largest single segment of cost.[7] The major craft workers, the *laneri*, the weavers, and the shearers, received for their labors 16 ducats (20%). All other workers including dyers and finishers shared 18 ducats (23%), and the merchants' share was 12 ducats (15%). If the entire tax burden on the wool industry had suddenly been lifted, Venetian cloths could have been the finest bargains in the marketplace. No wonder then that Venetian reports on the French wool cloth industry and its success in the Levant trade speak with undisguised envy of the support accorded the manufacturers by the French government, including tax privileges and subsidies for expor-

---

6. A.S.V., *Secreta, Materia Mista Notabile,* fasc. 133. Wood, wool, copper, and hides were among the chief contraband articles caught entering the city illegally. In one instance a smuggler offered his captor a bribe of 20 ducats to allow a boatload of copper to pass and unload in Venice. The smuggling problem intensified so severely in the first quarter of the seventeenth century that in 1617 customs agents on patrol were issued wheellock guns and given permission to fire on anyone offering resistance. In the 1620's all manufactures and modifications of small boats in the city's squeri had to be reported to the government on pain of five years in the galleys or ten in prison (A.S.V., *Cinque Savi,* n. s., b. 45, no. 306).

7. Bibl. Marc., *Ital.* VII, *Cod.* MDCCXLI (9638). The major taxes falling on wool cloths were the manufacturing tax (*dazio del purgo*), a tax on oil used in the cloth-making process, and the export tariff (*dazio d'uscida*); in addition there were surtaxes and payments by guildsmen to the galley-tax funds.

GOVERNMENT POLICY, OUTSIDE INFLUENCES, AND DECLINE

Table 5.1. The changing structure of Venetian tax revenues

	Tax income, by sources, in thousands of ducats and in percentage terms				
Year	Trade[a]	Consumption[b]	Terraferma[c]	Misc.[d]	Total
1587	707 (36%)	502 (26%)	690 (35%)	51 (3%)	1,950
1594	773 (37%)	537 (26%)	729 (35%)	48 (3%)	2,087
1602	896 (37%)	587 (24%)	842 (35%)	106 (4%)	2,431
1621	956 (25%)	961 (25%)	1,584 (41%)	323 (9%)	3,824
1633	631 (24%)	819 (31%)	1,088 (40%)	137 (5%)	2,675
1637	207 (11%)	598 (31%)	984 (51%)	123 (7%)	1,912
1641	601 (22%)	783 (29%)	1,142 (43%)	156 (6%)	2,682
1664	- 2,215 (59%) -		1,520 (41%)	- -	3,735
1670	590 (15%)	1,278 (33%)	1,799 (46%)	205 (6%)	3,872

Sources: For 1587-1641, *Bilanci Generali della Repubblica di Venezia;* for 1664, A.S.V., *Senato, Deliberazioni, Rettori,* filza 61, reports attached to *decreto* of Feb. 6, 1664, *m.v.*; for 1670, A.S.V., *Secreta, Materia Mista Notabile,* no. 106. Table totals differ slightly from documentary totals due to rounding error.

[a]Taxes on trade: Dazio del vin, dazio del sei per cento, dazio d'uscida, dazio di stagiera all'uscida, dazio d'intrada, dazio de panni di lana, impositione all'arte della seta, cottimo bailanze Constantinopoli, cottimo di Cipro, dazio veludi e pelli filadi, dazio di fontego dei tedeschi, dazio dell'ancorazo, soldo per lira de Levante, soldi per lira, dazio curami, dazio di pellami, dazio del transito, and lesser duties.

[b]Taxes on consumption: dazii della beccharia, del ferro, dell'oglio, dell'officio delle biave, del grassa, del vin a spina, de pesce, de piera, calcina, di legname, di legne, di frutte, transito di pesce, anguilla, del carbone, carte da giuoco, tabacco, osso di balena, candele, poste da vender vini & malvasia, quinto d'oglio, and net income from the salt monopoly.

[c]Incomes from the terraferma and dominions: incomes of the camere del Terraferma, revenues accruing to mainland regiments, limitazioni, tanse & decime del Terraferma, campatico, tassi di gente d'armi, decima del clero, dazio de uve passe.

[d]Miscellaneous: all other incomes, the most notable being incomes of the Ufficio dell'acque, incomes of other magistracies including the Provveditori di Comun and Rason Vecchie & Nuove, sales of merchandise in the Arsenal; taxes on officeholding, innkeeping, brokerage, contracts of sale, notarial services, decima del pro della camera d'imprestiti.

Surtaxes on duties (such as the "soldi per lira") have been prorated according to the income of the original duties.

GOVERNMENT POLICY, OUTSIDE INFLUENCES, AND DECLINE

tation.[8] The French knew that this was the way to encourage exports and bring bullion into the country. Venice, meanwhile, was unable to break away from her heritage of fiscalism founded upon market supremacy, even when that condition no longer existed.

The overall picture of the state budget for the seventeenth century shows a clear inverse relationship between yields from duties on commerce and manufacturing and from other revenue sources, above all the terraferma. Tax yields on trade actually fell, even as the amount of total revenues grew. Once the single largest share of state income, these sources fell to a position of lesser, but not negligible, importance. As this happened the state progressively called upon the territorial treasuries to compensate the shortfall and to support the increasing burden that war costs placed on the fisc. The trend to increased reliance on revenues from the mainland is visible long before the beginning of the War of Crete (table 5.1). The ordinary net incomes of Venice from the Camere del Terraferma jumped from about 500,000 ducats per year at the turn of the century to a level of 800,000-1,000,000 ducats beginning around the time of the 1620-1621 commercial crisis (table 5.2). These ordinary incomes derived from indirect taxes on mainland trade and consumption and did not include the non-periodic or extraordinary direct taxes such as the *tansa* and *campatico* which became so important a component of state finance during the war (table 5.3).

In Venice proper, taxes on consumption also rose in both absolute and relative terms, in keeping with general increases in the demands of the budget. But the early peacetime escalation of ordinary levies on the mainland confirms a policy of increased fiscal exploitation of the dominions to compensate for the failing customhouse—a policy that Luzzatto was convinced began in the fifteenth century with the first interferences in the Venetian commercial hegemony and the simultaneous expansion of empire in the Veneto.[9] Such exploitation is virtually a theoretical necessity if in fact the level of Venice's trade contracted and the level of her well-being did not. Certain well-documented patterns of investment and taxation lend credence to the

---

8. A.S.V., *Cinque Savi,* n.s., b. 125, fasc. 31. pt. 1, July 2, 1723, report of Barbon Morosini.
9. Gino Luzzatto, "L'economia veneziana dopo l'acquisto della terraferma," *Bergomum,* 58 (1964), 59-60.

GOVERNMENT POLICY, OUTSIDE INFLUENCES, AND DECLINE

Table 5.2. Ordinary revenues of Venice from Terraferma treasuries

Year	Net revenues (ducats)	Gross revenues (ducats)	Year	Net revenues (ducats)	Gross revenues (ducats)
1469	222,500	-	1633	939,438	1,076,319
1560	513,100	-	1637	828,345	965,226
1587	506,981	-	1641	1,009,068	1,145,949
1594	523,236	-	1664	863,055	1,090,039
1602	523,660	-	1670	-	1,200,479
1621	979,954	-			

Sources: For 1469 and 1560, Gino Luzzatto, "L'economia veneziana dopo l'acquisto della terraferma," *Bergomum,* 58 (1964), 59-60; for 1587-1641, *Bilanci generali della Repubblica di Venezia,* vol. I; for 1664, A.S.V., *Senato, Deliberazioni, Rettori,* filza 61, memorandum of the *Tre deputati sopra denaro pubblico,* attached to the *decreto* of Feb. 6, 1664, m.v. The datum includes revenues from Istria, Corfu, Zante, and Cefalonia. For 1670, A.S.V., *Secreta, Materia Miste Notabile,* no. 106; the budget is for 1669-1670, dated July 30, 1670. For the administrative details pertaining to terraferma treasuries, see the reports of the rectors, podestas, and regimental captains in A.S.V., *Senato, Secreta, Relazioni.*

Table 5.3. Direct taxes owed by the Terraferma during the early years of the War of Crete

Year	Tax quota (in thousands of ducats)				
	Sussidio ordinario	Campatico	Sussidio extraordinario	Tansa	Total
1645	100	190	-	-	290
1646	100	-	200	-	300
1647	100	190	-	-	290
1648	100	-	-	-	100
1649	100	-	200	-	300
1650	100	-	-	400	500
1651	100	190	-	-	290
1652	100	-	200	400	700
1653	100	-	-	-	100
1654	100	-	200	-	300
1655	100	480	-	-	580
1656	100	-	200	-	300
1657	100	-	200	-	300
1658	100	480	200	-	780
Total	1,400	1,530	1,400	800	5,130

Source: A.S.V., *Senato, terra,* filza 1081, January 1681, *m.v.*

theoretical conclusion but, leaving aside the state budget and turning to the broader question of private earnings, no well-developed argument has ever emerged to show that Venice extracted excessive income by exploitation of the terraferma after the crisis in commerce.

It is clear that land ownership by Venetians increased during the seventeenth century, but the complaint that trade was being abandoned in favor of *villegiatura* goes back to the 1400's.[10] It is also true that lands which came into Venetian hands were for the most part productive farms— "villas" in the Palladian sense of the word—not mere summering spots. The rent books of Venetian noble landholders show large incomes in money rents and in agricultural goods that were realized from a variety of land tenure arrangements used in combination to diversify the risks of agriculture.[11] Indications are, however, that actual rates of return on landed investment at current value were very low. Although historians have as yet come to no firm conclusions about Venetian land ownership in the terraferma, it seems likely that motives of diversification and preservation of capital, rather than the expectation of high rates of return, were paramount for noble investors in land.

Take, for example, the case of the Gozzi family which came to Venice from Bergamo in the early sixteenth century. They made so handsome a fortune in the silk trade, even during the years of crisis in the 1600's, that Alberto Gozzi (called Alberto della Seda) was able to purchase his nobility in 1646 for the requisite 100,000 ducats without endangering the family fortune.[12] In 1661 he owned about twenty-five houses, shops, and warehouses in Venice, large vineyards on the island of S. Erasmo, several mills, and about 1400 *campi* of improved land in various holdings on the terraferma.[13] His major investments, which were in textile trading companies, were fully active and profitable. On the whole, his management of family funds bears close

---

10. Angelo Ventura, "Aspetti storico economici della villa veneta," *Bollettino del Centro Internazionale di Studi di Architettura Andrea Palladio,* 11 (1969), 65.

11. *Ibid.,* p. 71. Land tenure contracts ranged from simple rent, paid in cash or kind, to the *boaria,* in which agrarian wage-workers were hired by the foreman (*gastaldo*) of the estate; the risk of bad harvest fell entirely on the landlord who was obligated to pay wages.

12. A.S.V., *Secreta, Archivio Proprio F. Balbi,* f. 21; *Miscellanea Codici,* III, *Cod. Soranzo,* 14.

13. A.S.V., *Dieci Savi sopra le Decime in Rialto,* b. 222, no. 1383 (*condizione di decima*).

resemblance to that of the old noble families in the early sixteenth century, except that banking and the long-distance galley trade do not figure in Gozzi family business. Wide diversification in commerce and the land characterized the Gozzi "portfolio."[14]

That Alberto was a perfect model of rational business behavior cannot be guaranteed, but if a successful record of investment is any measure then Alberto must surely qualify as an example of good decision making in difficult times. The balance sheets of his commercial companies show a pattern of consistent profitability from the early years of the seventeenth century to the time of his death in 1664. In the early years it was largely a family business with Alberto and his uncle Domenico operating a traditional silk manufacturing company, but as Alberto's connections expanded to Bologna, Lucca, Genoa, Verona, and especially Florence, he became a major partner in several other companies simultaneously. With outsiders to the family handling operations as minor partners he branched into other enterprises, among them paper-selling, wool cloth manufacture, the leather trade, and gold-thread making. The recorded profits of the various Gozzi firms were, on the whole, moderate. In the early years they often ran as high as 25 to 35 percent and almost never were they less than 6 percent per annum on original capital investments. A balance sheet of 28 December 1601—the earliest recorded for the company of Domenico and Alberto della Seda—shows an initial capital outlay of 11,530 ducats and a one-year profit of 7,376 ducats, 18 grossi, or about 64 percent. Profits were plowed back, and over the next decade the net worth of the company grew at a compound rate of nearly 13 percent per annum to 71,000 ducats in 1612 and ultimately to over 200,000 by 1620.[15] By contrast, on the death of Alberto in 1664 a liquidation of the Gozzi-Alberti Silk Company (housed on the Merceria S. Zulian) showed an increase in total value over six years of about 7,000 ducats on initial investments of 19,590 ducats, 15 grossi, or 5 1/4 percent compounded, a barely acceptable rate. By the last years of his life Alberto's total investments in commercial companies had declined (insofar as fragmentary records can show) from the

---

14. For comparison with older, and far wealthier nobles of a century before, see Lane, *Venice and History,* pp. 36-55: "Family Partnerships and Joint Ventures."
15. A.S.V., *Ospitali e Luoghi Pii Diverse, Commessaria Gozzi,* b. 556.

GOVERNMENT POLICY, OUTSIDE INFLUENCES, AND DECLINE

maximum level of about 250,000 ducats that he kept active in commercial investments in the second quarter of the seventeenth century.

It was chiefly during the years 1625-1650 that Alberto made significant purchases of real estate: agricultural holdings on the mainland, vineyards on S. Erasmo, rental properties in the city, and most notably the principal family residence in the SS. Apostoli parish, now known as the Palazzo Seriman.[16] Many of these purchases were made at public auction when default or criminal prosecution left lands in the hands of the *Sopragastaldi* or *Esator alle tanse e decime*. Alberto made heavy purchases of this nature immediately after the 1630-1631 plague when bargains were easy to come by. Often buying land in conjunction with his uncle Domenico, he rarely purchased any but the best quality developed lands (designated "Arativi, piantadi, videgadi"). However astute these transactions were from the standpoint of preserving and enhancing the family fortune, evidence strongly suggests that rates of return on these investments were very small. In 1622, by way of example, Domenico and Alberto purchased for 15,523 ducats a large plot of land on S. Erasmo, planted with gardens and vines, with about ten houses (ranging from straw huts to a *casa domenical*). The total rental income at the time of sale, valued at about 700 ducats, represented 4 1/2 percent return.[17] The following year a congregation of nuns in the S. Felice parish sold three large houses with four oil warehouses to Domenico and Alberto for 8,000 ducats, an investment yielding only 4 1/3 percent at the current rental value of 350 ducats. In 1661 the property brought in only 177 ducats in annual rents.[18] Incomes from landed investment on the terraferma were correspondingly low. Domenico and Alberto paid 105 ducats per *campo* for a parcel of arable land measuring nearly 6 *campi* which rented for a mere 9 *stara* of wheat and two pair of fowl.[19] *Livelli*, private loans secured by land, held by Alberto in 1661 paid an average of 6 percent on invested capital, and straight rental incomes corres-

---

16. *Ibid.*, b. 546, no. 9. The palace was acquired May 31, 1638, for 16,461 ducats.

17. *Ibid.* To arrive at the total rental value of the S. Erasmo property, I have estimated the rental value of the main house (*casa domenical*) at 160 ducats.

18. A.S.V., *Dieci Savi sopra le Decime in Rialto,* b. 222. On his tax form Alberto argued that the four oil warehouses did not in fact earn the 64 ducats he has declared, for they spend much time empty and expenses balance out income.

19. A.S.V., *Ospitali e Luoghi Pii Diverse,* b. 546, no. 9. A *campo* equals roughly half a hectare; a *staio* of grain, .8 hectoliters.

ponded more or less with this rate although returns varied considerably with land quality and the nature of the lease. By contrast, the seven mills that Alberto owned and subleased paid more handsomely, each yielding about 30 ducats per year on an approximate purchase price of 300 ducats.

In general, as the profitability of commercial investment diminished, low rates of return on land became less of an obstacle to agricultural investment, and the Gozzis, who had some terraferma holdings in the sixteenth century, expanded their mainland interests though not to the exclusion of commerce. The same may be said of the nobility in general. It is clear that investment in land was no *more* profitable than investment in commerce, so the shift cannot properly be explained solely in terms of maximization of current income, but neither is it true that land-buying was an unreasoned pattern of cowardice or negligence in the commercial sphere. In the early 1500's when Girolamo Priuli condemned the aristocrats of Venice who abandoned their maritime heritage and bought land for 20 to 25 ducats per campo (twice its value, he said), settling for meager returns of 3 to 4 percent, his angry criticism may have been justified by Venice's military failures but it was poor investment counselling. A century later that land was selling at 100 ducats per campo. Venetian investment in land was sensible as a hedge against commercial risk, but even more as a means of sustaining and augmenting family wealth through capital gains. It bore the added advantage that it could not be alienated from the family estate in future generations.[20] In the seventeenth century returns on landed investment were not high—roughly on a par with interest on mint deposits or the public debt in peacetime. But returns were certainly sufficient to justify maintaining wealth in this form. The Gozzi fortune was built on the silk trade but preserved by land ownership.

What then of exploitation, or the general effect of mainland property-holding on aggregate incomes in Venice? By mid-seventeenth century a quarter-million hectares of terraferma land were owned by Venetians, 70 percent of it by the patriciate.[21] From the standpoint

---

20. James C. Davis, *The Decline of the Venetian Nobility as a Ruling Class* (Baltimore, 1962), pp. 46, 67.
21. Woolf, "Venice and the Terraferma," pp. 184-185.

of productivity, Venetian ownership meant little. There were some interesting agricultural developments in the Veneto at this time, but there is no evidence that city landowners were particularly innovative. Their absentee status and encouragement of small-plot subdivision of agricultural estates was certainly no boon to technical progress.[22]

Venice might conceivably be thought of as a source of cheap capital for mainland agriculture because of the low rates of return that Venetians were willing to accept, but since Venetian "investments" in lands were really only transfers of ownership, not increments to the capital stock, this view must be rejected.

From the standpoint of income to the city of Venice the impact of the growth in Veneto land-ownership must have been sizable, even to the point of partially compensating for the losses the city suffered from declining industry and trade. Between the 1580's and the 1660's Venetian holdings rose by approximately 100,000 hectares from 150,000 to 250,000.[23] If all Venetian owners, hypothetically, had received the same proportionate returns as the Gozzi did—about 3,000 ducats per year on 600-700 hectares—Venetians would have received roughly a half-million ducats of income annually on these newly acquired lands. This figure has no basis in hard fact but it serves to show that the magnitude of incomes from the landholdings on the mainland was significant for the city. By comparison, the direct loss to Venice on an annual basis resulting from the decline in the production of wool cloths over the same period must have been on the order of a million ducats.[24] However crude these estimates may be, they satisfactorily demonstrate that increased land ownership was an important

22. Daniele Beltrami, *Saggio di storia dell'agricoltura nella Repubblica di Venezia durante l'età moderna* (Venice, 1955), pp. 70-73. Alberto Gozzi's tax form refers to expensive excavations (1500 ducats' worth) to defend the S. Erasmo littoral from inundation, but no improvements on mainland properties are mentioned. The property tax declaration of Gozzi possessions in the Polesine shows sizeable in-kind payments of maize (*formenton*) but as late as 1685-1690 maize was a very minor grain in rental payments from Paduan estates (A.S.V., *Dieci Savi sopra le Decime in Rialto,* reg. 467, pp. 215v and 234 r & v; *Ospitali e Luoghi Pii Diverse,* b. 939, fasc. 9).

23. Woolf, "Venice and the Terraferma," pp. 182, 185.

24. Output of the wool cloth industry fell from about 20,000 cloths per year in the 1580's to half that figure by the 1650's, the interval in which 100,000 additional hectares of land were bought by Venetians. At a unit price of 80 to 100 ducats per cloth, the annual loss to Venice from the 10,000-unit drop in production was on the order of 1,000,000 ducats, or about twice the estimated gains from annual returns on new land.

but not predominant factor in sustaining aggregate income in Venice during the commercial decline.

The Impact of the War of Crete

The War of Crete is an interruption of unmeasured consequence in the history of Venice during her transition from economic hegemony to relative decline. The twenty-four-year episode in the protracted Venetian-Turkish drama has already been mentioned as a possible cause of the extreme age of the Venetian work force toward the end of the century, and in connection with the growing tax burden on Venice and her territories. As we consider in turn the various institutional and non-market factors that may have contributed to Venice's economic difficulties, the War of Crete becomes an unavoidable issue. Yet contemporary sources tell us next to nothing about its effects on Venetian society. Oddly, the economic records of the government trade committees hardly ever mention the war. Our assessment of its impact must be, for the time being, the product of inference.

A reasonable way to approach the subject would be to divide the potential effects of the war into three categories: the direct costs of the war to the city and the empire; the indirect costs, meaning losses from the interruption of trade; and certain positive stimuli of the war such as the benefits of increased demand for war materiel and naval construction. The last category, economic benefits, can be dealt with summarily. After the 1630-1631 plague the Arsenal was in sorry shape. Before the plague about 1,500 workers came to the Arsenal daily. The holocaust reduced this number by "600 of the most valorous workers and masters." Also, many arsenalotti, like their colleagues in other crafts, departed Venice for foreign parts, notably Constantinople, Florence, and Naples. Certain naval stores were in desperately short supply; the Arsenal had on hand only one-third the necessary sail and canvas, and so little hemp for rope that the amount was deemed negligible compared to the need.[25]

The years between the low ebb of 1632 and the opening of hostilities were marked by a program of rebuilding. Arsenal expenses for labor

---

25. A.S.V., *Senato, deliberazioni, Rettori,* filza 3, report of the *Provveditori e Padroni all'Arsenale,* Mar. 31, 1632.

GOVERNMENT POLICY, OUTSIDE INFLUENCES, AND DECLINE

rose slowly between 1633 and 1641, and then at a quicker pace during the war years, so that by the last year of the war the Arsenal labor budget was 40 percent higher than in the 1630's.[26] The reactivation of the Arsenal to full strength must have provided a boost to employment for the entire construction sector of the economy. In time of need, house carpenters, private shipwrights (*squeraroli*), and many unskilled workers became part of its work force. Membership statistics show that most of those guilds which were in some way related to war production show a rise in numbers between the early years of the century and the later years of the war. Between 1603 and 1672 the number of *filacanevi* (ropemakers) more than tripled, and the guilds of the metalworkers (including weapons-makers), private shipwrights, fustian and canvas weavers, and house carpenters all showed sizable increases in membership (table 3.1).

Evidently the war, over its long duration, had some positive effect on the demand for labor and led to the revitalization of the Arsenal. Yet even as guild membership in war-related crafts was stimulated, the number of the city's gondoliers, bargemen, and small-boat operators—in sum, the transport sector of the city economy—fell drastically, possibly because of the manpower demands of the war fleets. This shortage of transport workers was probably more damaging to the productivity of the city economy than the tightening of the labor market was beneficial.

With respect to the direct costs to Venice of the War of Crete, little precision is possible. For one year at least we have some financial

---

26.   The Arsenal labor budget, 1587-1670 (in ducats)

Year	Amount	Year	Amount
1587	102,864	1633	108,000
1594	119,976	1641	115,445
1602	120,000	1664	150,000
1621	121,890	1670	159,920

Sources: 1587-1641, *Bilanci Generali,* vol. I; 1664, A.S.V., *Senato, Deliberazioni, Rettori,* filza 61; 1670, A.S.V., *Secreta, Materia Mista Notabile,* no. 106.

information. Two reports submitted for Senate consideration in 1664 attribute the year's budgetary deficit of approximately 1.5 million ducats to the state of war.[27] While annual war costs were surely greater than the budgetary shortfall, it must be reckoned that peacetime military expenditures were also high, so that the 1.5 million ducat estimate seems to be an accurate calculation of the added military expenses of the war. In 1641, a year of budget surplus, the total annual expense of the fleet was 500,413 ducats.[28] In 1664 the cost of the armada was about 1,050,000 ducats, of which 250,000 was for the military provisioning of Crete. The total does not include an additional 260,000 ducats for military expenses in Dalmatia. The rise in the expenses of the navy and other spending on the Mediterranean war was on the order of 500,000-750,000 ducats for one year.

Because, in great measure, the war was financed with the aid of heavy government borrowing, interest on the public debt became the second major component of increased wartime expenditures. In 1641, before the war, the public debt was about 8 million ducats and the annual interest payment was 410,000 ducats. In 1664 interest payments had risen to 960,000 ducats and in 1670 to 1,204,600.[29] Other war-related expenses were the increased costs of running the Arsenal and the hiring of local infantry and mercenary troops.[30] All together then, the extra wartime costs associated with the armada, the Arsenal, the debt service, and the army approach but do not exceed the 1.5 million ducat estimate for the year 1664.

How was the shortfall in the budget made up? Mocenigo reported the following measures: sales of official pardons, public lands, and public offices; the special galley-taxes and taxes on clerical incomes;

27. A.S.V., *Senato, Deliberazioni, Rettori*, filza 61. The reports, attached to the *decreto* of Feb. 6, 1664, *m. v.*, were prepared by Alvise Mocenigo and the *Tre Aggiunti al Denaro Pubblico* for a study of Mocenigo's recommendation about altering the size of the army and navy.

28. This included the pay and provisioning for 23 light galleys, 2 great galleys, and 27 smaller armed boats, plus 25,476 ducats for soldiers' pay in Candia (*Bilanci Generali*, I, pp. 566-573).

29. A.S.V., *Secreta, Materia Mista Notabile*, no. 106.

30. The cost of hired armies for the War of Crete does not show up readily in State budgets. In 1664 less than one-half million ducats were expended for troops in the terraferma and the dogado—less than half the charge in earlier years when Venice was fighting more on land than on sea.

donations; and deposits (i.e., borrowing) at 6-10 percent.[31] In the early years of the war, which were doubtless more costly than the year 1664 because of the greater intensity of naval war, direct taxes on the terraferma averaged 366,000 ducats annually, occasionally going as high as 700,000 ducats in a single year (table 5.3). Mocenigo's report indicates that these amounts must be discounted by as much as 25 percent because of non-payment; even so, the amounts are massive. And, since the expenditure of these funds took place largely in foreign parts (except for the interest payments and the Arsenal costs), the vast sums of money may be considered lost to the economy of Venice without coincident benefits of stimulating domestic demand.

By the close of the war the public debt had escalated to over 21 million ducats, not including 12.6 million ducats in ordinary obligations.[32] The mint held deposits at a variety of rates ranging from 4 percent to 14 percent, and the total interest payment was a major share of the state budget. In 1670, after the direct military cost of the war had ceased, the annual deficit was 1.2 million, about the same as the debt service cost for that year. Venetians were no novices at solving fiscal overloads of this sort. After the War of Cyprus (1570-1573) the government quickly apportioned a part of the yearly tax revenues toward the amortization of the debt, and ten years after the end of the war the liquidation was completed. Fiscal recovery was equally rapid after the War of Crete. On the 20th of February, 1671 (m.v.), the government consolidated the various "deposits" into a single perpetual annuity fund. Interest and amortization were combined, the interest was reduced to 3 percent, and the state began to pay off the debt. By dint of only slight increases in taxation and some cutbacks in spending, a quarter-million ducat surplus in the budget was realized exactly ten years after the termination of hostilities.[33]

The financial effects of the war, therefore, may be adjudged severe, but not long-lasting. The direct costs of the war weakened Venetian investment capabilities by siphoning funds into the war-chest, but the

---

31. A report of the early 1670's confirms the use of these measures, which were above and beyond the standard "extraordinary" forms of borrowing and taxation to meet wartime fiscal needs (see Sella, "Crisis and Transformation," p. 98).

32. A.S.V., *Senato, Affrancatione,* filza II; *ibid., Materia Mista Notabile,* no. 106. By ordinary obligations I mean interest-bearing accounts in revenue-producing state offices such as the Salt Office and the *Ternaria.*

33. *Bilanci Generali,* II, 54.

straitening was without persistence, and Venice shared in the general economic recovery of Europe after 1670, unimpeded by any sort of residual financial turmoil or incapacity.

The most severe economic hardship the war imposed on Venice may have been the indirect costs—specifically the interruption of trade with the Eastern Mediterranean. The Cinque Savi alla Mercanzia, when charged with explaining the decline of the woolen industry, reported in 1669: "The present war is one of the principal causes of its diminution, because the usual commerce to Constantinople, Smyrna, Syria, and Alexandria has been halted; whereas these before were major passage points for our cloth, now this rich trade is extinct and sales of cloth weakened."[34] This remark only prefaces their report, however. They go on to discuss other "prejudices" to the industry which bulk larger in their consideration as causes of competitive failure in woolens: the continued introduction of foreign cloths; the rivalry of clothmakers closer to home, especially the Paduans; and the black market in cloths wherein brokers bypassed the shops and sold fabric directly to Turkish merchants (war or no war!), undercutting traditional wholesalers. Although it is recognized that commercial intercourse with the Turks persisted to some degree throughout the war years, it was no compensation for the worsening of Venice's position in Eastern markets as the English, Dutch, and French consolidated their commercial hold on the Turkish market at Venetian expense.[35]

The War of Crete worsened Venice's already straitened commercial circumstances in the middle of the seventeenth century, but it was not a cause of economic decline. According to the indications we have of the effects of the war on the economy, it is safe to presume that had the war not happened, the motion of commercial change in the Mediterranean that had set in by 1620 would surely have continued, although there is no doubt that the key feature of this trend—the commercial take-over of the Mediterranean by Northern competitors—was abetted by the quarter-century of disruption that the Cretan war inflicted on Venetian commerce.

---

34. A.S.V., *Senato, Deliberazioni, Rettori,* filza 72, January 3, 1669, *m. v.*
35. Sella, "Crisis and Transformation," p. 98.

GOVERNMENT POLICY, OUTSIDE INFLUENCES, AND DECLINE

We have marveled at the demographic recovery of Venice after the plague of 1630, as the city was repopulated at the same pace as in the prosperous 1570's. Her speedy financial recovery from the War of Crete is hardly less marvelous, a perfect parallel to the recovery from the War of Cyprus in those same 1570's. The end of the Cretan war marked the end of the long downswing in Venice's commercial fortunes[36] and the beginning of a recovery phase in port activity and trade in line with the secular trend of the European economy. Neither the residual nor the long-term effects of the war were great. Like the plague of 1630 and the rash of piracy two decades earlier, the War of Crete was a short-run disaster with limited long-run impact.

The Policy of Competitive Response: Quality Control

The conquest of markets that had at one time been Venice's sole preserve was accomplished by England, Holland, and France, and the method was price competition. The North Atlantic won its economic supremacy, initially, in the Mediterranean marketplace, by selling traditional products. The new competitors captured a large market share by cost-cutting and underselling. Their devices were to steal the technology and then manufacture cheap but imitative versions of the standard commodities of international trade, driving out the old commercial monopolist. How did Venice meet this challenge? Did state policy prevent commercial disaster or encourage it?

We ought to try to answer these questions in a broad frame of reference. Venice is but a case history, for "trade rivalry" is a recurring theme in economic history. In the first century A.D. Roman peninsular industry succumbed in like fashion to the competition of the Gallic and Rhenish provinces; nineteen hundred years later Germany took over British industrial markets on a worldwide scale. Certain leitmotifs were common to all instances of trade rivalry. The original manufacturers held virtual world monopolies and their product quality was of the highest reputation. Inroads were first made by imitating the established product, but in a shoddier version that could sell for far less. The use of falsified trademarks was a common trick for associating the cheap competitor with the established article. The

---

36. *Ibid.*, p. 100.

only response that seems to have succeeded for the established manufacturer was to reduce costs—and standards of quality if necessary—to meet the challenger's price.

Market incursions by new European competitors into Venetian industrial hegemony followed this general pattern. They introduced cloths, soap, glassware and other products at bargain prices to Levantine and European markets[37] while the Venetians complained bitterly about the superficial resemblances of the new foreign goods to their own products.[38] Even instances of counterfeit trademarks and quality seals of San Marco were reported.[39] For the government this was frustrating to the point of outrage, for its foremost concern was the maintenance of the city's reputation for high-quality manufacturing. Not only were Venetian wares being undercut in prices, but cheap imitations, being passed off as of Venetian origin, were damaging the reputation that the city was finding so costly to sustain. But the state made no compromises concerning quality. It was anticipated that the historic reputation for quality would survive foreign attacks and stand Venetian manufactures in good stead in the long run. This belief may have been the greatest misjudgment of the commercial war that Venice fought. For the government, far from allowing a slippage in quality, actually increased its surveillance and the strictness of its control regulations during this period, causing further increases in costs. The Senate in the early seventeenth century promulgated a number of new quality regulations which contained attacks on the carelessness and avarice of manufacturers who no longer prided themselves on the quality of their work, but aimed at cheapness instead.

Among the toughest of the new regulations was the set of laws governing printing which were legislated by the Senate in 1603 and executed by the *Riformatori dello Studio di Padova.* These made several proofreadings a legal requirement for the state imprimatur, and the Riformatori were to appoint professional readers who would be

37. A.S.V., *Cinque Savi,* n. s., b. 121 (woolens); *Arte della Seta,* b. 119, fasc. 336, p. 16, and *ibid.,* b. 1, fasc. A, June 28, 1594 (silks); *Cinque Savi,* n. s., b. 145, fasc. 49, pt. 2, Aug. 24, 1651 (soap).

38. *Ibid.,* fasc. 1, no. 8; *Parti Veneziani,* no. 126, p. 412, Jan. 29, 1613, *m. v.*

39. *Ibid.;* A.S.V., *Cinque Savi,* b. 145, fasc. 1, no. 8; *ibid.,* b. 477, vol. I, June 18, 1546.

paid by the printers. Special attention was to be given to the quality of paper, ink, and type, and other quality inspections and tests were to be carried out periodically.[40] Similar laws were enacted in 1607 to monitor the silk industry. The laws were directed particularly against the employment at the looms of "Jews, Levantines, and other subjects who attend only to profit, caring little for making cloth of good quality, working instead on spoiled cloths and against the prescribed regulations." These offenses were said to be caused by expansion within the limits of the two and six loom rules which permitted weavers to work independently for their own profit.[41] From this, the condemnation concludes, "stems the discredit of our manufacture."[42]

The silk industry is actually somewhat of an exception to the industrial trends in seventeenth-century Venice. It is one case where maintenance of high quality may have actually benefited sales. Although troubled by difficult competition from France, from Bavaria, and from other Italian manufacturers, the industry prospered by increased specialization in the highest quality fabrics. To insure success in this, the silk merchants in 1608 went so far as to demand regulatory action by the government to insure quality standards.[43]

In the wool industry, regulations controlled every step of the manufacture of fabric to protect the reputation of *panni veneziani*, despite the growing failure of these fine cloths to sell against foreign competition. Manufacturers in Venice tried as best they could to diminish production costs within the limits of the law. Occasionally the bounds were exceeded. A common offense was overstretching by the tenterers to give a cloth the regulation width while economizing on warp threads. A *chiovarol* (tenterer) caught at this infraction could expect to spend eighteen months in the galleys "with his feet in irons."[44] A

40. *Parti Veneziani,* no. 20, p. 67, May 11, 1603. See also Horatio Brown, *The Venetian Printing Press: An Historical Study* (London, 1891), pp. 175-176.

41. See above, chap. 4, note 54.

42. A.S.V., *Cinque Savi,* b. 477, vol. 2, Aug. 27, 1607.

43. *Ibid.,* Oct. 24, 1608.

44. *Parti Veneziani,* no. 95, pp. 289-309, "Regolatione dell'Arte della Lana di Questa Città," Mar. 27, 1588, *capitolo* XXII. This was the first comprehensive set of wool regulations, the fruit of collaboration between the Cinque Savi alla Mercanzia, the Provveditori di Comun, and the Collegio del Lanificio. Complaints about overstretching were singled out for attention again, in the middle of the seventeenth century by the Provveditori di Comun (A.S.V., *Cinque Savi,* n. s., b. 126, fasc. 64, pt. 1, July 10, 1652).

special booth was set up in the wool office to measure certified cloths and count the threads. This went on causing loss of time and increased costs from 1656 to 1688 when the inspection was formally abolished.[45] In the woolen industry, as with all other Venetian manufacturing, there were no casual gradations of quality. The specifications for every characteristic of all grades of fabric were stipulated in the government-decreed regulations: the weight of the raw wool and its original quality, the number of warp threads, the length and width of the finished cloth, the type of dyestuff applied. Specifications were noted on the side and the head of the cloth, and if all were satisfactorily met, the cloth received the official seal of approval. Since any mixing of quality characteristics between types of cloth was forbidden, upper limits on low quality manufactures were as rigorous as lower limits on good qualities. In other words, strictures against using high quality wools and expensive dyes on light cloths were enforced with the same seriousness as laws against using cheap materials on fine heavy fabrics.[46]

At one time, early in the sixteenth century, Venetian wool manufacturers concentrated their efforts on the highest quality woolens, cloths of 100 and 80 portade, making only small amounts of the medium quality cloths (table 5.4). A radical change occurred during the 1530's and 1540's as the industry (and total output) grew and medium quality fabrics outnumbered first-rate cloths. Throughout the sixteenth and seventeenth centuries, as the industry prospered and then subsequently declined, the majority of woolen textiles produced were the so-called "ordinary cloths"—cloths of 60 and 70 portade. In the 1500's the woolen industry was able to shift from high quality to intermediate quality cloths under conditions of general market expansion,

---

45. A.S.V., *Arte della Seta,* b. 105, fasc. 130, p. 53, July 11, 1694.

46. The key measurement of wool cloth quality was the number of warp threads measured in *portade:* one *portada* being equal to 20 threads (*fili*). A "cloth of 100" (*panno di cento*) was the finest made, containing 2,000 warp threads. Cloths of 80, 70, 60, and 50 were also considered good to medium grades, but fewer than 50 portade were not permitted in regular Venetian cloths (Bibl. Marc., *Ital.* VII, *Cod.* MDCCXLI (9638), "Scrittura sulle fabbriche di panni," Jan. 19, 1612, *in. v.* The number of warp threads determined the weight and strength of the fabric. Frauds like overstretching were possible because premodern broadcloths, unlike modern woolens, were teaseled and sheared to bring up a fine, even pile or nap. The weave was not then visible as the surface of the cloth resembled felt or velour. Samples of early cloth are preserved in A.S.V., *Cinque Savi,* b. 491.

GOVERNMENT POLICY, OUTSIDE INFLUENCES, AND DECLINE

Table 5.4. Grades of wool cloth produced in Venice, 1516-1607

	Average annual cloth production		
Years	High quality cloth of 100 and 80	Intermediate quality cloth of 70, 60 and 50	Average annual total
1516-1519[a]	1,553.0	344.3	1,897.3
1520-1529	3,342.0	548.2	3,890.2
1530-1539	3,163.5	1,916.5	5,080.0
1540-1549[b]	3,225.5	4,546.6	7,772.1
1550-1559	3,048.2	10,119.0	13,167.2
1560-1561	3,654.0	12,553.0	16,207.0
1579-1589	1,099.4	18,734.2	19,833.6
1590-1594	478.8	22,753.4	23,231.2
1605-1607	49.3	19,819.3	19,868.6

Source: Bibl. Marc., *Ital.* VII, *Cod.* 1741 (9638).

[a]omits 1518
[b]omits 1543, 1544

but in the following century, when faced with vigorous, imitative competition, the industry was unable to respond. Manufacturers were denied the opportunity to make the same intermediate grades of cloth under looser quality standards, and this in large measure accounts for the competitive failure of the industry.

The state enforced quality control regulations in all other industries that produced for foreign consumption—even soaps bore an official *bolla* of quality. As Venetian merchants were well aware, freedom from such regulation was one of the main reasons that foreign competitors could undersell.

In 1700 the *capi di piazza* (merchants elected by their peers to represent the merchant community at large) in desperation described the Venetian woolen industry as a commerce in chains ("li mercanti esteri non vogliono mandare, ne li nostri mercanti far venire una mercantia, che rimane incatenata . . ."). The only remedy, they submitted, was to allow unregulated manufacture after the example of foreign countries, maintaining the old rules only for those who wished to continue working the old formulas.[47] But the state remained firm in its resolve to maintain the high standards on which the ancient reputation of Venice was founded, despite the cost that the economy paid in international trade.

Terraferma Competition

Competition from foreign countries was not the only external impediment to Venice's industry. Almost incredibly, Venetian mainland possessions emerged in the seventeenth century as the island city's stiffest competitors in many industries. From the standpoint of the government, this situation constituted a major dilemma; the difficulty was to strike a balance between economic oppression of the territories and sanction of an uncontrolled potential threat to the city economy from the territories. Compounding the quandary was the fact that state revenues from the mainland were considerable—more in fact than tariff incomes.[48] This meant that purposeful policies of constraining terraferma enterprise would have been unsound from a fiscal as well as a political point of view. Venice could only allow her mainland economic policy to follow a course of very limited and selective controls. For the most part this meant prohibiting certain competitive products from entering the port of Venice, but since most of the mainland's manufactures were destined for local and transalpine markets, the overall effect of the prohibition was small.

The problem of terraferma competition was not a new one in the seventeenth century. Years before, certain industries had taken firmer root in the mainland than on the island because of natural advantages. The first of such industries was metalworking which proved to be more economical when located near the supplies of raw materials. The city metalworking guilds had been threatened by terraferma competition as early as the fourteenth century when the Great Council prohibited most worked iron products from entering the city.[49] Mainland forges drove Venetian barrelhoop makers to extinction. Brescia

---

47. *Ibid.,* n.s., b. 83, fasc. 158, Mar. 11, 1700.
48. See *Bilanci Generali,* I, 486-491, 562-566, and above, table 5.1.
49. A.S.V., *Cinque Savi,* b. 56, insert to memorandum of Aug. 30, 1719, on ironmongery. The law prohibiting the entry of nails, anchors, etc. is of Mar. 23, 1354.

GOVERNMENT POLICY, OUTSIDE INFLUENCES, AND DECLINE

became the arms and armor center of north Italy. As a result of these developments the Venetian smith was forced to limit his craft to the fabrication of small articles for domestic use.

During the seventeenth century silk manufacture in Venice was threatened by mainland competition. Raw silk that at one time came to the island for spinning was diverted to terraferma water-driven mills.[50] Worse, the weaving operation too had begun to move to incipient mainland centers in Padua, Vicenza, and Rovere de Trento.[51] By mid-century the silk manufacturers, merchants and weavers, felt the effect of a severe reduction in their numbers and in the output of the city industry. The principal reason, they asserted, was the introduction of silk manufacturing in the terraferma. In response to their supplications, the Senate prohibited it in the mainland dominions, but looms still remained operational, particularly in Vicenza and Bergamo throughout the century.[52] Subsequently silk cloth manufacture never posed a serious threat to the island industry, which showed marked revitalization in the second half of the century.[53] This may well be an instance where active state intervention made the difference between life and death of the Venetian industry.

Like the workers in the silk industry, woolen manufacturers felt the keen threat of mainland competition whose key advantage as the Venetians saw it was neither factor costs (cheaper land or labor) nor location; the issue was their freedom from the regulated quality control that governed island manufacture.[54]

During the seventeenth century, the exodus of woolworkers from Venice reached major proportions. Almost all the departees went to the terraferma, principally to Padua. Apparently some Venetian merchant-manufacturers succumbed to the temptation to invest in the

---

50. A.S.V., *Milizia da Mar,* b. 543, fasc. *filatogi,* Sept. 6, 1696.

51. A.S.V., *Arte della Seta, b.* 109, fasc. 203, p. 22, June 20, 1608. The document notes that the number of (operational?) looms in Venice had been reduced from 2300-2400 to 1600-1700 (cf. Sella, *Commerci,* p. 125, table I).

52. A.S.V., *Arte della Seta,* b. 123, fasc. 382 *extra, supplica* of Aug. 17, 1666.

53. By 1689 over 5500 looms were operational in Venice. In 1675 less than 500 looms were working in the terraferma (*ibid., fasc.* 394 *extra, p.* 89).

54. A.S.V., *Cinque Savi,* n.s., b. 120, fasc. 296, pt. 1, Oct. 3, 1711: "To [the Turkish Wars and the interruption of Mediterranean commerce] must be added the increasing [woolen] manufactures of the terraferma, which abandon the usual formalities regarding nap, selvage, warp threads, and others . . . the terraferma merchants are earning more from those advantages that are forbidden to merchants of this city."

mainland enterprise soon after the contraction in island wool-cloth making set in, for in 1636/1637 such investments were prohibited.[55]

The old specialty of the terraferma wool industry was *panno basso,* woven of local wools and meant mostly for regional consumption.[56] Far from being competitive with Venice, this manufacture was reserved exclusively for mainland domestic industry. The majority of terraferma woolens were panni bassi for most of the seventeenth century, but mainland production of *panni alti* made with imported wools gradually expanded to the point where it far outstripped Venetian output.

Bergamo was the largest mainland production center of wool cloths at the end of the century. Her annual production during the twenty-five year period from 1685 to 1710 (table 5.5) exceeded by far the maximum number of cloths *ever* produced in one year by Venice herself. Of panni alti alone, when Bergamo was producing ten to fifteen thousand cloths at the beginning of the eighteenth century, island production was at a level of only two to three thousand pieces.[57]

Still other Venetian industries such as leatherworking, printing, and waxworking, were subject to mainland competition. Even the flourishing craft of mirrormaking was hit in its early years by transfers of men and materials to Padua and Vicenza.[58]

These accounts of terraferma competition, fragmentary as they are and based primarily on Venetian viewpoints, provide at best an incomplete glimpse into a complex situation. Too long has the mainland been regarded as merely the farmyard and the playground of Venice. From nearby Padua to distant Brescia powerful industrial enterprise seems to have flourished even as Venetian industry contracted. Government policy—if there *was* a general policy covering this problem— was either ambivalent or ineffective. All that is certain at this stage of inquiry is that too little is known about non-agricultural enterprise on the Venetian mainland. Generally speaking, the commercial policy of Venice during these years of economic difficulty was conservative. It was the aim of the state to return the city to the happy days of indus-

---

55. A.S.V., *Provveditori di Comun,* b. 53, Feb. 20, 1636.
56. Sella, *Commerci,* p. 58, n. 1.
57. *Ibid.,* p. 118.
58. Correr, *Mariegola dei specchieri,* no. 35, p. 19, *capitolo* XXVI.

GOVERNMENT POLICY, OUTSIDE INFLUENCES, AND DECLINE

Table 5.5. Wool-cloth production in Bergamo, 1685-1710

Year	High quality cloths (*panni alti*)	Low quality cloths (*panni bassi*)	Total cloths
1685	10,130	23,986	34,611[a]
1690	-	-	31,026
1691	-	-	36,760
1692	-	-	32,391
1693	-	-	32,846
1694	-	-	30,466
1695	-	-	39,665
1696	-	-	33,374
1701	14,396	21,522	35,918
1702	13,588	23,218	30,588
1703	15,026	-	-
1704	13,724	23,218	36,942
1705	15,498	24,018	39,516
1706	14,131	23,099	37,230
1707	14,664	18,686	33,330
1708	10,318	18,267	28,585
1709	9,611	17,000	26,611
1710	9,638	15,197	24,835

Source: A.S.V., *Cinque Savi,* b. 121, fasc. 85, pt. 1.

[a]Sella (*Commerci,* p. 57) gives total terraferma production in 1685 as 49,944 cloths, nearly 70 percent of which were made in Bergamo.

trial power and market hegemony, chiefly by maintaining quality standards and excluding foreign competitive products from the port of Venice.[59]

One does not have to speculate about reasons for conservatism in Venice during these years of challenge, for with a record of six centuries of commercial success, it would have been hard for her suddenly to abandon old and established methods. The success of Venetian

59. A list of prohibited imports accompanying a tariff of 1753 included: hats, buttons, printing type, paper, wigs, rosaries, hides, silk cloths, fustians, gloves, knitted goods, ironwork, molasses, glass products, worked gold or silver, woolen cloth, combs, costume jewelry, and buffalo hides. The only forbidden exports were raw materials for soap, wax, glass, and book manufacture (A.S.V., *Tarife Mercantile,* b. 1, tariff of May 29, 1753).

state finance in the past had in large measure been due to the tax imposed on merchandising, so that only foreigners and the wealthiest of Venetians were the major contributors to the "ordinary" (regular) source of state revenue. This fiscal policy guaranteed intense government concern about manufacturing. Traditionally the commercial success of Venice was linked to the city's reputation for reliability not only as a carrier and a banker, but as a producer as well. Products bearing the seal of San Marco—be they books, cloths, soaps, or whatever—could be relied upon for uniformly high standards of quality. In the European marketplace, and especially in the Mediterranean emporium, expediency would seem to have dictated cost reductions at the time when cheap competitive products made Venetian goods nearly unsalable. But despite some pressure to permit reductions in cost and quality, the government would have none of it. Old quality standards were bolstered with new and tougher regulations to counteract the natural tendency to cut corners. Even in this extraordinary situation when territorial dominions were causing hardship in the city by low-cost competition, the government, which in this case had the absolute power to control the conditions and guarantee the results, would not act in contravention of the old territorial relationship with the mainland.

From a purely commercial standpoint, the government's conservatism was an obvious failure. Costs remained too high to enable Venetian goods to recapture lost ground, and with high taxes and severe quality regulations imposed by the state, cost reductions were unattainable. Increasing the intensity of quality control was clearly a mistaken response.

The international activity of the port of Venice diminished. Her foreign markets became the preserves of other northern commercial powers. The Mediterranean, once Venice's maritime dominion, became the stamping ground of the new powers. Their southern trade was a mercantilist's dream.[60] Importing Mediterranean raw materials for their home industries in their own ships, bypassing Venice, they returned to sell the finished product of their manufactures.

Yet from a larger perspective, Venetian state policy must be viewed more sympathetically. First, it must be remembered that Venice's

---

60. Davis, "England and the Mediterranean," p. 125.

means of reducing costs to competitive levels were circumscribed because of the higher wages earned by Venetian workers. The state finance program did not fail or inflict excessive hardship on the citizenry despite a shrinking revenue base. Thirdly, the unique and satisfactory political relationship between Venice and her dominions was preserved in spite of the lessening of Venice's power and the economic threat from the mainland. Although the government formulated no new general policy to counteract the industrial and commercial reverses of the seventeenth century and consequently failed to respond positively to the economic crisis, the political and socio-economic status quo was preserved. The Serenissima adjusted calmly to a new role in the European economic order.

A Final Word on Decline

A great deal of thought and much research has been devoted by many historians to describing and explaining the economic decline of Venice in the seventeenth century. While it would be simplistic, even callous, to deflate this examination into a mere semantic issue there are still basic contradictions in the possible definitions of "decline" that demand resolution.

Of relative decline there can be no doubt. Commercially Venice fell from undisputed world leadership to insignificance over the span of 150 years (1550-1700). Her carrying trade was blasted and the port was reduced from the foremost international emporium to a regional harbor. Venice's commercial presence in foreign markets in Turkey, England, and the Low Countries evaporated. This was the most real of all possible declines for contemporary Venetians, who revered, even if they did not remember first-hand, the days of Venice in her great mercantile glory.

Industrially, the "before and after" picture is equally grim. Employment in the major manufacturing industries was reduced during the course of the century to approximately the same proportion of total employment that had preceded Venice's industrial expansion of the sixteenth century—a retrogression of 150 to 200 years. Correspondingly, output statistics of major industries—woolen manufacture, shipbuilding, and soapmaking, for example—show marked reductions.[61] High costs and efficient competition set Venetian manufactures at a disadvantage in world markets. Venice fell from industrial world leadership to virtual unimportance within a century, overshadowed by the growing industrial might of the North Atlantic.

The relative decline of Venice was due to three interrelated facts: (1) commercial and industrial competition which robbed Venice of her market for exports; (2) an aging labor force (after 1650) which lowered productivity; (3) mistaken government policy in the fields of tariffs and quality control regulations which forced up the prices of Venetian exports at a time when prices should have been driven down.

In a sense the last two factors must be assigned a secondary role, for even had the labor force been more vital and the state less intransigent Venice would in all probability have diminished anyway. The change in markets was inexorable and Venice's location, her prime commercial advantage, could no longer have served her. But with her established manufacturing tradition Venice might have competed favorably in Europe's new markets and might have avoided industrial collapse had it not been for the falling quality of the labor force and the incapacity of government to react to economic change.

More elusive is the notion of "absolute decline." Did economic reverses in the seventeenth century cause a decline in the population or in the gross product (or income) of the city? Population remained at a constant level over the century, exhibiting a remarkable capacity for recovery from the short-term ravages of plague and famine. The overall level of employment too remained stable during the years of vicissitude. Money wages rose during the century, while prices did not. Real income therefore did not fall; in fact it may actually have risen slightly if money wages increased as living costs remained constant. The output of the economy as a whole, GNP in modern terms, measures not merely the few industrial giants, but all goods and services produced, from the major city industries to the petty manufactures, crafts, and services. This is the best and most general indicator of economic performance, for it most directly relates to the standard of

---

61. For wool figures, see Sella, *Commerci,* pp. 117-118; for shipbuilding, Lane "Venetian Shipping," pp. 42-46; for soap, see above, chap. 4, and for silk, which was the exception, chap. 5.

living of the populace. By means of shifts away from big industry to island-directed or regional enterprise, no fall in aggregate income occurred. There was therefore, in an absolute sense, no decline in the Venetian economy.

Furthermore, Venice's achievement in maintaining a livable—even comfortable—economic status quo throughout a period of commercial reverses is especially impressive because of the ease with which adjustments were made. The employment census shows that reductions in those parts of the labor force associated with declining sectors were compensated by movement into a diversity of other occupations. Transitional crises were avoided and the overall level of employment remained stable.

Equally remarkable was the success of the economy at maintaining stable output without sustained growth—a situation which seems nearly impossible in the economy of today. This success owes much to the characteristics of premodern technology. Capital equipment was so small a factor of production that the manufacture of investment goods was not in itself a major enterprise. As part of their trades, carpenters, metalworkers, and the users of equipment themselves built the looms, presses, vats, mills, and other requisite machinery and structures along with the consumption goods that they ordinarily made. The important implication of this absence of exclusive capital-goods industries is that when growth terminated for Venice in the first quarter of the seventeenth century and net investment in industry approached zero, the structure of employment was not drastically affected. With no separate capital-goods industry there was little displacement of workers, and the distributive function of the economy as a whole went undamaged.

For a clearer understanding of the Venetian problem in the seventeenth century we can draw a casual comparison to Great Britain from about 1850 to the time of World War I. There are several basic resemblances. Both Venice in her time and Britain in hers were world leaders in commerce, industry, and economic influence. Both unwillingly shared their techniques with incipient competitors. Over their respective hundred-year spans, both countries succumbed to the incursions of newcomers into market preserves that were once exclusively theirs, and eventually world leadership was lost to them. Yet in the long run neither was worse off. Neither population nor real income—the ultimate consequences of economic events—diminished. For late-Victorian Britain, population and industrial production continued to grow, although at reduced rates. For early modern Venice there was no such further growth; rather there was a gentle transition to continued stability in the new role of regional port. Neither in Venice nor in Britain was "pure economic decline" a reality, and yet the loss of hegemony, of economic power to control the destiny of a larger than national sphere was sorely missed by both. Both often defined their new condition as decline.

In the purest economic sense, Venice did not decline. If income and population levels are constant, a sustained decline in output cannot have occurred. Admittedly, it may not be wise to rest the case on purely economic grounds. The loss of economic hegemony shows up in no indicators, but it may have been more crucial to a Venetian of the period than the price of a loaf of bread. There is really no ultimate definition of decline. If the nation was more sensitive to the loss of leadership in the world than to the movements of gross product, then perhaps the definition of decline that economic logic dictates must defer to the sensible reality of the times. Still, for the historian, it would seem an abdication to permit past sentiments to make such judgments. If Venice suffered decline, it troubled her spirits more than her body.

The ability to adjust smoothly, and without major dislocations or lasting poverty, from an atmosphere of ebullient growth to a stationary economic condition was the great achievement of the economy of the city of Venice during the seventeenth century.

Appendices
Bibliography
Index

APPENDIX I
Principal Arti
of Venice
in the Seventeenth Century

ACQUAROLI water-porters: suppliers of fresh water to bakers, dyers, etc.
ACQUAVITERI distillers, liquor sellers
BARBIERI barbers
BARILERI coopers: makers of large barrels and wooden vats
BASTASI stevedores: there were three separate guilds, one for each of the three points of entry and exit for all goods legally traded in the city—the *Fonteco dei Tedeschi* (the German mercantile center), the *Doana da Mar,* and the *Doana da Terra*
BATTIORO ALLEMANI goldleaf beaters
BATTIORO STAGNOLI chemists and paint manufacturers, also known as *colori:* some members of this guild also worked with tin and lead, making bullets and beating tin leaf for mirrors
BATTIORO CON SCUOLA gold thread makers, also known as *tiraoro*
BECHIERI butchers: made an "open profession" in 1680's; included, for tax accounting purposes, the slaughterers' guild, *scortegadori da bovi*
BIAVAROLI grain and flour sellers
BOCCALERI potters
BOMBASERI cotton, linen, and canvas merchants: the "putting-out" employers of the *tesseri fustagno*
BOSSOLERI turners, also known as *tornidori*
BOTTERI coopers: makers of small barrels or "butts" (*botte*)
BRONZERI, *see* FABBRI
BURCHIELLI boatmen: their organizations not classed as arti
CALCINERI quicklime-sellers
CALDERERI, *see* FABBRI
CALEGHERI, ZAVATTERI, ZOCCOLERI shoemakers and cobblers; the *zoccoleri,* judging by their name, specialized in the high-heeled shoes (*zoccoli*) peculiar to Venetian fashions
CAPPELERI E BARETERI hatters
CASAROLI cheesesellers
CASSELERI box and crate makers
CENTURERI beltmakers
CERCHIERI barrelhoop makers
CESTERI basketmakers
CHIODAROLI wool cloth tenterers (stretchers)

APPENDIX I

CIMADORI wool cloth shearers

CIMOLINI raw wool shearers

CONZACURAMI tanners

CORDAROLI, *see* FILACANEVI

CORDOVANI leather merchants: "putters-out" to tanners

CORIDORO, *see* DEPENTORI

CORIERI couriers: *corieri di Roma, portalettere di Padova,* and *portalettere di Vicenza* were three separate guilds

CORONERI wood and bone carvers: principally of rosaries

CRIVELLADORI, PESADORI E MESURADORI DI FORMENTO grain sifters, weighers, and sellers: three separate arti

DEPENTORI painters: an agglomerate guild composed of these formerly independent arti: (1) *depentori* or *pittori,* painters; (2) *miniadori,* miniaturists; (3) *coridoro,* leather gilders (*cuoio d'oro*); (4) *indoradori,* gilders and frame-makers (*soazeri*); (5) *desegnadori,* pattern designers (for cloth)

DESEGNADORI, *see* DEPENTORI

DRAPPIERI cloth retailers: of smaller than full-bolt pieces

FABBRI metalworkers: an agglomerate guild composed of these formerly independent arti: (1) *fabbri,* ironworkers; (2) *caldereri,* copperworkers (makers of copper caldrons); (3) *schiopeteri,* gunsmiths; (4) *stadieri,* scale makers; (5) *bronzeri,* bronzeworkers; (6) *lattoneri,* brassworkers; (7) *stagneri,* tinworkers; (8) *peltreri,* pewterworkers; (9) *conzalavezi,* tinkers; (10) *strazzaferi,* used-iron dealers; (11) *far chiodi,* nailmakers; (12) *mercanti di ferrarezza,* hardware dealers

FAR CALZE DI SETA silk stocking makers: guild was formed in the 1680's when the method for making stockings was brought to Venice

FAR CHIODI, *see* FABBRI

FENESTRERI glaziers

FILACANEVI ropemakers

FILATOI silk throwsters

FORNERI bakers

FRECERI arrowmakers: guild died out by the early 1600's

FRITOLERI fried foods sellers

FRUTTAROLI fruit and vegetable sellers; *erbaroli,* vegetable sellers, were incorporated into this arte

FUSTAGNERI, *see* TESSERI FUSTAGNO

GALINERI poultry sellers

GARBELLADORI spice sifters and sellers

GARZOTTI wool cloth teaselers: generally grouped with *cimolini* for tax-accounting purposes

GASTALDIA DI S. NICOLO the community of fishermen in Dorsoduro which, although not officially a guild, had some degree of internal organization as well as liaison with the government in the person of an elected *gastaldo,* "the Doge of the Nicoletti." Most of the fishermen of Venice (excluding the Lido and lagoon islands) lived in or around S. Nicolo dei Mendigoli, one of the poorest parishes in the city.

GUA CORTELLI   knife grinders

INDORADORI, *see* DEPENTORI

INGUCCHIADORI   knitters

INTAGIADORI   wood carvers

LANERI   wool workers, composed of: *verghezini* wool beaters, *scartazini* wool carders, *pettenadori* wool combers

LASAGNERI   pasta sellers

LATTONERI, *see* FABBRI

LAVORANTI ALLA CAMERA DEL PURGO   wool cloth cleaners and examiners

LIBRERI DA STAMPA   printers and booksellers, also *compositori* compositors, *fonditori* type founders

LIBRERI DI CARTA BIANCA   stationers and account-book makers; also sellers of terraferma-produced paper

LIGADORI DI FONTECO   packers at the German mercantile center

LINAROLI   linenworkers

LUGANEGHERI   pork butchers

MANDOLERI   almond and condiment sellers

MANGANERI   wool cloth manglers (pressers)

MARANGONI DI CASA   house carpenters

MARZERI   dry-goods retailers: an agglomerate guild of shopkeepers who sold domestic cloth for clothing, hats, gloves, trimmings, hardware, stockings, combs, mirrors, and imported hardware

MERCANTI DI FERRAREZZA, *see* FABBRI

MERCANTI DI LEGNO   lumber merchants

MERCANTI DI MALVASIA   imported wine (malmsey and others) merchants

MERCANTI DI PANNI DI LANA   wool merchants: "putters-out" to all the wool guilds

MERCANTI DA VIN   domestic wine merchants

MINIADORI, *see* DEPENTORI

MURERI   masons

ORESI (*orifici*)   goldsmiths and jewelers: for tax-accounting purposes sometimes includes *gioiellieri* jewelers, *diamanteri* diamond merchants, *ochialeri* spectacles sellers. Masters are classed as *maestri negotianti* or *maestri di manufatture*

ORTOLANI   market-gardeners, principally on the Giudecca, the Lido, and in Cannaregio

OSTI   hotelkeepers

PANATAROLI   breadbakers

PASSAMANERI   ribbon and trimmings makers

PATERNOSTRERI   glass rosarybead makers: terminology for other glass bead makers (*margariteri, perleri* [*delle perle false*], *suppialume*) varies with type of bead and with date

PEATERI   bargemen

PELICERI   furriers

PELTRERI, *see* FABBRI

PESCE, COMPRAVENDE   fish sellers

APPENDIX I

PESTRINERI   milk vendors
PETTENERI DA TELLA   wool cloth comb makers
PETTENERI DA TESTA   haircomb makers
PISTORI   bakers
PITTORI, *see* DEPENTORI
PORTALETTERE DI PADOVA *and* VINCENZA, *see* CORIERI
PORTATORI DI VIN   wine porters
SABBIONERI   sand dealers
SAGOMADORI DA OGLIO   oil bottlers and sellers
SALUMIERI   dried fish sellers
SANSERI   brokers in two separate guilds: *sanseri in Rialto* and *sanseri in Fon-
   teco dei Tedeschi.* Exchange brokers (*sanseri di cambii*) were a separate
   organization, not included among the arti.
SAPONERI   soapmakers
SARTORI   tailors
SCALCHI E CUOGI   waiters and cooks
SCALETERI   biscuit bakers
SCHIOPETERI, *see* FABBRI
SCORTEGADORI, *see* BECHIERI
SCORZERI   hide processors, sometimes known as *scorzeri alla Zuecca,*
   because their craft was isolated to the Giudecca for sanitary and olfactory
   reasons
SONADORI   musicians
SPADERI   swordsmiths: included, for tax-accounting purposes, the guild of
   coltreri (knifemakers)
SPECHIERI   mirrormakers: originally a branch of the *marzeri,* the mirror-
   makers broke away in the 1560's and prospered independently
SPICIERI   retail spice dealers
SQUERAROLI   private boatbuilders: accounted as a separate group of ship-
   wrights (distinct from arsenal workers) as early as 1539; formally incor-
   porated as an *arte* in 1606 (Lane, *Ships and Shipbuilders,* p. 85)
STADIERI, *see* FABBRI
STAGNERI, *see* FABBRI
STRAMAZERI, *see* STRAZZAROLI
STRAZZAFERI, *see* FABBRI
STRAZZAROLI   used clothing and rags dealers; includes *stramazeri* (mattress
   makers)
TAGIAPIERA   stonecutters
TAMISI E CRIVELLI   sieve and screen makers
TELLAROLI   cotton cloth merchants
TENTORI   dyers: divided into *tentori di seta* silk dyers, *tentori di arte mazor*
   dyers skilled in working in scarlet and kermes, and *tentori da guado* dyers
   in woad and baser dyestuffs
TERRAZERI   pavers
TESSERI FUSTAGNO (FUSTAGNERI)   linen, fustian and canvas weavers
TESSERI PANI DI LANA   wool cloth weavers
TESSERI DI TELLA   weavers (cotton and various other non-apparel cloths)

TESTORI DI SETA   silkweavers
TOSCHANI   silk cloth merchants: sometimes known as *mercanti di seta; "tos-chani"* reflects the belief that the silk industry was brought to Venice by Tuscan-Lucchese silk merchants
TRAGHETTI   various organizations of gondoliers: not arti, strictly speaking
VAROTERI   furriers
VAZINERI   scabbard makers
VERIERI   glass workers: on the island of Murano
ZACHERI   armorers
Arsenal Guilds
CALAFATI   caulkers
MARANGONI ALL'ARSENALE   shipwrights
REMERI   oarmakers

Source: This list has been compiled principally from the lists of guilds made by the Milizia da Mar, the government committee charged with recruiting oarsmen for the state galleys. From these lists the Milizia da Mar apportioned the "draft call" or associated taxes among the arti, whose ultimate responsibility it was to supply crewmen. There were, however, guilds that for one reason or another were not included in this levy. Major ones (arsenal guilds, wool merchants, hatters) have been included in this listing. Others, such as notaries, teachers, lawyers, minor brokers, and boatmen are of relatively small numerical consequence.

For further materials dealing with guild listings and terminology see: A.S.V. *Inquisitorato alle Arti,* b. 2, Arti di Venezia (1797), which may be found reprinted in A. Sagredo, *Sulle consorterie delle arti edificative a Venezia* (Venice, 1858); G. Boerio, *Dizionario del Dialetto Veneziano* (Venice, 1867); P. Molmenti, *La storia di Venezia nella vita privata dalla origini alla caduta della Republica* (Bergamo, 1927-29).

For a similar listing of Veronese guilds, see: Amelio Tagliaferri, *L'economia Veronese secondo gli estimi dal 1409 al 1635* (Milan, 1966); M. Cortelazzo, "Glossario," *Bollettino dell'Istituto di Storia della Società e dello Stato Veneziano,* 3 (1961), 254-279.

APPENDIX II
*A Critical Note
on the Population
of Venice in 1655*

Regrettably, an important source of population statistics for Venice in the year 1655 has been omitted from the demographic history of the city for over fifty years. The forgotten document, which is actually an addendum to a population table for the year 1586, is located in the Marciana Library (Venice), Italian manuscripts, Class VII, Codex 2211 (10049), page 42 (see frontispiece).

The general omission of the 1655 estimate from the population history of Venice stems from an article by Karl Julius Beloch entitled "La popolazione di Venezia nei secoli XVI e XVII" published in the *Nuovo archivio veneto,* n.s. 3 (1902). This was the first modern examination of demographic sources for these two centuries. Beloch examined and rejected the 1655 population estimate because of similarities of certain numbers to those of a doubtful population table of 1593 (*Cod. Cicogna,* 1102, p. 64). The numbers of servants (*massere*), monks (*frati*), and institutionalized poor (*poveri d'ospitali*) are identical in both documents and Beloch believed this must be more than coincidence. He concluded that the 1655 estimate is probably a "corrected edition" of the 1593 population statistics, *composed* in the year 1655. Further noting that the physical location of these data is between estimates for 1586 and 1606 in the Marciana codex 2211, Beloch inferred that the true date of the addendum must fall between these years.

These are insufficient grounds for disallowing the statistics, for while it must be recognized that the compiler of the 1655 estimate may have "borrowed" occasional conventional figures from the census of 1593, differences between the two sets of statistics outweigh by far the similarities and obviate the possibility that they both represent the same year. While, for example, the number of monks is identical for both years, the estimate of priests in 1655 is roughly twice that of 1593 and the estimate of the number of Jews in the city is four times greater for the year 1655 than in the 1593 figures (for 1593, 1,043 Jews; for 1655, 4,870). This last point is particularly important for it gives a clue to the true document dates. While through the sixteenth century the Jewish population of Venice verifiably remained at a level of between one and two thousand, there is known to have been a large influx of European Jews into the city in the seventeenth century. Simone Luzzatto, the author and religious leader (1583-1663), claimed in his *Discorso circa il stato de gl'Hebrei et in particolare dimoranti nell'inclita Città di Venezia* (Venice, 1638), "stimo gl'Hebrei esser vicino al numero di sei mila in circa . . . " (p. 28). Luzzatto can be given some leeway for exaggeration but an estimate of six thousand leaves small doubt of the growth of the Jewish community since the sixteenth century. There is evidence of continued influx in mid-century with the arrival of refugees from the Chmielnicki pogroms in Eastern Europe (Attilio Milano, *Storia degli ebrei in Italia* [Turin, 1963], p. 312).The "ebrei" figure of 4,870 is most unlikely for 1593, most reasonable for 1655.

The simple fact that the presentation of 1655 figures is entitled unequivocally, "Nota di tutte le Anime esistenti nella Città di Venezia nell'Anno 1655" makes Beloch's supposition still more improbable. The physical location of the statistics as an addendum to the 1586 "Nota" is of no significance. The compiler merely used the columnar breakdown of the page to insert his numbers, saving himself the effort of constructing a new table.

Population studies of Venice since Beloch's article of 1902 have omitted the 1655 statistics. In his general history of Venetian population, Beltrami ignores these figures in his table of total city population, but he inexplicably employs the subtotals for 1655 in his sex-composition and age composition tables (*Storia,* pp. 59, 82, 86).

(a) *Inventory of the Shop of Bortolo Bruni, Printer*[1]

1673, 6 September, in Venice

Inventory of books belonging to the estate of the deceased
Mr. Bortolo Bruni

RED AND BLACK BOOKS

303	Offici B.M.V. In 24 of 13 pages	- pages	3939
336	Diurni Romani 16 of 27 1/2 pages		9240
670	Misse Defunctorum of 5 pages		3350
716	Officia B.M.V. 32 large of 9 pages		6444
590	32 small of 9 pages		5310
991	Diurni Romani 24 of 17 1/4 pages		17094
500	Officia Sti. Francesci pro Diurnale, 24 of 2 pages		1000
			46377

They total 9 bales, 2 reams and 15 quires.[2]

BLACK BOOKS

1800	Grammatiche Emanuel 16 of 15 pages	-pages	27000
396	Magistri Stupini 16 of 6 pages		2376
455	Direttore de Religiose del Sales, 24 of 5 pages		2275
218	Circulus Aureus 12 of 15 pages		3270
150	Devotione del Martigiani 32 of 8 pages		1200
750	Goffredo del Tasso 24 of 15 1/2 pages		11625
			47746

---

1. A.S.V., *Giudici Petizion,* b. 378/43, no. 35.
2. 1 bale (*balla*) = 5000 pages; 1 ream (*risma*) = 500 pages; 1 quire (*quinterna*) = 25 pages.

They total 9 1/2 bales and 10 quires.

We the undersigned have valued the above red and black books at 40 ducats per bale, and the black books at 15 ducats per bale

    I, Paolo Baglioni so affirm with my oath
    I, Nicolo Pezzana so affirm with my oath

The total of red and black books, 9 bales, 2 reams and 15 quires @ 40 ducats per bale equal	Duc. 371
The total of black books, 9 1/2 bales, and 10 quires @ 15 ducats per bale equals	Duc. 143 d 4
	Duc. 514 d 4

1673, 18 September, in Venice

Appraisal of the printshop of the deceased Mr. Bortolo Bruni, appraised by us, Messrs Bortolo Tramontin and Giovani Cagnolini, so appointed to do this in good faith as follows

New nonpareil weighing 363 lbs. @ D. 14 per 100	D.	60 £ 1
for casting of above	D.	60 £ 1
Old nonpareil tin [3] weighing 313 lbs. @D. 14 per 100 lbs.	D.	43 £ 2
Testin, new, tin weighing 313 lbs. @ D. 14 per 100 lbs.	D.	43 £ 2
for casting of above	D.	56
For *Testin, Garamonzin, Garamon magro,* all old, weighing 1273 lbs. @ D. 13 per 100 lbs.	D.	165
For *Garamon* weighing 381 lbs. for tin with casting @ D. 16 per 100 lbs.	D.	60
Silvio Tondo and cursive, the tin weighing 406 lbs. @ D. 18 per 100 lbs. with casting	D.	72 £ 5
Corsivo filosofia, old, weighing 200 lbs.	D.	24
Canonzin Corsivo e Tondo, new, weighing in tin 318 @ D. 20 per 100 lbs. with casting	D.	63
Canon Grosso con Canto the tin weighing 825 lbs. @ D. 20 per 100 lbs.	D.	165
Canto per il Messal, e Canto piccolo, weighing 348 @ D. 15 per 100	D.	52 £ 1
Testo Parangon per il Messal the tin weighing 491 lbs. @ D. 15 per 100 with casting	D.	73 £ 3
Garamon Grasso, new, weighing 300 lbs. @ D. 16 per hundred	D.	48

3. "Stagno" typemetal, a combination of lead, tin, and antimony, is more frequently called "lead" (piombo).

APPENDIX III

for casting of above	D.	32
Cases of miniatures of two lines for printing weighing 113 lbs. with casting	D.	20
Various tin equipment weighing 369 lbs. @ D. 12 per 100	D.	44 £ 2
for casting of above	D.	40

Sum D. 1122 £ 4:12

Old tin 100 lbs.	D.	12
Boxes no. 50	D.	25
Typecases and small boxes	D.	7
Bookshelves and benches	D.	10
Iron oven	D.	35
9 cases of miniatures and wooden figures	D.	80
A printing press of red and black [books?] with iron screw and bronze plates and equipment	D.	80
Another printing press with bronze screw and plates	D.	50
Another press with iron screw and plates	D.	80
Another new press with iron screw and plates, brand new	D.	40
Two caldrons, one for ink, the other for washing, and a washing stand	D.	8

Sum	D.	387
above Sum	D.	1122 £ 4:12

D. 1509 £ 4:12

D. 1509 *d* 18

I, Bortolo Tramontin, printer, have appraised the above together with those signed below, and I so affirm with my oath.

(signatures)

(b) Inventory of the Shop of Giacomo Pesanti, Silk Dyer[4]

1658, 15 October, in Venice

In the Shop

One great caldron and three caldrons of copper	£ 328 s 12
One copper ladle, 2 copper buckets, 2 copper vats weighing lbs. 40 at 30 *soldi* per lb.	£ 60
Three andirons for the furnace	£ 10
Una Forada da herba [?]	s 10
Un Anzin da Pozzo [?]	s 10
Eight shop benches, some good, some broken	£ 37 s 4
Six basins	£ 12 s 8
Two tubs for brazilwood dye	£ 12 s 8
Two tubs for woad	£ 24 s 16
Two baskets	£ 4
A barrel	s 10
A cask of lemon juice	£ 4
Two barrels	£ 6
A bronze mortar with pestles	£ 155
A brazilwood cutter	£ 1
Two stirrers, two others, broken, and an ax	£ 2
Doi storti in Corve [?]	£ 24 s 16
Six cloths	£ 2
A brazilwood ax	£ 2
Four silk fabrics	£ 3
Tubes and various other shop equipment	£ 31
Wood	£ 31
A small scale	£ 8
230 lbs. indigo at 30 *soldi* per lb. less the weight of the barrel 30 lbs.	£ 300
786 lbs. brazilwood @ 8 ducats per 100 lbs.	£ 389 s 16
534 lbs. orchil @ £ 3 s. 2 per lb.	£ 1655 s 8
240 lbs. *bonicel* at *soldi* 6 per lb.	£ 72

---

4. A.S.V., *Giudici Petizion*, b. 367/32, no. 32. Dyestuffs are measured in *libbre sottile*, equivalent to .301230 kilograms (Sella, *Commerci*, App. A, p. 101).

APPENDIX III

600 lbs. *suodeno* @ 8 ducats per 1000 lbs.	£	29 s 14
Gum weighing (with the barrel) 240 lbs. @ 3 ducats per 100 lbs. less the barrel 50 lbs.	£	37 s 4
5 empty barrels	£	5
8 lbs. indigo	£	32
A sieve for crimson and another for gall	£	1
4 buckets, good and also broken	£	4
4 baskets		s 4

A credit of 70 ducats from Pietro Bulghera Alle tre Re for dyeing

A debit of 172 ducats 2 *grossi* to Steffano Alberti for orchil.

Sum   [£   3,287]

BIBLIOGRAPHY

NOTE ON THE MAJOR CENSUS SOURCES

The documents housed in the State Archives of Venice are generally arranged and catalogued according to the branch of government in which they resided (or might have resided) during the days of the Republic. There are major exceptions to this arrangement, such as the immense archive of notarial records and the records of the Scuole Grandi, but for the most part the repositories of documents follow the administrative organization of the state bureaucracy. The procedure in locating records, therefore, is often quite straightforward, sometimes convoluted, and occasionally unpredictable. For example, the private business papers of the Gozzi family (chap. 5) are found in the archive of the hospitals and almshouses (A.S.V., *Ospitali e Luoghi Pii Diverse*) because they accompanied a financial bequest to a hospital upon the death of the last heir to the family name and property. For records relating to the labor force and its structure the route is indirect. Although there were several agencies concerned in one way or another with guilds and workers— the Justices of Industry (Giustizia Vecchia) and the Board of Trade (Cinque Savi alla Mercanzia), to name just two—it is in the archive of the Naval Personnel Administration (Collegio alla Milizia da Mar) that one finds the most complete records of guild membership for the early modern period. Since the chief responsibility of the Milizia da Mar was the raising of galley crews to man the reserve fleets, this office periodically monitored the membership of those arti which bore ultimate responsibility for supplying oarsmen. As Lane points out (*Venice: A Maritime Republic,* pp. 314, 318, 476), the obligation of the guilds to furnish conscripts (or money to pay for conscripts) was deemed so vital to the national defense that guild membership became practically obligatory for artisans and shopkeepers, and the question of whether new guilds might be formed often revolved around the process of naval recruiting.

The records of the Naval Personnel Administration are found in a variety of forms. For certain observation years in my examination of guild membership, information about all the guilds was available in prepared lists made by Milizia da Mar officials. For other years material was collected from individual guild reports on membership filed with that agency; in still other cases I have derived membership data from the recruitment quotas by statistical projection. The archives of the Milizia da Mar are not well organized. Most of the materials used in this study are arranged in loose bundles ordered alphabetically. Misplacements are frequent. The archive has been subject to severe water damage and the ink on many pages has been eroded by water and fungus to the extent that writing is fully visible only with the aid of ultraviolet light. For these reasons, and because the materials of the census will, I hope, be of some future value to historians, I have made elaborate identification of the sources which would seem redundant in less complicated circumstances—the lengthy notes to tables 3.1 and 3.2 are the awkward but necessary result.

The principal sources of guild membership material for each observation year in the employment census are:

1539: A.S.V., *Mil. Mar,* no. 705: a levy list in ledger form; Museo Civico Correr, Cod. *Donà dalle Rose,* b. 228, pp. 198-202: a levy list differing slightly from *Mil. Mar,* no. 705. Where differences between the two lists occur, I have used the *Mil. Mar,* no. 705 figures because of indications that this was the final listing. A call-up of 1581 for 50 galleys used the 1539 carata, doubled, and correspondence to the 705 list is exact.

1595: Correr, Cod. *Donà dalle Rose,* b. 228, pp. 227-231: a census summary giving total membership, able-bodied men, the levy list of 1595, and an earlier levy list known as the "obbligo vecchio." The latter is mentioned in several documents, always without an associated date. It corresponds to exactly double the 1539 levy: that is, the 1539 total is for a crew of 25 galleys, the obbligo vecchio is for a 50-galley fleet.

1603: A.S.V., *Mil. Mar,* no. 707: a multiple levy list for "obbligo vecchio," 1595, 1603, and 1610; *ibid.,* no. 708: a partial census summary appears on the front cover of this fascicle; total membership and able-bodied men are given for 22 guilds.

1610: A.S.V., *Mil. Mar,* nos. 707 and 723: levy lists.

1612: A.S.V., *Mil. Mar,* no. 540, fasc. *bombaseri:* a levy list included in the census summary of 1660.

1618: [no records extant]

1638: A.S.V., *Mil. Mar,* no. 540, fasc. *bombaseri:* a levy list included in the census summary of 1660.

1660: A.S.V., *Mil. Mar,* no. 540, fasc. *bombaseri:* a full census summary giving total membership, able-bodied men, and breakdown by guild ranks. Also given are levy lists for 1595, 1612, and 1638. This important document bears no date but is readily identifiable as the census summary of 1660. Dated guild rolls for 1660 correspond to the summary totals. The blank column in the summary entitled "Carata 1660" was meant to be filled in on the basis of the census results. The curious location of the document in the bundle of guild rolls of the bombaseri is probably due to the fact that the summary contains information about bombardieri (see chap. 3, n. 6) and was therefore alphabetized with bombaseri materials. A.S.V., *Senato, terra,* filza 883: a levy list for 1660; A.S.V., *Archivio delle Arti, Fabbri,* b. 110, *Registro termination e sententie,* pp. 106-107: a levy list; A.S.V., *Mil. Mar,* nos. 538-557: these buste contain individual guild rolls which give total membership, able-bodied men, guild ranks, and ages. Rolls survive for the years 1660, 1672, 1690, 1695,

1705, and 1714 in varying states of completeness.

1672: A.S.V., *Mil. Mar,* no. 273, Jan. 16, 1696 (*m.v.*): a levy list for 1673 with all woolworking guilds excluded; A.S.V., *Senato, terra,* filza 883, Jan. 1673: a levy list; A.S.V., *Archivio delle Arti, Fabbri,* b. 110, *Registro termination e sententie,* pp. 112-114: a levy list; A.S.V., *Mil. Mar,* nos. 538-557: guild rolls.

1690: A.S.V., *Mil. Mar,* no. 273, Jan. 16, 1696 (*m.v.*): a levy list with all wool-working guilds excluded; A.S.V., *Mil. Mar,* nos. 538-557: guild rolls for 1690 and updates for 1695.

1705: A.S.V., *Mil. Mar,* nos. 538-557: guild rolls.

1714, 1739: A.S.V., *Mil. Mar,* no 241: levy and *tansa* lists.

An unidentifiable levy list appears as part of a bound volume of manuscripts entitled *Milizia Veneta 1462-1557,* Bibl. Naz. Marciana, *Ital.* VII, *Cod.* 1213 (8656), p. 65. It is undated and corresponds to no known listing. The call-up was for 50 galleys.

A second major source of information about employment in seventeenth-century Venice are the Board of Health censuses which were taken by the parish priests on a door-to-door basis and organized by sestiere and parish. In these "anagrafi dei piovani," household heads are identified by their occupation, and additional demographic data about each household is included. The raw census data are accessible in Venetian archival repositories under the following rubrics:

Year	Sestiere	Location of documents
1607	S. Polo	Correr, *Donà,* 351
1624	S. Marco	Correr, *Donà,* 352
	S. Marco	*Donà,* 352 (abstract)
	S. Polo	*Donà,* 352
	S. Croce	*Donà,* 352
	Dorsoduro	*Donà,* 352
	Castello	*Donà,* 352
	Dorsoduro	*Donà,* 354 (abstract)
1633	Castello	A.S.V., *Provveditori alla Sanità,* 568
	Cannaregio	*Provveditori alla Sanità,* 568
	S. Polo	*Provveditori alla Sanità,* 569
	S. Marco	*Provveditori alla Sanità,* 569
1642	Castello	A.S.V., *Provveditori alla Sanità,* 570
	Cannaregio	*Provveditori alla Sanità,* 570
	S. Marco	*Provveditori alla Sanità,* 571
	S. Croce	*Provveditori alla Sanità,* 571
	Dorsoduro	Correr, *Donà,* 351

For succeeding years in the late seventeenth and eighteenth centuries, see A.S.V., *Provveditori alla Sanità,* b. 572-575.

186

BIBLIOGRAPHY

WORKS CONSULTED

Antonelli, Antonio. *Spechio di direcione delli pesi, valute, prezii, e pagamenti dell' armte da Mar, e Terre, del Serenissimo Dominio Veneto, et altre particolarità.* Venice: 1727.

Aspetti e cause della decadenza economica veneziana nel secolo XVII. Venice: Istituto per la Collaborazione Culturale, 1961.

Aston, Trevor, ed. *Crisis in Europe 1560-1660.* Garden City, N. Y.: Doubleday, 1967.

Aymard, Maurice. *Venise, Raguse, et le commerce du blè pendant la seconde moitè du XVI siècle.* Paris: S.E.V.P.E.N., 1966.

Beloch, Karl Julius. "La popolazione di Venezia nei secoli XVI e XVII." *Nuovo Archivio Veneto,* n.s. 3 (1902), 5-49.

Beltrami, Daniele. "La composizione economica e professionale della popolazione di Venezia nei secoli XVII e XVIII." *Giornale degli economisti e annali di economia,* n.s.10 (1951), 69-86, 155-179.

‾‾‾‾‾‾ *La penetrazione economica dei veneziani in Terraferma: forze di lavoro e proprietà fondiaria nelle campagne venete dei secoli XVII e XVIII.* Venice-Rome: Istituto per la Collaborazione Culturale, 1961.

‾‾‾‾‾‾ *Saggio di storia dell'agricoltura nella Repubblica di Venezia durante l'età moderna.* Venice-Rome: Istituto per la Collaborazione Culturale, 1955.

‾‾‾‾‾‾ *Storia della popolazione di Venezia dalla fine del secolo XVI, alla caduta della Repubblica.* Padua: Cedam, 1954.

Bilanci generali della Repubblica di Venezia. 3 vols. Venice: R. Commissione dei documenti finanziarii della Repubblica di Venezia, 1903-1912.

Boerio, Giuseppe. *Dizionario del dialetto veneziano.* 3d ed. Venice: 1867.

Born, Wolfgang. "Scarlet." *Ciba Review,* 7 (1938), 206-227.

Braudel, Fernand. *La Méditerranée et le monde méditerranéen à l'époque de Philippe II.* 2d ed. 2 vols. Paris: Colin, 1966. My references are to this edition. The English translation by Siàn Reynolds (New York: Harper & Row, 1974) has become available just as this study goes to press.

‾‾‾‾‾‾ "La vita economica di Venezia nel secolo XVI." In *La civiltà veneziana del rinascimento,* pp. 81-102. Venice: Centro di cultura e civiltà della Fondazione Giorgio Cini, 1958.

‾‾‾‾‾‾ and Spooner, Frank. "Prices in Europe from 1450 to 1750." In *Cambridge Economic History of Europe,* vol. IV, pp. 374-486. Cambridge: Cambridge University Press, 1967.

Brolio d'Ajano, Romolo. "L'industria della seta a Venezia." In *Storia dell' economia italiana,* edited by Carlo Cipolla. Turin: Einaudi, 1959.

Brown, Horatio E. *The Venetian Printing Press: An Historical Study.* New York: 1891.

Brunello, Franco: *L'Arte della tintura nella storia dell'umanità.* Vicenza: Neri Pozza, 1968.

Bulferretti, L. "L'oro, la terra, e la società (Un'interpretazione del nostro seicento)." *Archivio Storico Lombardo,* ser. 8, 4 (1953), 5-66.

Carus-Wilson, E. M. "An Industrial Revolution of the Thirteenth Century."

Economic History Review, 11 (1941), 39-60.

Cipolla, Carlo, *The Economic Decline of Empires.* London: Methuen, 1970.

_____ "The Economic Decline of Italy: The Case of a Fully Matured Economy." *Economic History Review,* 2d ser. 5 (1952) 178-187. Revised and reprinted in Brian Pullan (ed.), *Crisis and Change in the Venetian Economy in the Sixteenth and Seventeenth Centuries,* pp. 127-145. London: Methuen, 1968.

Coleman, D. C. "An Innovation and Its Diffusion: The New Draperies." *Economic History Review,* 2d ser. 22 (1969), 417-429.

Contento, Aldo. "Il censimento della popolazione sotto la Repubblica Veneta." *Nuovo Archivio Veneto,* 2d ser. 19 (1900), 5-42, 179-240.

Cortelazzo, Manlio: "Glossario." *Bollettino dell'Istituto di Storia della Società e dello Stato Veneziano,* 3 (1961), 254-279.

Cozzi, Gaetano. *Il doge Nicolo Contarini. Ricerche sul patriziato veneziano agli inizi del seicento.* Venice-Rome: Istituto per la Collaborazione Culturale, 1958.

Davis, James C. *The Decline of the Venetian Nobility as a Ruling Class.* Baltimore: Johns Hopkins Press, 1962.

Davis, Ralph. "England and the Mediterranean, 1570-1670." In *Essays in the Economic and Social History of Tudor and Stuart England,* edited by F. J. Fisher, pp. 117-137. Cambridge: Cambridge University Press, 1961.

De Roover, Florence Edler. "Lucchese Silks." *Ciba Review,* 80 (1950), 2902-2930.

De Roover, Raymond. "A Florentine Firm of Cloth Manufacturers." *Speculum,* 16 (1941), 3-33.

_____ "Labour Conditions in Florence around 1400: Theory, Policy and Reality." In *Florentine Studies; Politics and Society in Renaissance Florence,* edited by Nicolai Rubenstein, pp. 277-313. London: Faber & Faber, 1968.

Diderot, Denis. *A Diderot Pictorial Encyclopedia of Trades and Industry; Manufacturing and the Technical Arts in Plates Selected from* L'Encyclopédie, ou Dictionnaire Raisonné des Arts et des Metiers *of Denis Diderot.* Edited by Charles Coulston Gillispie. New York: Dover, 1959.

Dobb, Maurice. *Studies in the Development of Capitalism.* London: Routledge & Kegan Paul, 1963.

Doren, Alfred. *Studien aus der Florentiner Wirtschaftsgeschichte: I. Die Florentiner Wollentuchindustrie vom 14. bis zum 16. Jahrhundert.* Stuttgart: J. G. Gotta'sche, 1908.

Easterlin, Richard A. *Population, Labor Force, and Long Swings in Economic Growth.* New York: National Bureau of Economic Research, General Series 86, 1968.

Fanfani, Amintore. "Il mancato rinnovamento economico." In *La civiltà veneziana del settecento,* pp. 27-68. Venice: Centro di cultura e civiltà della Fondazione Giorgio Cini, 1960.

_____ *Storia del lavoro in Italia dalla fine del secolo XV agli inizi del XVIII.* Milan: Giuffrè, 1943.

BIBLIOGRAPHY

Fisher, F. J. "London's Export Trade in the Early Seventeenth Century." *Economic History Review,* 2d ser. 3 (1950-1951), 151-161.

Garzoni, Tommaso. *La piazza universale di tutte le professioni del mondo.* Venice: 1605.

Gasparetto, Astone. *Il vetro di Murano dalle origini ad oggi.* Venice: Neri Pozza, 1958.

Great Britain. *Calendar of State Papers and Manuscripts, Relating to English Affairs, Existing in the Archives and Collections of Venice, and in Other Libraries of Northern Italy.* Edited by Rawdon Brown et al. London: 1864.

Guareschi, Icilio. *Storia della chimica.* Turin: Unione Tipografico-editrice, 1907.

Hall, A. R. "Scientific Method and the Progress of Techniques." In *Cambridge Economic History of Europe,* vol. IV, pp. 96-154. Cambridge: Cambridge University Press, 1967.

Heyd, W. *Histoire du commerce du Levant au Moyen Age.* Leipzig: 1885-1886.

Hirsch, Rudolf. *Printing, Selling and Reading 1450-1550.* Wiesbaden: Otto Harrassowitz, 1967.

Hobsbawm, E. J. "The Crisis of the Seventeenth Century." In *Crisis in Europe 1560-1660,* ed. Trevor Aston, pp. 5-62.

Howell, James. *A Survey of the Signori of Venice.* London: 1651.

Isard, Walter. *Methods of Regional Analysis: An Introduction to Regional Science.* Cambridge, Mass.: MIT Press, 1960.

Kuznets, Simon. *Modern Economic Growth; Rate, Structure, and Spread.* New Haven: Yale University Press, 1966.

Landes, David S. "Social Attitudes, Entrepreneurship, and Economic Development: A Comment." *Explorations in Entrepreneurial History,* 6 (1954), 245-272.

Lane, Frederic C. "The Mediterranean Spice Trade: Further Evidence of Its Revival in the Sixteenth Century." *American Historical Review,* 45 (1940), 581-590. Reprinted in Lane, *Venice and History,* pp. 25-34, and in *Crisis and Change,* ed. Brian Pullan, pp. 47-58.

_____ "The Merchant Marine of the Venetian Republic." In Lane, *Venice and History,* pp. 143-162. Translation of "La Marine marchande et le trafic maritime de Venise à travers les siècles," in *Les Sources de l'histoire maritime en Europe du moyen age au XVIII siècle,* pp. 7-37, edited by Michel Mollat. Paris: S.E.V.P.E.N., 1962.

_____ *Navires et constructeurs à Venise pendant la Renaissance.* Paris: S.E.V.P.E.N., 1965. Revised edition of *Venetian Ships and Shipbuilders of the Renaissance.*

_____ "The Rope Factory and Hemp Trade of Venice in the Fifteenth and Sixteenth Centuries." *Journal of Economic and Business History,* 4 (1932), 830-847. Reprinted in Lane, *Venice and History,* pp. 269-284.

_____ "Venetian Shipping during the Commercial Revolution." *American Historical Review,* 38 (1933), 219-239. Reprinted in Lane, *Venice and History,* pp. 3-24, and in *Crisis and Change,* ed. Brian Pullan, pp. 22-46.

_____ *Venetian Ships and Shipbuilders of the Renaissance.* Baltimore: Johns Hopkins Press, 1934.

_____ *Venice: A Maritime Republic.* Baltimore: Johns Hopkins Press, 1973.

_____ *Venice and History: The Collected Papers of Frederic C. Lane.* Baltimore: Johns Hopkins Press, 1966.

Laslett, Peter. *The World We Have Lost.* New York: Scribner's, 1965.

Leggett, William F. *Ancient and Medieval Dyes.* New York: Chemical Publishing Co., 1944.

Leix, Alfred. "Dyes of the Middle Ages." *Ciba Review,* 1 (1937), 19-22.

Luzzatto, Gino. "La decadenza di Venezia dopo le scoperte geografiche nella tradizione e nella realtà." *Archivio Veneto,* 5th ser. 54 (1954), 162-181.

_____ "L'economia veneziana dopo l'acquisto della terraferma." *Bergomum,* 58 (1964), 57-71.

_____ *Storia economica di Venezia dall'XI al XVI secolo.* Venice: Centro Internazionale dell Arti e del Costume, 1961.

_____ "Le vicende del Porto di Venezia dal primo medio evo allo scoppio della guerra 1914-1918." In Gino Luzzatto, *Studi di storia economica veneziana,* pp. 1-36. Padua: Cedam, 1954.

Luzzatto, Simone. *Discorso circa il stato de gl'Hebrei et in particolare dimoranti nell'Inclita Città di Venezia.* Venice: 1638.

Lyber, A. H. "The Ottoman Turks and the Routes of Oriental Trade." *English Historical Review,* 30 (1915), 577-588.

Mandich, Giulio. "Formule monetarie veneziane del periodo 1619-1650." In *Studi in onore di Armando Sapori,* pp. 1143-1184. Milan: Cisalpino, 1957.

_____ "Primi riconoscimenti veneziani di un diritto di privativa agli inventori." *Rivista di diritto industriale,* 7 (1958), 101-155.

_____ "Le privative industriali veneziane, 1450-1550." *Rivista di diritto commerciale,* 34 (1936), 1-39.

Melis, Federigo. *Aspetti della vita economica medievale; Studi nell'Archivio Datini di Prato.* Siena: Monte dei Paschi di Siena, 1962.

Milano, Attilio. *Storia degli ebrei in Italia.* Turin: Einaudi, 1963.

Molmenti, Pompeo. *La Storia di Venezia nella vita privata dalle origini alla caduta della Repubblica.* 7th ed. Bergamo: Istituto Italiano d'Arti Grafiche, 1927-1929.

Mood, Alexander M., and Graybill, Franklin A. *Introduction to the Theory of Statistics.* 2d ed. New York: McGraw Hill, 1963.

Mosto, Andrea da. *L'Archivio di Stato di Venezia, indice generale storico, descrittivo ed analitico.* 2 vols. Rome: Biblioteca d'Arte Editrice, 1937.

Nani-Mocenigo, Mario. *Storia della marina veneziana da Lepanto alla caduta della Repubblica.* Rome: Ministero della Marina, 1935.

Nef, John U. *Industry and Government in France and England, 1540-1640.* Memoirs of the American Philosophical Society, XV. Philadelphia, 1940.

_____ "The Progress of Technology and the Growth of Large-Scale Industry in Great Britain 1540-1640." *Economic History Review,* 5 (1934), 3-24.

Neri, Antonio. *L'Arte vetraria distinta in libri sette.* Florence: 1661.

BIBLIOGRAPHY

Pancotto, Angelo. "Le Condizioni dei garzoni a Venezia dalla fine del secolo XVI alla fine del secolo XVIII." Unpub. diss., Istituto Universitario di Economia "Ca'Foscari." Venice: 1945-1946.

Papadopoli-Aldobrandini, Nicolo. *Le monete di Venezia descritte ed illustrate.* 2d ed. 3 vols. Bologna: Forni, 1967.

Phelps Brown, E. H., and Hopkins, S. "Seven Centuries of Building Wages." In *Essays in Economic History,* edited by E. M. Carus-Wilson, II, 168-178. New York: St. Martin's Press, 1966.

Pullan, Brian S. "Poverty, Charity and the Reason of State: Some Venetian Examples." *Bollettino dell'Istituo di Storia della Società e dello Stato Veneziano,* 2 (1960), 17-60.

———— *Rich and Poor in Renaissance Venice; The Social Institutions of a Catholic State, to 1620.* Cambridge, Mass.: Harvard University Press, 1971.

———— "Service to the Venetian State: Aspects of Myth and Reality in the Early Seventeenth Century." *Studi secenteschi,* 5 (1964), 95-148.

———— "Wage-Earners and the Venetian Economy, 1550-1630." *Economic History Review,* 2d ser. 16 (1964), 407-426. Reprinted in *Crisis and Change,* ed. Brian Pullan, pp. 146-174.

————, ed. *Crisis and Change in the Venetian Economy in the Sixteenth and Seventeenth Centuries.* London: Methuen, 1968.

Putnam, George Haven. *Books and Their Makers during the Middle Ages.* 2d ed. New York: Hillary, 1962.

Romano, Ruggiero. "Una crisi economica 1619-1622." *Rivista Storica Italiana,* 74 (1962), 480-531.

———— "Economic Aspects of the Construction of Warships in Venice in the Sixteenth Century." In *Crisis and Change,* ed. Brian Pullan, pp. 59-87. First published as "Aspetti economici degli armamenti navali veneziani," *Rivista Storica Italiana,* 66 (1954), 39-67.

———— "Encore la crise de 1619-1622." *Annales: Economies, Sociétés, Civilisations,* 19 (1964), 31-38.

————; Spooner, F.; and Tucci, U. "Le finanze di Udine e della Patria del Friuli all'epoca della dominazione veneziana." *Memorie Storiche Forogiuliese,* 44 (1960-61), 235-267.

Rosetti, Giovanni Ventura. *PLICTHO de larte de tentori che insegna tenger panni telle banbasi et sede per larthe magiore come per la comune.* Venice: 1540.

Sagredo, Agosto. *Sulle consorterie delle arti edificative a Venezia.* Venice: 1858.

Sanuto, Marino. *I Diarii.* 58 vols. Venice: Deputazione (R.) veneta di Storia Patria, 1879-1903.

Sardella, Pierre. "L'épanouissement industriel de Venise au XVIe siècle." *Annales: Economies, Sociétés, Civilisations,* 2 (1947), 196.

Scarpa, V., ed. *La scrittura inedita del mercadente del secolo XVII: Francesco Alborelli Cassiere della Camera del Purgo sulla pannina veneziana.* Venice: 1856.

Scoville, Warren C. *Capitalism and French Glassmaking, 1640-1789.* Berkeley: University of California Press, 1950.

Sella, Domenico. *Commerci e industrie a Venezia nel secolo XVII.* Venice-Rome: Istituto per la Collaborazione Culturale, 1961.

_____ "Crisis and Transformation in Venetian Trade." In *Crisis and Change,* ed. Brian Pullan, pp. 88-105. Revised version of "Il declino dell' emporio realtino," in *La civiltà veneziana nell'età barocca.* Venice: Centro di cultura e civiltà della Fondazione Giorgio Cini, 1959.

_____ "Industrial Production in Seventeenth-Century Italy: A Reappraisal." *Explorations in Entrepreneurial History,* 2nd ser., 6 (1969), 235-253.

_____ "The Rise and Fall of the Venetian Woolen Industry." In *Crisis and Change,* ed. Brian Pullan, pp. 106-126. Revised version of "Les mouvements longs de l'industrie lainierè à Venise." *Annales: Economies, Sociétés, Civilisations,* 12 (1957), 29-45.

Sestan, Ernesto. "La politica veneziana del Seicento." In *La civiltà veneziana nell'età barocca.* Venice: Centro di cultura e civiltà della Fondazione Giorgio Cini, 1959.

Singer, Charles, et al. *A History of Technology.* 5 vols. Oxford: Oxford University Press, 1954-1958.

Smith, H. G. "Cornelius Drebbel and English Scarlet Dyeing." *Ciba Review,* 7 (1938), 231-33.

Stella, Aldo. "La crisi economica veneziana nella seconda metà del secolo XVI." *Archivio Veneto,* 5th ser. 58 (1956), 37-69.

Supple, Barry. *Commercial Crisis and Change in England, 1600-1642.* Cambridge: Cambridge University Press, 1964.

Tagliaferri, Amelio. *L'economia Veronese secondo gli estimi dal 1409 al 1635.* Milan: Giuffrè, 1966.

Tenenti, Alberto. "Aspetti della vita mediterranea intorno al seicento." *Bollettino dell'Istituto di Storia della Società e dello Stato Veneziano,* 2 (1960), 3-16.

_____ "Luc'Antonio Giunti il giovane stampatore e mercante." In *Studi in onore di Armando Sapori,* pp. 1021-1060. Milan: Cisalpino, 1957.

_____ *Piracy and the Decline of Venice, 1580-1615.* Translated by Janet and Brian Pullan. London: Longmans, 1967.

United Nations, Department of Social Affairs. *The Determinants and Consequences of Population Trends.* New York: U.N. Publications, 1953.

Usher, Abbot Payson. *A History of Mechanical Inventions.* Boston: Beacon Press, 1954.

Ventura, Angelo. "Aspetti storico economici della villa veneta." *Bollettino del Centro Internazionale di Studi di Architettura Andrea Palladio,* 11 (1969), 65-77.

White, Lynn, Jr. *Medieval Technology and Social Change.* Oxford: Oxford University Press, 1967.

Wilson, C. H. "Cloth Production and International Competition in the Seventeenth Century." *Economic History Review,* 13 (1960), 209-221.

BIBLIOGRAPHY

_____ "Trade, Society and the State." In *Cambridge Economic History of Europe,* vol. IV, pp. 487-575. Cambridge: Cambridge University Press, 1967.

Woolf, S. J. "Venice and the Terraferma: Problems of the Change from Commercial to Landed Activities." *Bollettino dell'Istituto di Storia della Società e dello Stato Veneziano,* 4 (1962), 415-441.

Zecchin, Luigi. "L'Arte muranese dal 1674 al 1718 secondo i capitoli della Mariegola." *Giornale economico* [Venice (Province): Camera di commercio, industria, ed agricoltura di Venezia], 1959.

_____ "La rivendita dei vetri in Venezia citta fra il XIII e il XVIII secolo." *Giornale economico* [Venice (Province): Camera di commercio, industria, ed agricoltura di Venezia], 1958.

Zompini, Gaetano. *Le Arti che vanno per via nella città di Venezia; inventate ed incise da Gaetano Zompini.* Venice: 1785.

INDEX

Ancona, 11
Antwerp, 12
Apprenticeship, 42-46, 86, 87, 95, 122
Arsenal, 8, 16n, 79, 80-81, 99n, 117n, 149-151; labor budget of, 150; workers of, 23, 26, 69, 149
Arti, 14, 171-175. *See also* Guilds

Bakers, 79, 96
Barbers, 98
Barrel-hoop makers, 125, 159
Basketmakers, 107
Beloch, K. J., 40, 176, 177
Beltrami, D., 78n, 177
Bergamo, 144, 160, 161, 162
Birth rates, 34
Boatmen, 43, 96, 150
Bombardieri, 51n, 64
Brescia, 159-160
Butchers, 98

Capital equipment, 5, 99, 100, 107-108, 116-121, 127, 166
Carpenters, 98, 166
Castello (sestiere), 78-81
Chemical industries, 6, 8, 98, 99, 100
Cinque Savi alla Mercanzia, 16n, 115, 139, 153, 183
Cittadini, 24, 78
Cloth-of-gold, 109
Collegio alle Arti, 16n, 17
Collegio da Milizia da Mar, 19, 23, 49-53, 175, 183
Commerce, 2-3, 5, 10-13, 104-106, 126, 139, 164; fiscal aspects of, 139-142; impact of War of Crete on, 153; investment in, 145; taxation of, 104, 140-142
Commercial Revolution, 12
Competition: commercial and industrial, 10-12, 140, 142, 163, 165; Northern, in Mediterranean, 3, 4, 5,
10-12, 104, 153-155; terraferma, 159-164
Constantinople, 2, 10, 149
Coopers, 21, 107, 125
Costs of production, 17-18, 47, 112-113, 116, 126-130, 163; government control of, 16, 19, 134; taxes as a component of, 140

Death rates, 34
Dorsoduro (sestiere), 78, 79
Dry-goods retailers (*marzeri*), 20n, 21, 98, 102
Dyeing, 8, 99, 109, 113-115, 126, 130, 140; shops for, 121, 181-182

Economic decline, 1, 3, 4, 5, 6, 11-13, 138, 164-167
Economic growth, 1, 5, 166
Economic nationalism, 138
Employment, 20-32, 42, 47, 102-106, 122; distribution of, 76-77, 78-81, 96-106; in textile industry, 103
Employment census, sources and derivation of, 49-57, 183-185
England, 1, 3, 9, 101, 105, 109, 114, 153, 154, 164, 166; Mediterranean trade of, 10, 11, 116; wages in, 134-136
Experimentation, industrial, 112-116
Exports, 3, 6-9, 102-106, 137, 139, 165; prohibited, 109, 162n

Fishing, 79, 80
Florence, 10, 127, 149
Food processing and selling, 96, 98
France, 1, 101, 105, 109, 137, 153, 154, 156; encouragement of exports in, 141-142
Furniture making, 9, 105
Furriers, 96
Fustian cloth, 7; weavers, 16-17, 94-95

HARVARD HISTORICAL MONOGRAPHS

46. Carroll Wright and Labor Reform: The Origin of Labor Statistics. By James Leiby. 1960.
47. Chōshū in the Meiji Restoration. By Albert M. Craig. 1961.
48. John Fiske: The Evolution of a Popularizer. By Milton Berman. 1961.
49. John Jewel and the Problem of Doctrinal Authority. By W. M. Southgate. 1962.
50. Germany and the Diplomacy of the Financial Crisis, 1931. By Edward W. Bennett. 1962.
51. Public Opinion, Propaganda, and Politics in Eighteenth-Century England: A Study of the Jew Bill of 1753. By Thomas W. Perry. 1962.
52. Soldier and Civilian in the Later Roman Empire. By Ramsay MacMullen. 1963.
53. Copyhold, Equity, and the Common Law. By Charles Montgomery Gray. 1963.
54. The Association: British Extraparliamentary Political Association, 1769-1793. By Eugene Charlton Black. 1963.
55. Tocqueville and England. By Seymour Drescher. 1964.
56. Germany and the Emigration, 1816-1885. By Mack Walker. 1964.
57. Ivan Aksakov (1823-1886): A Study in Russian Thought and Politics. By Stephen Lukashevich. 1965.
58. The Fall of Stein. By R. C. Raack. 1965.
59. The French Apanages and the Capetian Monarchy, 1224-1328. By Charles T. Wood. 1966.
60. Congressional Insurgents and the Party System, 1909-1916. By James Holt. 1967.
61. The Rumanian National Movement in Transylvania, 1780-1849. By Keith Hitchins. 1969.
62. Sisters of Liberty: Marseille, Lyon, Paris and the Reaction to a Centralized State, 1868-1871. By Louis M. Greenberg. 1971.
63. Old Hatreds and Young Hopes: The French Carbonari against the Bourbon Restoration. By Alan B. Spitzer. 1971.
64. To the Maginot Line: The Politics of French Military Preparation in the 1920's. By Judith M. Hughes. 1971.
65. Florentine Public Finances in the Early Renaissance, 1400-1433. By Anthony Molho. 1971.
66. Provincial Magistrates and Revolutionary Politics in France, 1789-1795. By Philip Dawson. 1972.
67. The East India Company and Army Reform, 1783-1798. By Raymond Callahan. 1972.
68. Ireland in the Empire, 1688-1770: A History of Ireland from the Williamite Wars to the Eve of the American Revolution. By Francis Godwin James. 1973.
69. Industry and Economic Decline in Seventeenth-Century Venice. By Richard Tilden Rapp. 1976.